ANATOMY OF MALICE

JOEL E. DIMSDALE

Anatomy of Malice

THE ENIGMA OF THE NAZI WAR CRIMINALS

Yale

UNIVERSITY PRESS

NEW HAVEN & LONDON

Excerpts from *Nuremberg Diary* copyright © 08-22-1995 books-contributor-g-20m-20gilbert.
Reprinted by permission of da capo, a member of the Perseus Books Group.

Yale University Press books may be purchased in quantity for educational,
business, or promotional use. For information, please e-mail sales.press@yale.edu
(US office) or sales@yaleup.co.uk (UK office).

Additional information, including references, links, and discussion guide,
is available at www.anatomyofmalice.com

Set in Scala type by Newgen North America.
Printed in the United States of America.

Library of Congress Control Number: 2016930154
ISBN 978-0-300-21322-5 (hardcover)
A catalogue record for this book is available from the British Library.

This paper meets the requirements of ANSI/NISO Z39.48–1992 (Permanence of Paper).

10 9 8 7 6 5 4 3 2 1

CONTENTS

Beginnings in a Land of Manure and Blood

WHEN THE WIND BLOWS FROM THE EAST, there is a gentle wafting of manure and blood that settles over Sioux City, Iowa. It is not unpleasant, and it reminds one of the agricultural richness of the area. Growing up there in the 1940s and 1950s was about the most secure environment imaginable, tucked away in the vastness and fastness of America, surrounded by thousands of square miles of prairie and Great Plains and remote from threatening borders.

And yet, there were shadows. William Faulkner said, "The past is never dead; the past is not even past." Sioux City became home to many concentration camp survivors, attracted there by its beautiful, gentle rolling hills, its agricultural richness, and its isolation from a world they knew, a world that was in no way secure. My brother saw it first as a ten-year-old boy, when he was on his paper route, and glimpsed a tattoo on the forearm of a neighbor. The neighbor, it seems, was embarrassed by this revelation, and my brother didn't know what it meant. My mother, usually at no loss for words, was uneasy and sparing in her explanation.

I think I must have been six or seven when I learned what shadows haunted our neighbors. I was on an after-dinner walk with my dad, who was a local doctor. It was March or April, and the ground in the neighboring park was soft from the melting snows and the land smelled fresh. It was Passover, and my father was upset about a house call he had made that week. One of his patients had developed severe angina. That in itself was not enough to upset my dad. He took care of everybody and was accustomed to death. What was different for this patient was the timing of his illness. He was a concentration camp survivor who had witnessed the murder of his entire family on Passover in another land of rolling hills, blood, and manure. His religion told him to rejoice in his liberation on Passover; he knew better.

In those days before Adolf Eichmann was captured, people preferred not to know about the Holocaust. Robert Jay Lifton famously remarked in *Death in Life: Survivors of Hiroshima* (1968) that survivors of massive trauma typically elicit a fear of contagion from the people they meet subsequently. Still, it was hard for me to dismiss the Holocaust, since in small towns, one is privy to many secrets and ghosts.

As a little boy, I hadn't thought much about evil. Television was still new, the programing scanty, and the news lasted only fifteen minutes. I grew up with stick-finger thin ideas of evil from the comic books—the Joker, Lex Luther, Doctor Doom. This was not a world where evil was nuanced. Instead, it was "the other," demonic, and utterly different from the citizens and the heroes of the comic strip. Thus, it comes as no surprise that I—like most people in the 1940s and 1950s—thought that the Nazis who designed and ran the concentration camps were depraved and utterly foreign to human nature.

The Executioner in my Office

Years passed. After college, I joined an archaeological expedition, digging far below the surface of the twentieth century and sorrowfully unearthing layers of ashes that indicated other violence, millennia before. I went to graduate school in sociology to learn more about how social forces shape our lives and went to medical school to learn how to heal people.

I probably would have left the Holocaust behind had I not received a call from one of my parents' friends, inviting me to dinner to celebrate my beginning medical school. She took me to one of Sioux City's old family-run restaurants and—over a midwestern comfort-food kind of dinner with caramel sweet rolls as a starter, meat loaf, baked potatoes, overcooked string beans, and Folgers coffee—she told me about her life in the concentration camps. She said that she hadn't talked about it before but she was getting old and wanted someone to know. She too had lost her entire family in the war but had built a new life in Iowa that seemed so utterly normal except for the nightmares that haunted her every night. We talked for hours, and the restaurant's celebrated caramel sweet rolls didn't rest easy on my stomach that night.

With my interests in history and social forces, it was no surprise that I eventually became a psychiatrist, nor was it a surprise that I started studying concentration camp survivors to learn how they coped with their imprisonment and survival. In 1974, I published an article on the coping behavior of Nazi concentration camp survivors. The article briefly captured the interest of local media, and the news coverage resulted in an encounter that shaped my subsequent research interests.

I was in my office in the attic of a little isolated building on the Massachusetts General Hospital grounds. There was a loud knock on my door, and I was startled because I wasn't expecting anyone and the building had few visitors. A stocky man walked in, saying without any preamble, "I am the executioner and I have come for you." He sat down on my sofa, gestured to a gun case, and I said a quiet little prayer to myself. When he opened the case, I saw that it was not a gun case after all but rather a document case with scrolls of World War II documents. "I was the Nuremberg executioner and these documents prove that I am who I say I am." He went on to tell me that he was proud of his job and that while still being professional about it, he enjoyed hanging the criminals. "They were scum, Dimsdale, and you need to be studying them, not the survivors."

Chance Meetings

One doesn't forget such an encounter. I didn't act on it, but it lurked there in the back of my mind. Then, another chance meeting happened. I was at a dinner party in Gainesville, Florida, where I met the renowned Rorschach expert Molly Harrower. It was Molly who told me the story of the Rorschach testing of the Nuremberg war criminals and the mystery and controversy that to this day swirls around this topic.

This book tells a dark story that stretches from Germany to Switzerland and, oddly, from New Jersey to California. I didn't rush to write this book; I didn't want to. It was just too dark, but the story kept haunting me, and as I got older, I couldn't fend it off any longer. So, this book traces the legacy of Nuremberg and what I have come to learn about evil, what I have called the "anatomy of malice."

THE PROTAGONISTS

Burton C. Andrus, warden of Ashcan and Nuremberg

Gustave Gilbert, American psychologist

Hermann Göring, Reichsmarshall, head of the Luftwaffe

Molly Harrower, American psychologist and Rorschach expert

Rudolf Hess,* deputy Führer

Robert Jackson, Supreme Court Justice and lead American prosecutor at Nuremberg

Douglas Kelley, American psychiatrist

Robert Ley, head of the German Labor Front

Hermann Rorschach, Swiss psychiatrist

Julius Streicher, editor, *Der Stürmer*

*Hess is a relatively common German surname. When written in English, it is typically spelled as Hoess, Höss, or Hess. This can lead to some confusion because there were two war criminals named Rudolf Hess. This book focuses on Rudolf Hess the deputy Führer. The "other" Rudolf Hoess was the Auschwitz camp commandant who was tried and executed in a subsequent war crimes trial.

Introduction

Whoever desires to found a state and give it laws, must start with assuming that all men are bad and ever ready to display their vicious nature.

> —Niccolò Machiavelli, *The Prince*

The only thing necessary for the triumph of evil is for good men to do nothing.

> —attributed to Edmund Burke

What Drives Malice?

WHEN WORLD WAR II ENDED, the Allies had multiple motives in dealing with the captured Nazi leaders. Their punishment was a crucial part of the de-Nazification of Germany. Secondarily, the Allies hoped that a war crimes trial might deter future leaders from committing war crimes and genocide.

In addition to these goals, there was an overwhelming desire to understand what kind of people could have steered Germany on such a lethal course. Paradoxically, many of the Nazi leaders were well-educated individuals steeped in the Western intellectual tradition. How could they? This goal of "understanding" the leaders was not an explicit aim of the Nuremberg trials, but it was a prominent undercurrent. The trial wasn't so much a "Who done it?" as it was a "Why did they do it?" and "How could they?" The assumption was that the defendants were beasts, monsters, something wholly "other," which could be revealed and confirmed by careful investigation. The popular press was alive with theories, and historians as well as social scientists rushed in to offer their explanations. There were, however, quieter voices pointing out that evil is in the nature of man. And then there were voices from psychiatry, neurology, and psychology that viewed the Nazis' behavior in a different context. Strikingly, these latter experts tried to get data to test their assumptions. "It was a reflection of diseased brains," said one school of thought. "It reflected severe psychiatric disorder," said another. "It reflected normal people who had made bad choices," offered a third.

How could the war criminals do what they did? Were they suffering from a psychiatric disorder? Were they criminally insane, delusional, psychopaths, sadists? Countless scholars have offered opinions about the Nazis' behavior, based on their ideas about the nature of society and individual behavior. Many have made brilliant contributions by delving into the abundant archival material. Rather fewer scholars have directly interviewed the perpetrators, but they have generally examined the rank and file as opposed to the leaders of the Third Reich.[1]

In trying to understand the Nazis' behavior, we are thus faced with an enormous blind spot—the leaders themselves. We have interviews with their subordinates, but they claimed to be cogs in the machinery of the state.[2] Of course, we are all cogs, shaped by many forces, but some of us turn larger wheels. If there is "agency" (that is, responsibility), one needs to turn to higher echelons of government—exactly the people on trial at Nuremberg.

As a psychiatrist, my expertise is in listening to, diagnosing, and treating patients, and I have practiced in remarkably diverse settings: in intensive care units surrounded by ventilators, in prisons that seemed to have been designed by Franz Kafka, in psychiatric asylums for the wealthy where peacocks strolled complainingly across the grounds. I have worked in moldering state hospitals that somehow resisted collapsing, interviewed patients in emergency rooms so filled with screams and sirens that it was difficult to hear—and everywhere I worked there was a chart. Doctors are historians; we leave notes behind, not just because of our fallible memories, but also to guide future care. There is an art to writing and reading those notes because they are invariably telegraphic, but there is a hidden grammar and logic to them. When I read the medical and psychiatric notes from Nuremberg, I thus filter them through my own clinical experience and regard them as a conversation with colleagues from the past. What are they trying to tell me about the patient? What is being left unsaid?

The Nuremberg doctors left cryptic and contradictory notes about their observations of the Nazi leaders. I have tried to decipher their records and to examine them anew from the vantage point of the twenty-first century.

Access to psychiatric records of governmental leaders is rare. There is one enormous exception, but the investigators are largely forgotten. Psychiatrist Douglas Kelley and psychologist Gustave Gilbert were ordered to the Nuremberg jail to assess the inmates' competency to face trial and to bolster their morale. Covertly, they were also advisers to the prison warden and the prosecution. But each also had a personal agenda: they had the audacious idea of employing Rorschach inkblot tests to characterize the nature of the Nazi leaders' malice. They spent many hours (Kelley claimed eighty hours per defendant) interviewing the defendants in their cramped prison cells, giving them psychological tests and observing their behavior in the trial. In short, they had extraordinarily intensive observations on the leaders of Nazi Germany. This book recounts the story of what they discovered about four of the defendants whose malice was rooted in different soils: Robert Ley, Hermann Göring, Julius Streicher, and Rudolf Hess.

These observations by Kelley and Gilbert were not easy on either of them; both men emerged marked by their experiences encountering malice so closely. It is one thing to study such malice from a distance, but to sit on a narrow cot with such criminals day in, day out, looking at them, listening to them, smelling them, was deeply troubling. The stress of it undermined Kelley's and Gilbert's collaboration, stoked their personal differences and jealousies, led to intrigue, lawsuits, and recriminations. Regardless, their discoveries and quarrels have shaped how we understand the anatomy of malice today. Contemporary researchers, haunted by the ghosts of Nuremberg, have performed some of our most prominent studies of this uncomfortable topic.

In telling this story I have relied on many different types of information. There are a number of valuable books in this area, but I have drawn on other sources as well.[3] Extensive press accounts give an indication of how popular culture regarded the Nuremberg war criminals. In addition, practically everyone who participated in the trial wrote memoirs that are rich in detail. Some of these memoirs have been published, but others were classified or locked in special collections. Information from these various special collections forms the heart of this book.[4] Seventy years after the trial, Nuremberg lurks in the background and provides a lens for viewing the abundant examples of contemporary malice.

Discordant Voices

I was frankly surprised to discover the extent of disagreements among all these sources. I was naive. I have attended meetings on the Holocaust that have deteriorated into violent arguments and denunciations—everything short of throwing chairs. Discordant voices are the rule, not the exception, in any historical examination, but when it comes to mass murder, the quarrelsomeness increases exponentially.[5]

Memory, even in the best of circumstances, is fragile and subject to forgetting, distorting, and lying. People puff themselves up and offer rationalizations, sometimes consciously and sometimes not. These difficulties are particularly prominent in understanding the diaries and autobiographies of the Nazis.[6] The novelist Rose Macauley frames the problem beautifully: "We have to grope our way through a mist . . . , and we can never sit back and say, we have the Truth, . . . for discovering the truth . . . means a long journey through a difficult jungle."[7]

This history is a thicket, complicated by the need to interpret language that itself has changed over time. When we read a hospital record or a psychiatric evaluation from seventy years ago, the words have a different connotation. As I shall discuss in Chapter 2, we are not even sure how to understand Göring's cardiac difficulties in jail since the term "heart attack" had a much looser meaning then. This confusion in understanding historical medical conditions is even more pronounced in psychiatry. Our efforts at systematizing a diagnostic nomenclature are relatively recent; the first edition of psychiatry's *Diagnostic and Statistical Manual* (DSM) appeared in 1952. In 1945, there was no DSM at all and no widely agreed upon way of understanding, describing, or treating psychiatric problems. As a result, reading the psychiatric records of that era is a daunting task; similarly, there was no well-established approach to administering and coding the Rorschach test at that time.[8] For all these reasons it is challenging to understand terminology and inferences made so long ago. The words simply do not mean the same thing.

The Organization of This Book

When I was nine, my father gave me my first microscope. I learned that the best way of viewing a slide was to examine it repeatedly, switching back and forth from low to high magnification. Years later, I got my first stereo microscope, which allowed me to look at the same image from slightly different points of view. All of a sudden, I could see depth and perspective.

I have spent years studying the war criminals from one vantage point to another, at low magnification (their public personas) versus high magnification (during psychiatric interviews). We catch a glimpse of them in detention and in the Nuremberg courtroom, low-magnification perspectives. However, we also have high-magnification views of the Nazi leaders—notes from the Nuremberg psychiatrists and psychologists about their extensive personal interviews and psychological testing of the war criminals.

This book is organized in four sections that move forward and backward in time. Part I provides historical context, the run-up, so to speak, to Nuremberg and how the Nazi genocide came to haunt our ideas of the nature of malice. Part II details the Nuremberg events in the public eye of the courtroom as well as in the private darkness of the defendants' prison cells. Part III focuses on four of the war criminals who exemplify radically varied origins of malice. Twenty-two individuals were indicted at the first Nuremberg trial. I selected four for extended study because they posed distinctly different diagnostic challenges. To get a sense for the contours of malice in the Nazi leaders, I selected defendants who had different portfolios of responsibility in the war and who behaved at Nuremberg in decidedly diverse fashion. Part IV returns to the central question of this book: How do we understand malice? Does it reside in all of us, or are certain individuals distinctly different in their capacity for malice?

The psychological testing of the war criminals lay hidden and unpublished for decades, mired in a toxic mélange of ambition, betrayal, and ideological differences. These forgotten records allow us to examine how contemporary psychiatry and psychology understand malice—its social psychological, psychopathological, and neurobehavioral roots—and how encounters with malice influence our ideas of humanity.

Trying to understand is not the same thing as condoning or condemning. Readers who believe that the Nazi leaders were homogeneous, aberrant monsters might as well put this book down now because, as this book will make clear, they were certainly *not* homogeneous. They were malicious, grasping human beings, but they differed profoundly from one another. This book clarifies the nature(s) of their malice, tracks the toxic effect of the trial on the investigators themselves, and examines how this history has shaped contemporary research.

This is a very extensive and contentious scholarly area, marked by careful assessments as well as innuendo and acrimony. I hope this book helps guide the reader to "the general vicinity of historical truth."[9]

PART ONE

RUN-UP TO NUREMBERG

The Holocaust:
How Was This Genocide
Different from All the Rest?

I'd like to call them all by name,
But they took away the list, and there is nowhere to find out.
For them I have woven a broad shroud
From their poor, overheard words.
      —Anna Akhmatova, "Requiem," 1940

During the first try, my hand trembled a bit as I shot, but one gets used to it. By the tenth try, I aimed calmly and shot surely at the many women, children, and infants. I kept in mind that I have two infants at home whom these hordes would treat just the same, if not ten times worse. . . . Infants flew in great arcs through the air, and we shot them to pieces in flight, before their bodies fell into the pit and into the water.
      —German policeman writing home about shooting
      Jews in the Ukraine, October 1941

The Blood Lands of Europe

WHEN I WAS LITTLE, I HAD A PRETTY sketchy idea about death. I had an even vaguer idea about large numbers. Coming from a region where the four-footed mammals vastly outnumbered the two-footed mammals, I had no idea what "millions" of deaths could mean.

I also had rather limited models of malice. Every Saturday afternoon I would walk to the Uptown Theater, pay a quarter, and watch Westerns or monster movies. The monsters back then were never human. Usually, they were large, angry animals—spiders, say, and who knew what went on in their nasty arachnid brains? The alternatives to the large, angry animal monsters were zombies, and it was obvious that their brains weren't right. As I got older, I learned about offscreen monsters—people who were consumed by rage, jealousy, and sheer nastiness. The scope of the killings in the blood lands of Europe defies comprehension. How can thinking human beings resort to such malice?

I grew up to be a psychiatrist, not a historian, but I sit with patients and take histories all day long. What motivated my patient's actions? What did the patient do with his or her life? What were the consequences of these life choices? I have tacitly asked similar questions about the war criminals who are the focus of this book, but these questions also help in framing the unique nature of the Nazi genocide more broadly.[1]

When World War II finally ended, forty million men, women, and children were dead in Europe. That people die in war is expected—that is, after all, the point, to achieve aims through violence—but two-thirds of these deaths were noncombatants.[2]

Although noncombatant deaths in warfare are not unique, usually they involve people who happened to be in the wrong place at the wrong time. Sometimes, however, as a matter of policy, states conduct genocide against whole peoples—soldiers and civilians alike. Most countries and cultures have resorted to genocide at some point in their history, and in most cases this was simply blood lust. When people's arms grew tired, they stopped killing. The Holocaust, however, was different. It was a genocide characterized by sustained killing operations, orchestrated with stunning attention to detail, by one of the most civilized countries in the world. It was also one of the largest mass killings ever known. In his brilliant book *Bloodlands*, Timothy Snyder pointed out the immense scope of the killing: "On any given day in the second half of 1941, the Germans shot more Jews than had been killed by pogroms in the entire history of the Russian empire."[3]

I used to wonder: What kind of individuals could design such a killing machine? I still do.

I also wonder whether people remember.

One week before invading Poland, Adolf Hitler urged a merciless campaign and is reported to have said: "Who . . . speaks today of the annihilation of the Armenians?"[4] Whether the quotation is accurate as reported, it highlights a distressing point. If no one remembers genocide, can it be said to have occurred? It's akin to the proverbial question "If a tree falls in the forest and no one is around to hear it, does it make a sound?" In the case of the Jews, Poles, Armenians, Bangladeshis, Tutsi, Cambodians, people from Darfur, and all of the other victims of the countless other campaigns of mass killings, it is clear that survivors do remember, but how well does the rest of the world remember?

I hesitated about providing a broad overview of the Holocaust in this book because some readers will already be knowledgeable, but I have learned not to make assumptions. Many years ago, I asked Jewish Sunday school students what the "final solution of the Jewish problem" meant and if they could name two concentration camps. They couldn't, and their lack of knowledge was not unusual.

During the Adolf Eichmann trial, when news coverage was so extensive, investigators polled hundreds of adults in Oakland, California, about their perspectives on the trial.[5] Sixteen percent of the respondents were unaware of the trial at all. The investigators pressed further. Among the 384 people who knew that there was an ongoing trial, 59 percent indicated that Eichmann was a Nazi. The rest guessed that he was a communist, a Jew, or "other," or they had no absolutely no idea who he was, even though they knew he was on trial for something. The researchers also studied which sorts of people paid attention to news about the trial. Whites were more likely to know about the trial but less likely to know about the Freedom Riders, who were also in the news at the time. Conversely, African Americans were less likely to know about the trial, but almost all of them had heard of the Freedom Riders. In other words, people disregarded news that was not salient or relevant to them.

People ignore, deny, forget, or never learn. In one of his final publications, the historian Raul Hilberg issued a sobering challenge: "The fact is that Holocaust research is now in a kind of 'ghetto,'" a highly specialized corner of historiography.[6] As I write these words today, seventy years have passed since the Nuremberg war crimes trial. I suspect that some readers will not be clear about what led up to the trial or why the debates about the Nazis' psychiatric diagnoses became so all-consuming and sulfurous. This chapter, then, provides a broad overview.

Rationale for the Mass Killings

The Nazi machinery of destruction targeted many types of people—Jews, Roma, Slavs, homosexuals, Jehovah's Witnesses, the mentally infirm—but principally the Jews. This book is more of a meditation on diagnoses than motivations. It is beyond the scope of this book to examine the complexity of Nazi motivations that drove the murders.[7] Indeed, for some, these analyses of motivation have been an anathema. Witness the statement of the poet Yitzhak Katzsnelson: "I utterly repudiate every reason or formula that . . . 'scholars' . . . put forward to explain this abomination. I despise whoever utters such stupidity and nonsense. . . . What possible connection . . . can this political economy have with the criminal wantonness which this beast in human form metes out to us?"[8]

Nonetheless, three dominant features coalesced to make the Jewish genocide particularly devastating: anti-Semitism grounded in religious tradition, social Darwinism, and the ruination that followed World War I.

For centuries, anti-Semitism had been stoked in the churches. The Jews were accused, at best, of spurning Christianity and, at worst, of being Christ killers. They were readily identifiable by unusual customs in dress, diet, and holidays. In many countries, they were coerced into centuries-long occupational patterns that made them reviled, and they were forced to live apart. Jews were objects of fear and loathing, targets for projected feelings of rage and aggression. When a violent crime was committed, it was assumed that "the Jews" had done it, not just "done it," but "done it" out of pure intentionality, malice, and depravity. Paradoxically, as the Austro-Hungarian Empire started modernizing and lessening some of the anti-Jewish restrictions, popular anti-Semitism increased. No longer were the Jews sequestered; instead, there was a collision of cultures, and anti-Semites felt under assault because of their increased interactions with Jews. With assimilation, people feared a malign, hidden influence of Jews who blended in with the surrounding culture.[9] The fact that some Jews prospered was an additional source of outrage.

Social Darwinism comprised the second toxic strand that contributed to the Nazi genocide. Following the discovery of the New World, Europeans were increasingly struck by the disparities in race and culture as well as the disparate living conditions of newly encountered peoples. The thinking was that non-Europeans who lived in less developed cultures did so because that was all that they were capable of—they had bad genes. On the other hand, the people who thrived had better genes and were more fit. Any taint of a different race, no matter how miniscule, was assumed to carry with it a genetic proclivity to disease and backwardness. If one culled animals to improve the breed, why not cull humans to eliminate undesirable traits or groups?

Race was carried in the blood. This belief added new meaning to the term "blood crime." If you carried the wrong blood, you were like a carrier of cholera who would bring death and destruction to those around you. It made no difference if you converted to Christianity sincerely; the "fact" was that you carried the evil in your blood, and that evil was beyond redemption.

Enormous scholarly efforts were dedicated to recognizing hidden racial characteristics. Once race was diagnosed, it was simply a matter of eugenics to design a better world: don't let "them" breed or at least make sure they bred only with each other so that any racial stigmata would be obvious for all to see. In only a matter of time, so the prevailing belief went, the inferiors would be bred out and one would have a strong society.

What is interesting about the eugenics argument is that the target group kept shifting from more easily distinguishable groups like blacks to other groups that were less easy to recognize: Jews, Roma, Slavs, Poles. The eugenics ideology focused on other subgroups as well: mentally handicapped individuals, psychiatric patients, homosexuals, and criminals. If all of these people could be rounded up, they could not infect others. If all could be sterilized, then the genetic contamination would cease, once and for all. It was a small but logical step from sterilization to killing. Wouldn't it be better to eliminate these diseases (that is, people) and get it over with more quickly?

The third factor that engendered the Nazi mass killings was the chaos following World War I. That war, so incredibly costly in lives and resources, ended with Germany's defeat. Not only had Germany lost the war, but it faced devastating and humiliating financial terms from the Versailles settlement. Germany's government could not counter the massive inflation and ruin, and millions of Germans brooded. Oddly, the Jews were viewed as in league with both the communists on the left and the capitalists on the right. Clearly, they must have conspired together to take their revenge on Germany. Clearly, they must be punished.

In those days of fiscal uncertainty and scarcity, there was not enough food to share with so-called useless eaters and vermin. Thus, Hitler's vision was to obliterate all the undesirables and to provide the purified Aryan nation with the freed-up space and confiscated resources so that a resurgent Germany could rule the world in security and plenty. With a strong leader, he believed that Germany would march from humiliation to triumph and complete its manifest destiny by expanding east into a fruitful land that had been cleared of all nondesirables. It was an intoxicating idea that swept the nation.

The Steps to Genocide

Whatever their motivations, it was the *behavior* of the Nazis that brought them to trial, and it was the peculiar nature of the killing and the killers' responses to the acts of murder that kindled the psychiatric speculations. With an old-fashioned pogrom, all you needed was a permissive government, a precipitating excuse, a massive discrepancy in the size and power of the two groups, and reasonably cooperative weather. In a matter of days or weeks, you could kill a significant number of people and then get on with your business. For a modern, coordinated genocide that aimed to eliminate large multitudes of people, the rules for pogroms needed radical revision.

The Nazi genocide relied on meticulous attention to detail. Justice Robert Jackson, lead American prosecutor, opened the Nuremberg trial by stating: "This war did not just happen—it was planned and prepared for over a long period of time and with no small skill and cunning. . . . Whatever else we may say of those who were the authors of this war, they did achieve a stupendous work in organization."[10]

Historians such as Ian Kershaw have argued that the genocide wasn't all planned and driven from the top down but that the mass killings also relied on considerable improvisation from the bottom up.[11] What struck Justice Jackson and most observers was the amount of bureaucratization that undergirded the killings. To understand the participation of the vast rank and file in this process, one needs perspectives from sociology and industrial psychology. The machinery of destruction was powered by a bureaucracy that relied on familiar tools of precision, speed, and administration. As historian Zygmunt Bauman has argued: "The . . . success of the Holocaust was due in part to the skillful utilization of 'moral sleeping pills' made available by modern bureaucracy and modern technology."[12]

Detailed laws were written to define and identify the enemy and specify under what circumstances exceptions could be considered. The breadth of these laws was staggering. Jews were forbidden to have radios, bicycles, drive cars, have pets, go fishing, use the telephone, visit non-Jews. The lists went on and on and are exhausting to read. One Jewish business owner in Rotterdam, for instance, was informed: "I refer to your letter of 17/12/1943 and I inform you that your firm's name has been erased from the trade register and will henceforth be excluded, until you have yourself sterilized. In the meantime you are not allowed to exercise your profession."[13]

Laws were passed to strip the undesirables of citizenship and to ensure that the media supported the Nazi efforts. Bills were passed to fire all Jewish civil servants and professors and to expel all Jewish students from the universities. The military followed suit with its Jewish soldiers. Jewish-owned businesses were confiscated, and intimate relations between Jews and Christians were prohibited. Additional laws were passed to empower the police and army to support the killing efforts.

After removing Jews from all social and commercial contact with others, the next step was to force them out of their homes to specific areas or ghettoes, which became increasingly more restrictive in terms of movement and access to food. At one point, the Warsaw ghetto held 445,000 Jews in an area of 1.3 square miles. In terms of housing density, the average occupancy was 7.2 persons per room.[14]

The Nazis considered transporting the Jews elsewhere, deporting them to some country far away—Madagascar, to be precise—but retreated from that plan because of the time it would take and the expense of the operation. They also worried that these "racially infected deportees" might not stay put in Madagascar. Finally, aspirations aside, Germany lacked sufficient navy and shipping resources to transport *all* of its undesirables.

To transport victims to killing fields or to concentration camps would go more smoothly if the victims were already weakened or did not understand their fate. Thus, most prisoners, already apathetic from starvation and imprisonment and numbed by their encounters with brutality, more or less cooperated by boarding trains for "resettlement." They wondered, "Could the concentration camps be any worse than their life in the ghetto?"

The gas chambers were the culmination of the death factory efforts. By capitalizing on duplicity, the Nazis could march thousands of inmates to their death every day with minimal resistance. A marching band greeted arriving inmates.[15] Street signs en route to the gas chambers at Treblinka read Himmelfahrt Strasse (Street to Heaven), and the entrance to the showers (gas chambers) was indicated with a large, reassuring Star of David replete with a Hebrew inscription underneath: "This is the gateway to G—d. The righteous shall pass through." The newly arrived victims were stripped and marched to the showers, the doors were closed, and they died within twenty minutes from a shower of cyanide gas.[16]

For the Nazis, the hardest part of the killing was the destruction of the gassed bodies. The crematoria required considerable design experimentation in terms of airflow, chimney height, and other practical matters. There were also difficulties optimizing the body stacking to assure a rapid burn. The Nazis experimented and found that multiple bodies burned more rapidly and evenly if women, because of their higher fat content, were stacked at the bottom of the pyre.[17]

Bizarre medical experiments were performed on concentration camp inmates. Some were frankly sadistic, while many were both cruel and pointless (such as injecting inmates' lungs with tuberculosis bacilli to see how quickly the disease developed). As the war neared an end, anxious to cover up the evidence, the Nazis stepped up the killing in these medical research facilities. In a Hamburg facility, SS doctors rushed to kill children who had been victims of medical experiments. When drugs didn't finish them off, the children were hanged.[18]

The Nazis also conducted research on so-called racial science. In one study, reported at the Nuremberg war crimes trials, scientists lacked sufficient skulls of "Jewish-Bolshevik commissars" and complained that the scarcity of fresh skulls was hindering their work. "Only very few speci-

mens of [such] skulls are available. . . . The war in the East now presents us
with the opportunity to overcome this deficiency. By procuring the skulls
of the Jewish-Bolshevik commissars, who represent the prototype of the
repulsive, but characteristic subhuman, we have the chance now to obtain
scientific material." The best way of obtaining these skulls was to keep
inmates alive until a medical doctor could arrive and take the necessary
photographs. Then, "following the subsequently induced death of the Jew,
whose head should not be damaged, the physician will sever the head from
the body."[19]

Children were shot in front of their parents so that the parents would
know that their lineage had ended. Then the parents were shot. Some
guards enjoyed inflicting pain, and a smaller subset of sadists apparently
derived sexual gratification out of inflicting pain.[20] The vast majority of
killers merely regarded their work as "a job," made easier by alcohol and
habituation.

I mention such details because they bring into stark focus the central
question of this book: What kind of people could do this, not just once or
twice, but day in, day out, for months or years at a time? A minority (about
10 percent) asked to be transferred from the slaughter operations to the
front.[21] Some were sadists, but the rest of the hands-on killers reacted with
varying amounts of alcoholism, enthusiasm, or indifference. As historian
George Kren and psychologist Leon Rappoport concluded, the unhappy fact
"is that the overwhelming majority of SS men, leaders as well as rank and
file, would have easily passed all the psychiatric tests ordinarily given to
American army recruits or Kansas City policemen."[22]

All of this killing required the organizational skills of the desk murderers—the people who designed and ordered the killing from a distance.
These were the individuals on trial for their lives at Nuremberg.

To carry out killing on such a vast scale, the Nazis needed thousands
of individuals. They needed architects to design the concentration camps.
How wide should the roads be from the railroad terminus to the selection
point? What was the best way to schedule train transports to the killing
centers? What were the tradeoffs between shipping armaments to the
front versus cargo (people destined to be exterminated) to the camps? How
strong should the gas chamber doors be to contain the doomed prisoners?

How could one increase the production of lethal gas chemicals from the pharmaceutical companies without jeopardizing production of medications for the troops? This ministerial attention to detail was one of Germany's strong suits and a topic of special interest at Nuremberg.

The historian David Bankier highlighted one of the lesser-known examples of this attention to detail—Joseph Goebbels's efforts to shape propaganda messages for the Germans. Head of the Ministry of Enlightenment and Propaganda, Goebbels was a pioneer in the quality assurance movement. He meticulously deployed survey teams to towns throughout Germany to learn how best to shape his message. What did people think if police dispatches referred to prisoners as vermin instead of communists?[23] Euphemisms were developed to find acceptable terminology for the killing: *liquidiert* (liquidated), *erledigt* (finished off), *Aktionen* (actions), *Sauberung* (cleansing), *Aussiedlung* (resettlement).[24]

Raul Hilberg famously calculated the costs of the various killing campaigns. In the early days of the war, revenue from the expropriation of Jewish property and various punitive taxes more than exceeded the overhead and personnel costs for murdering the Jews. However, as the war dragged on and no additional revenues could be extracted, the net costs skyrocketed. It was expensive to build the killing camps and slave labor facilities, transport the prisoners to the camps, guard and kill them, and then burn the corpses.[25] Removing so many from the labor force was a disaster for Germany, and there were spirited, angry debates within Hitler's cabinet whether it was more productive to kill the inmates or use them to support the Reich's labor needs.[26] Even using the inmates for slave labor didn't make sense. Fritz Sauckel, one of the labor ministers, thought the policies were folly: "Underfed slaves, diseased, resentful, despairing and filled with hate, will never yield that maximum output which [is needed]."[27] But he did nothing to stop the killings. At a time when Germany could least afford the costs of the Final Solution, the Nazis persisted in killing; it was an obsession that made no economic or strategic sense.

Logical or not, the Nazis kept on killing. As a psychiatrist, I have seen an enormous amount of irrational self-destructive behavior. Why should it surprise me if an entire nation gets derailed and intoxicated by malice that was so clearly destructive to its own interests?

The Killers' Reaction to Their Labors

The Nazis experimented with various ways of killing. Their initial efforts focused on handicapped children, psychiatric patients, and other so-called useless eaters. It was hard work and morale was low, so the workers in one euthanasia factory celebrated their ten thousandth killing with a party, wrapping the corpse in flowers before cremating it.[28]

The Nazis tried gassing inmates in specially designed vans that killed the passengers with carbon monoxide. This worked, but the guards didn't like it. It took too long, the drivers heard the screams and moans of their passengers, it was hard to extricate the twisted bodies from the vans, and the guards became demoralized and started drinking more. Next, they put people in barns and set the buildings on fire. That worked, but it was slow and there were only so many vacant barns available. In the East, Nazi soldiers in *Einsatzgruppen* (task forces) shot vast numbers of people in the woods, forcing victims to dig their own graves and wait to be shot. Indeed, more people were shot by these mobile killing squads than were killed in the extermination camps themselves.

The murders haunted the executioners in their dreams, which they tried to blot out with drugs and alcohol. SS leader Heinrich Himmler visited one killing site and said, "Look at the eyes of the men in this Kommando, how deeply shaken they are! These men are finished for the rest of their lives. What kind of followers are we training here? Either neurotics or savages!" He tried to buck up their morale by reminding the killers that there was combat everywhere in nature and one must defend oneself against "vermin."[29] Hans Frank, head of the general government, tried to reassure the killers: "Gentlemen, I must ask you to rid yourselves of all feeling of pity. We must annihilate the Jews wherever we find them in order to maintain the structure of the Reich as a whole."[30]

The psychic toll on the killers was brought up at Nuremberg. Otto Ohlendorf, leader of the Ukrainian *Einsatzgruppe*, testified that the killing "was, psychologically, an immense burden to bear" and that "the burial of the victims was a great ordeal for the members of the *Einsatzkommandos*."[31] Himmler's SS doctor reported that even SS general Erich von dem Bach-Zelewski suffered from flashbacks about shooting Jews.[32]

The stressful nature of mass killing had a curious effect on the murderers: they distorted, revised, and rationalized what really happened. The political theorist Hannah Arendt summarized the implicit rationalizations used by the killing squads: "Instead of saying: What horrible things I did to people!, the murderers would . . . say: What horrible things I had to watch in the pursuance of my duties. How heavily the task weighed upon my shoulders!"[33]

The Final Tally

This was not your typical bloodlust killing. The concentration camps were built all across Europe (fig. 1). These were not isolated or rare installations; there were more than forty thousand camps—slave labor camps, ghettos, concentration camps, prisoner of war camps, and euthanasia centers scattered across greater Germany and points east. The different categories of camps varied enormously in terms of their lethality. Slave labor camps

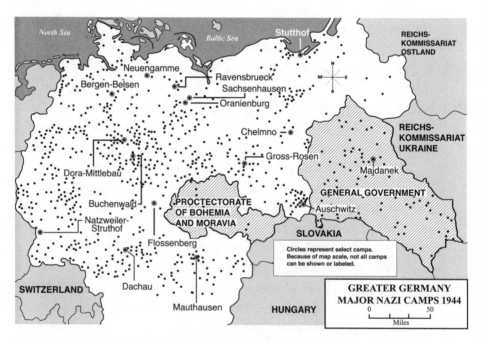

Fig. 1. Location of major Nazi camps in Greater Germany, 1944. (Reprinted with permission from the United States Holocaust Museum)

killed people slowly from overwork and starvation. Slave workers at one of the I. G. Farben camps were told that they had not come there to live but "to perish in concrete," and their life expectancy in fact averaged only three to four months.[34] On the other hand, extermination camps killed people with alarming alacrity; Nazi soldiers could unload hundreds of detainees from railcars and complete their murder and cremation within two hours flat.

When the war ended, the Nazis had murdered six million Jews and millions of other noncombatants—Poles, Russians, Ukrainians, and Byelorussians— as well as two hundred thousand Roma, three thousand Jehovah's Witnesses, seventy thousand mentally ill patients and disabled children, and ten thousand homosexuals.[35] These are difficult numbers to grasp, and historians still struggle to find a way of representing the enormity of the numbers. The number is HUGE, whether it is three million or thirteen million. If you stacked the murdered bodies head to toe and assumed an average height of five and a half feet, the bodies would stretch 6,250 miles, and that would be just the Jewish bodies.[36] Another way of summarizing the killing is to point out that by the end of the war, 75 percent of the concentration camp survivors were in fact the sole surviving members of their families.

The horrors of these mass killings have transfixed many a scholar and led to vituperative debates. The noted critic George Steiner observed: "I am not sure whether anyone . . . who spends time and imaginative resources on these dark places can . . . leave there personally intact." Noting that the camps are the transference of hell from below the earth to its surface, he continued: "The camp embodies, often down to minutiae, the images and chronicles of Hell in European art and thought. . . . We find the technology of pain without meaning, of bestiality without end, of gratuitous terror. For six hundred years the imagination dwelt on the flaying, the racking, the mockery of the damned, in a place of whips and hellhounds, of ovens and stinking air."[37] Steiner's statement was eerily true for those people who studied the war criminals at Nuremberg. There would be grim reverberations indeed in the lives of those who worked in such dark places.

With a crime of this magnitude, there would be retribution, but the Allies were unsure how to proceed. As a first step, the captured Nazi leaders had to be isolated somewhere until the Allies could sort out what to do with them. This sequestration offered the first glimpse into the psychology of the war criminals, and questions were immediately raised.

The Gathering at Ashcan

"Suppose," the Colonel commented, "someone had written a play . . .
and put all these characters on the stage when the curtain went up.
The playbill would have read, 'A jail in Luxembourg in June, 1945.'"
—John Kenneth Galbraith, writing about Ashcan, 1945

From Spa to Prison Camp

AS THE WAR WOUND DOWN, the Nazi leaders were corralled and tucked away
out of view. Nerves were raw from the sufferings of the war and the horror
of the mass killings. It was prudent to hold the Nazi leaders under tight security lest Nazi sympathizers try to free the prisoners or Nazi victims lynch
them, or lest the prisoners follow Hitler's example by killing themselves. All
three were serious possibilities.

The Nazi leaders' holding tank could not have been more surreal. The
young John Kenneth Galbraith sensed it right away—the utter improbabil-
ity of the thing. It was almost a play, with villains and champions appearing
scene by scene. On the champions' side were Warden Burton Andrus and
psychiatrist Douglas Kelley. On the other side were three of the four war
criminals who are the focus of this book (Hermann Göring, Robert Ley,
and Julius Streicher).[1]

Ground zero for this unlikely drama was the little village of Mondorf-
les-Bains in the Grand Duchy of Luxembourg, ten miles south of the city

Fig. 2. The Palace Hotel before World War II. (Reproduced with permission from John Dolibois, *Pattern of Circles: An Ambassador's Story* [Kent, OH: Kent State University Press, 1989])

of Luxembourg. The luxurious Palace Hotel had been in use since mid-nineteenth century as a spa resort (fig. 2). Its recent history was more complex. In the 1930s, refugees such as pianist Arthur Rubinstein fled here from the Nazis. In the early days of the war, vacationing Nazis stayed there for rest and recuperation. By 1945, US troops had taken occupation and were constructing fifteen-foot-high barbed-wire fences, watchtowers, and searchlights ringing the perimeter of the four-star resort.

The Palace Hotel had now morphed into Central Continental Prisoner of War Enclosure Number 32, code-named Ashcan.[2] Security was so tight that getting in required "a pass signed by God, and then somebody [had] to verify the signature."[3] In April 1945, a contingent of German POWs—cooks, barbers, hotel managers—moved into Ashcan to prepare the building for the arrival of high-ranking Nazi detainees. The luxury furnishings were removed and replaced with military cots, and as a suicide precaution, the glass windows were replaced with screens and bars.

Ashcan wasn't exactly a jail. Technically, it was a prisoner of war camp, and prisoners were free to circulate within its confines. It had somewhat the feel of an elegant, old university fraternity house, but with extras—guards carrying machine guns and the ever-present barbed-wire fences and search-lights. By mid-May 1945, Ashcan was ready to welcome its many guests. I can imagine the intense curiosity the prison staff must have felt when their guests arrived at the Palace Hotel.

Warden Andrus

On May 20, 1945, Colonel Burton C. Andrus was assigned as the com-mandant of Ashcan (fig. 3).[4] He first came under fire at the age of two months when his father, also a West Point graduate, had taken the family to live on the Indian frontier in the 1890s.[5] By the time Warden Andrus arrived at Mondorf-les-Bains fifty years later, he had completed an illustri-ous military career in the cavalry in World War I. During that war he had

Fig. 3. Burton C. Andrus, warden of Ashcan and Nuremberg. (National Archives)

developed a reputation for effective prison administration, imposing strict discipline on a previously chaotic military stockade in Georgia. At the end of World War I, he became a prison officer at the Presidio in Monterey, California. Following the war, he continued in the cavalry in a variety of postings.

Continuing his service in World War II, Andrus focused on air-ground coordination, security of the New York port, and traffic regulation in Europe. To our eyes, "traffic regulation" evokes images of speed cameras and radar traps. Then, however, that benign-sounding office oversaw the vital movement and coordination of troops and transport on the bombed-out roads of Europe.

That spring in 1945, Andrus was somewhat surprised to be summoned to the American embassy in Paris, where General Dwight D. Eisenhower ordered him to assume command of Ashcan.[6] On arriving at the camp, he saw security holes and immediately beefed up the perimeter with electric alarms on the fence, new and well-trained guards, camouflage netting, and more machine guns. With his previous experience in prison administration, he also focused on the conditions inside the fence. He needed doctors, adequate kitchen and sanitation facilities, and supplies, and he needed rules, clerks to type them up, and teleprinters for communication. Andrus was a very thorough man.

Many of the high-ranking Nazis arrived at Ashcan with suicide on their mind. They had the examples of Hitler, Goebbels, and Himmler, and some had already attempted suicide before arriving. Hans Frank had barely survived his attempt, slashing his wrist, arm, side, and throat, while Nazi foreign minister Joachim von Ribbentrop was so deeply depressed that the other prisoners worried about him. As a result, Andrus ordered thorough searches of every prisoner on arrival; he found razor blades taped to the soles of men's feet and vials of cyanide and other contraband in their clothes. He confiscated scissors, neckties, suspenders, batons, and all sharp instruments—anything that could be used for self-harm. Ultimately, his efforts to block suicide were doomed to failure.

Andrus made the prisoners' state of mind a chief concern. It was not that he liked them; indeed, he regarded them with considerable distaste. Rather, to his way of thinking, suicide was an act of insubordination—rule breaking—and he ran a tight ship. Suicide in these circumstances would also be a propaganda nightmare, suggesting a desperate response to barbaric treatment or else a successful act of defiance. In addition to these strategic concerns about suicide, Andrus was always a professional. Wardens look after their charges and guarantee their safety until such time that they are released (or executed). Thus, Andrus staffed Ashcan with morale officers. No one was going to die on his watch until he said so.

Göring Arrives

Reichsmarshall Hermann Göring had written to the US Army on May 7, 1945, announcing his intention to surrender, and by the next night, Göring was in American custody. He surrendered under highly unusual circumstances, for Hitler had sentenced him to death for disloyalty several weeks earlier. As a result, even in American captivity, Göring feared that the SS would kill him, and, strange as it may seem, for that first day, the American military allowed Göring's staff to accompany him and even keep their arms to protect him.

The next day, he was flown from the small alpine town of Kitzbühel, Austria, to Germany. It was an anxious flight because the pilot was unsure if the small two-seater plane could safely carry a man of Göring's heft. Once he got the plane off the ground, the pilot relaxed, later commenting, "[Göring] acted as though he was going on a sightseeing tour . . . and he was showing me where he grew up."[7]

When Göring landed, he expected to be treated as a head of state, and conflicts immediately ensued about his status. It was a foretaste of things to come. Göring eventually arrived at Ashcan on May 20, 1945. As Warden Andrus noted, "He brought with him sixteen matched monogrammed suitcases, a red hatbox and his valet," and he had red nail polish on his fingernails and toenails. He also brought along approximately twenty thousand paracodeine pills, noting that he required forty pills a day "for his heart." After some discussion, Göring admitted that he used the paracodeine, a morphinelike derivative, to treat his long-term morphine addiction.[8] His addiction dated back to the 1923 Munich Putsch, when he was shot in the leg and developed chronic pain. He had been hospitalized in 1925 in Sweden and again in Germany in 1927 because of his addiction.[9]

In addition to his medical problems, Göring presented other challenges. A search of his accompanying baggage revealed a vial of cyanide buried in a tin of Nescafé and a second vial sewn into one of his uniforms. He would need to be watched.

Göring had expected to be housed in a luxurious spa while details of the German demobilization were worked out. Instead, he was greeted by Warden Andrus, whom he instinctively despised. The warden, as the expression goes, "loved his job." He was a bit of a martinet, and observers noted that "when he walked, he marched!"[10] He used to say, "Hell, I was fourteen years old before I learned that God's last name wasn't 'Damn.'"[11] Göring, with his taste for luxury and cynicism, had no patience for Andrus's straight-laced persona. Sparks flew immediately when Andrus and Göring met. Andrus considered Göring a "simpering slob" and described him contemptuously, noting "the blubber of high living wobbling under his jacket."[12]

Göring was the key detainee. When he arrived at Ashcan, the five-foot, six-inch Göring weighed in at 264 pounds. He was perspiring profusely, was short of breath and tremulous, and had an irregular heartbeat. He was so obese that the first chair he sat in collapsed. He gave a history of numerous "heart attacks" over the preceding years. This notation of heart attacks was my first indication of how difficult it would be to pin down the medical and psychiatric history of the Nuremberg war criminals. In 1945, before the widespread availability of electrocardiograms and blood tests for cardiac enzymes, "heart attack" could mean anything from palpitations to sudden death. In Göring's case, it probably denoted arrhythmias, no doubt worsened by anxiety and drug withdrawal. It is also possible, however, that they were panic attacks. His medical evaluation at Ashcan notes that the "frequent, recurrent heart attacks [were] manifested by pericardial distress, dyspnea, profuse perspiration, and nervousness," all of which can also be found in panic attacks.[13]

A few days after his arrival, on May 26, Göring was started on a slow reduction in his paracodeine dose. He developed bronchitis on May 31, and the drug taper was suspended for a few weeks. On July 19, he complained of headaches and sleeplessness. By the end of that month, he had dropped twenty pounds, but his blood pressure was soaring. Andrus noted, "He whined and wailed as he saw one tablet less in each second handful. . . . By 12th August we had him completely free of the drug habit."[14] Throughout it all, Göring continued to have "heart attacks," and Andrus came under fire from his superiors, who were concerned that their prisoner might die before trial. Between Göring's increasing cardiac symptoms and pressure from his superiors, Andrus was worried. No, he didn't like Göring; he just didn't want anything to happen to him at Ashcan on his watch. So Andrus requested the addition of a physician on his staff with expertise in medicine, drug addiction, and heart disease. Army doctor Douglas Kelley seemed to fit the bill, and he was flown in to Mondorf-les-Bains on August 4, 1945.[15] His orders were cryptic: "You are to contact Captain Miller at . . . Palace Hotel at Mondorf Lesbains . . . Captain Miller will give you specific instructions as to your mission."[16]

Douglas Kelley: A Most Unusual Psychiatrist

During the war, Douglas Kelley, MD, was chief psychiatrist at the US Army 130th general hospital in Belgium, where he established an effective program for treating combat exhaustion. He was a decidedly unusual and eccentric man who was well respected both for his accomplishments and for his personality. It was an easy matter to transfer him to Mondorf-les-Bains. Kelley was a brilliant, garrulous raconteur, able to hit it off well with all sorts of people. However, he could be glib, and he loved the spotlight, which antagonized others, particularly later during the politically sensitive war trials.

Kelley had grown up in Truckee, California, a descendant of the pioneering McGlashan family, who included many lawyers and judges. He was quite literally a genius, having been part of the famous Terman study of gifted youth (fig. 4). He was interested in forensic psychiatry, was skeptical of scammers and malingerers, and defined mental illness narrowly. And, oh, was he a talker! He had a remarkable gift of gab and could quickly assess people's strengths and vulnerabilities. Among other talents, he was also a professional magician and, after the war, was even vice president of

Fig. 4. Douglas M. Kelley, circa 1945. (Reprinted
with permission from Douglas Kelley)

the Society of American Magicians. And did I mention that Douglas Kelley
happened to be a world-renowned expert in the Rorschach?

Robert Ley Arrives

Two more war criminals need to be introduced before we leave Ashcan
for Nuremberg. Contemporary readers may be unfamiliar with Robert Ley,
but he was one of the highest-ranking Nazi leaders captured. On May 16,
1945, Ley was apprehended in his pajamas in the town of Schleching, near
Berchtesgaden, where he was hiding under the name of Dr. Ernst Distel-
meyer. He tried to poison himself on capture, but the bottle was knocked
out of his hands. Then, when he was searched, troops discovered a cyanide
capsule hidden in his ring. On his arrival at Ashcan, Ley was allowed to
change from his pajamas to khakis, but even so, he "looked like a Bowery
bum who had got into an induction center while on a toot."[17]

In the early days of the Nazi Party, Ley had been a beer hall hooligan,
but by the end of the war he had acquired an incredibly large portfolio of

responsibility. He was yet another editor of yet another anti-Semitic newspaper, but his main claim to fame was heading up the German Labor Front. He destroyed the independent labor unions (and their leaders, of course), built a labor force that was aligned with Nazi war plans, and helped organize slave labor to support the war effort. His closeness to Hitler shielded him from charges of arrogance and incompetence. Ley was a dreamer, with little follow-through and spotty organizational abilities, and his domain of dreams was broad—including the Volkswagen as a car for the masses; banks, travel agencies, and cruise ships dedicated to the workers; and total worker surveillance to ensure their reliability.

Ley had a severe stammer that dated back to World War I, when his plane was shot down. He was unconscious for hours, and when he wakened from his coma, he couldn't talk at all. Thereafter, unless he'd had a few drinks, he spoke with hesitancy. This is not an uncommon phenomenon; perhaps it contributed to his alcoholism. With alcohol on board, his speeches were not particularly clear in terms of content, but they were effective as emotional rabble-rousing.

He led a troubled life.[18] He had a track record of embarrassing the Nazi Party because of his very public embezzlements and drunkenness. Ley quarreled constantly with other high party officials in an effort to expand his empire. Albert Speer called him a "vulgar drunkard," and Alfred Rosenberg complained of Ley's "organizational gigantomania." Others used saltier language, calling him a "geistloser Schwatzer" (mindless bullshitter).[19]

Throughout it all, Ley was unpredictable. He loved his second wife, Inge, so much that at one dinner party, he tore her clothes off so that his guests could admire her body.[20] Inge soon had had enough; between his behavior and her drug addiction, it was too much. She shot herself in December 1942. Ley's behavior deteriorated. He became even more erratic, and his staff worried about his violent temper and out-of-control drinking. Himmler was so concerned that he asked his private physician to treat Ley. The physician soon gave up, noting that after a month, he "had not once found Ley sober when he made his house calls."[21]

At Ashcan, few of the other leading Nazis would have anything to do with Ley. There had been too many turf struggles with him, and his alcoholism and corruption were too much even for Göring. Ley's interrogations at Ashcan were difficult. When questioned, he would get carried away with the topic, shouting, stammering, and pacing the room. Throughout the interrogations, Ley argued that he could be useful to the Allies by organizing their working classes, just as he had done so effectively in Germany. His offers were declined.

Julius Streicher Arrives

One week after Ley arrived at Ashcan, newspaper publisher Julius Streicher, also known as "Jew-Baiter Number One," was captured by American troops in Waidring, just over the Austrian border from Berchtesgaden.[22] Streicher had been masquerading as an artist named Joseph Sailer and was indeed painting a scene of the Alps when he was apprehended. When he arrived at Mondorf-les-Bains days later, he complained that in the interim, he had been tortured by black soldiers who forced him to drink out of the urinal and burned his feet with cigarettes—all while Jews photographed him.[23]

Paradoxically, at Mondorf, Streicher claimed a change of heart toward the Jews. "An American came in with a pitcher of cocoa and some biscuits. He set them on a table and stepped back. 'This is from me to you, Mr. Streicher. I am a Jew.' I broke down and cried. . . . I have always said there were no good Jews, but this has proved to me that I am wrong."[24] The change of heart about Jews must have been transient, because Warden Andrus wrote: "He was so obsessed with hatred that when he mentioned the word 'Jew' he trembled visibly."[25]

Other staff at Ashcan noted how Streicher bragged about his accomplishments and would start ranting, volubly carried away by excitement. He felt that other Nazis had cheated him out of getting credit for inspiring the Nuremberg laws.[26]

Streicher was a tactless, uncouth man whom the other internees detested. He was obsessed with sex, bragging that if people wanted to see how strong he was, they should make a woman available to him in prison. At one point, when he was asked to undress for a physical examination, the female interpreter started to leave the room. "Streicher leered at her and said, 'What's the matter? Are you afraid of seeing something nice?'"[27] This was not a man who cared about making a good impression.

Tact had never been Streicher's strong suit. During the war, he gossiped that Göring was not man enough to have a child and that Göring's daughter, Edda, must have been a product of artificial insemination. What's worse, he published the rumor in *Der Stürmer*. Göring had him arraigned in front of the Nazi Party Arbitration and Investigation Committee. The Nazi judge presiding over the trial stated, "We were ready to stop that sick mind once and for all."[28] Because of this accusation and his many shady business transactions, in 1940, Streicher was confined to house arrest on his farm for the rest of the war.[29]

Life at Ashcan

The status of the detainees was uncertain. Were they in protective custody, war criminals, prisoners of war? They had not been indicted or charged with any crimes. Rather, they were being held as POWs and thus had less restricted activities than they would in a formal prison. In Ashcan, the detainees regarded their sequestration as temporary until the terms of the Allied victory could be nailed down. In the months of their detention, intelligence officers frequently interrogated them, but the detainees had plenty of time to pace on the long veranda, to think, and to gossip. Despite its somewhat Spartan furnishings, the prison resembled a retreat center. A famous photograph captures the detainees in a posed moment as "the Class of 1945" in front of the hotel (fig. 5).

The detainees were eager to talk. They were bored, worried, and accustomed to being in the center of things. "They felt neglected if they hadn't been interrogated by someone for several days. If you were interrogated a lot, it meant you were important."[30] Some talked out of guilt, but as John Dolibois, the Ashcan intelligence officer, put it, "[Their] favorite pastime was casting blame." These comments help us understand the detainees' unusual openness to psychiatric interviews and psychological examinations.

Göring constantly chafed against the rules and regarded Andrus as a petty tyrant. He called him "that pompous fireman" because of Andrus's proclivity to tour the camp wearing his highly polished red helmet. Andrus was fit to be tied: "They are perverts, dope fiends and liars. When Dr. Frank got here he was wearing a pair of lace panties. Goering brought

Fig. 5. The "Class of 45" detainees at Mondorf-les-Bains, Luxembourg.
Julius Streicher, top row extreme right; Robert Ley, row beneath
second from right; Hermann Göring in front row center.
(Reprinted with permission from Associated Press Images)

an apple-cheeked 'valet' with him. When Ley got here he had a gonorrheal stricture and complained that he couldn't live without women. When [Wehrmacht commander Wilhelm] Keitel got here we took his baton away from him and he went all to pieces and wrote a letter to Eisenhower. These are the eagles who planned and executed world war."[31]

From the distance, the detainees were all high-ranking Nazis, and it could be assumed that they saw things similarly. In reality, they were a disparate lot—generals, cabinet members, industrialists, propagandists. Many held longtime grudges against one another. Göring insisted that he was the senior commander of the internees, but Admiral Karl Dönitz, not Göring, was Hitler's named successor. Wilhelm Frick (Reich minister of the interior) complained that Göring treated him like a little boy.[32] Streicher complained that Goebbels had cheated him out of receiving credit for the Nuremberg race laws. Göring complained that Goebbels and Ribbentrop turned Hitler against him.[33] Almost all of the other Nazis shunned Streicher. Dönitz and several others immediately moved their chairs and refused point-blank to sit with him because they regarded him as a sadist, rapist, and loathsome pornographer.[34]

Streicher's only friend at Mondorf was Ley, and they were known as the "Bobbsey twins," not just because they sat together but also because they resembled each other physically.[35] Through it all, Streicher paced with the rest of them on the hotel veranda, but he alone would stand at attention, salute, and shout out, "Heil Hitler!"[36]

Ashcan Is Emptied

After roughly three months, Ashcan was closed on August 12, 1945, and the building reverted to the Palace Hotel. The detainees (as well as Warden Andrus and psychiatrist Kelley) were transferred to Nuremberg. There they were joined by the detainee Rudolf Hess, psychologist Gustave Gilbert, and prosecutor Justice Robert Jackson. We will make their acquaintance in Chapter 4. A brief interlude, however, is necessary in order to consider how a war crimes trial came about in the first place and why in Nuremberg.

What became of Ashcan? In 1988, the Palace Hotel was torn down and a new hotel, Mondorf Domaine Thermal, occupies the site today.[37] As a contemporary guidebook describes it, "This health resort is known for its idyllic location, with vineyards and woods to the east and the Lorraine Hills to the west."[38] Not a word about Ashcan.

PART TWO

NUREMBERG

3

The Nuremberg War Crimes Trial: What Do We Do with the Criminals?

[The trial] can hold up a mirror to Germany and help her to solve her own perplexing mystery—that mystery which, in Nuremberg and the countryside around it, is set out in flowers. . . . It is difficult not to conclude that a people who so love flowers must love all beautiful and simple things. The . . . landscape continues this protestation of innocence, this artless seduction. Where the pine trees rise from the soft, reddish bed of scented pine needles, . . . and the miller's little blond son plays with the gray kitten among the meadowsweet by the end of the millpond, there can surely be no harm. There is, of course, evidence to the contrary.

—Rebecca West, "Extraordinary Exile," September 7, 1946

The wrongs which we seek to condemn and punish have been so calculated, so malignant, and so devastating, that civilization cannot tolerate their being ignored, because it cannot survive their being re-peated. That four great nations, flushed with victory and stung with injury, stay the hand of vengeance and voluntarily submit their cap-tive enemies to the judgment of the law is one of the most significant tributes that Power has ever paid to reason.

—Justice Robert Jackson, opening address, International
Military Tribunal, November 21, 1945

The Purpose of the Trial

WHILE THE GUESTS AT ASHCAN were walking the veranda of the Palace Hotel that long summer, the Allies were hammering out the details of what
would develop into the International Military Tribunal. The conversations
had been ongoing since 1943 but kept breaking down. What should be done
with the captured leaders of the Third Reich? History provided no rules for
what to do with defeated wartime leaders. Napoleon Bonaparte was exiled
and imprisoned on the island of Elba, and Kaiser Wilhelm II abdicated and
spent his remaining years in exile after World War I. Such leniency rankled,
particularly in the shadow of the concentration camps.

It was no surprise, then, that the Allies disagreed about having a trial at
all. The Russians saw no need for one and favored quick executions in a
back alley. At the Tehran conference in 1943, Joseph Stalin proposed execut-
ing between fifty thousand and a hundred thousand German military officers. Winston Churchill was so incensed by the suggestion that he threatened to walk out, and Franklin D. Roosevelt broke the tension by joking that
perhaps only forty-nine thousand would need to be shot.[1] The three leaders'
positions on these points waffled as the war wound down. At a subsequent
meeting, Churchill proposed that the Nazi leaders be summarily shot, but
Stalin of all people replied: "In the Soviet Union, we never execute anyone
without a trial."[2] Some Americans thought that selective trials were a waste
of time and that it would make more sense to execute LOTS of Germans. Joseph Pulitzer thought that one and a half million was about the right number.[3] Over time, though, US leaders decided that a public trial was necessary
not only to punish the Nazi leaders but also to unmask their brutality.

Ultimately, the International Military Tribunal was created. The Third
Reich had destroyed any notion that justice could be found in the German
court system, and the international trials were designed to demonstrate that
law and justice had returned to Germany. All the same, the attitude of the
Russians throughout the trials was more or less accurately characterized as:
"Can we kill them now?" Early in the proceedings, there was a formal re-
ception for court personnel, and Andrey Vyshinsky, Stalin's prosecutor for
the Purge trials, proposed a toast "to the prisoners and their march [from]
the Palace of Justice to the gallows."[4] The trial hadn't even started yet. Were

the judges supposed to raise their glasses to such a toast? Russian legal scholar Aron Trainin opined: "In meting out punishment to the Axis War Criminals, Russia would not permit herself to be restricted by traditional legalisms."[5]

Even after agreeing to a trial, the Allies were uncertain about its wisdom. Would it not appear to be merely another show trial? Wasn't this just an instance of victors' justice? Given the Russians' role in the mass murders in Poland and Ukraine, would the Allies be viewed as hypocrites in their judgment and revenge against the Nazi defendants? It would take the Allies all summer long in 1945 to thrash out these details. Not least among their disputes was the venue for the trial.

The disagreements among the Allies foreshadowed the corrosive conflicts that came to dominate Nuremberg. So much horror was revealed that its caustic effects spilled over onto everyone in attendance—the lawyers, judges, guards, interpreters, witnesses, and, certainly, prison psychiatrists and psychologists. Those emotional reverberations would come to haunt the psychiatric assessment of the prisoners.

There is a term for it—countertransference—which needs some explanation. I teach medical students and have heard a recurring lament over the years: "Why is it that I am so exhausted when I am on my psychiatry clerkship? I don't get it; the call schedule is light and the patients aren't dying, but after listening all day, I leave the ward feeling like I could scream." When you sit with a patient, you cannot help having an emotional response to what the patient discloses. Novice therapists are sometimes taken aback by these emotional reverberations, and they don't know how to deal with them. Over the years, I've treated thousands of patients, but even if I had seen ten times that many patients, had I been assigned to Nuremberg, I don't think my clinical experience would have prepared me for encountering the horror so close up.

Nuremberg: Site for the International Military Tribunal

All this monstrosity was unveiled in a place previously famed for its beauty and culture. Nuremberg had a centuries-long reputation for toy making—lovely porcelain dolls, artfully constructed wooden toys, tin models, absolutely captivating toy trains and steam engines. The Nazi Party changed all that. Storm Troopers rallied in vast plazas and amphitheaters. Thudding boots, hoarsely shouted oaths, waving torches, and banners of black and red and white pushed the toys aside. When the Reichstag convened there in 1935 to pass the Nuremberg racial laws, the city was already home to scurrilous Nazi propaganda newspapers. It would soon have a large armaments industry dependent on slave labor and its very own concentration camp, Flossenbürg. The toys were gone. In their place came war, and by the war's end, Nuremberg was no more. Repeated bombing sorties had destroyed over 90 percent of the buildings; an estimated thirty thousand bodies rotted in the ruins. The place stunk with death and gloom. Nuremberg had disappeared into the night and fog.

Ironically, the Nuremberg Palace of Justice survived relatively unscathed and became ground zero for the Trial of the Major War Criminals before the International Military Tribunal (fig. 6). Conveniently adjacent to the Nuremberg courthouse, a large prison had also survived the bombings. The extensive destruction surrounding these buildings provided a natural security perimeter for the trial.

In addition to these concrete advantages, Nuremberg was the symbolic center of Nazi Germany. If one were to go to "the belly of the beast" of Nazi Germany for a trial, there would be few venues better than Nuremberg. It was thus both a pragmatic and deeply symbolic venue for the trial. But what kind of trial?

The Legal Team: Quarrels and Grudges

Supreme Court Justice Robert Jackson was chosen as the lead American prosecutor (fig. 7). Jackson grew up in rural New York. He never attended college, and his legal training consisted of one year at Albany Law School, followed by a legal apprenticeship. His law practice flourished, and he became noted for his eloquence. He began his federal service in 1934 and worked his way up from general counsel of the Bureau of Internal Revenue to assistant attorney general, solicitor general, and attorney general. In 1941, he was appointed an associate justice of the United States Supreme Court.[6]

Fig. 6. Aerial view of the Nuremberg Palace of Justice, November 20, 1945. The
Nuremberg Palace of Justice is the large building in the center; at right is the
courthouse. Behind the palace is the prison (surrounded by a semicircular wall).
Historical and Special Collections, Harvard Law School Library. (National Archives)

President Roosevelt died on April 12, 1945. By coincidence, the next day,
Jackson was scheduled to give a lecture on "the rule of law among nations."
He told his audience that although he had no objections to summary executions, he worried that they would make martyrs of the Nazi leaders if
executions were used in place of a trial. As to having a trial, he spoke about
his concerns regarding jurisdiction and application of international laws
"by which standards of guilt may be determined." He concluded with this
telling observation: "You must put no man on trial before anything that
is called a court . . . if you are not willing to see him freed if not proven
guilty."[7] There were ears in that audience.

Fig. 7. Justice Robert H. Jackson. (National Archives)

Two weeks later, President Harry Truman asked Jackson to take a leave of absence from the Supreme Court and to lead the US prosecution. In the next month, there were so many squabbles within the government and in the press concerning the mission of the tribunal that Jackson threatened to resign if the hard-liners tried to undercut the legal proceedings. The newspapers called him "soft on Germany." Still, Jackson prevailed, assembled his team, moved to Europe, and began to amass the evidence. On June 7, 1945, he published his persuasive justification for the war crimes trial:

> What shall we do with them? We could, of course, set them at large without a hearing. But it has cost unmeasured thousands of American lives to beat and bind these men. To free them without a trial would mock the dead and make cynics of the living. On the other hand, we could execute or otherwise

punish them without a hearing. But undiscriminating executions or punishments without definite findings of guilt, fairly arrived at, . . . would not set easily on the American conscience. . . . The only other course is to determine the innocence or guilt of the accused after a hearing as dispassionate as the times and horrors we deal with will permit. . . . We are put under a heavy responsibility to see that our behavior during this unsettled period will direct the world's thought toward a firmer enforcement of the laws of international conduct, so as to make war less attractive to those who have governments and the destinies of peoples in their power.[8]

Jackson spent the summer of 1945 gathering evidence and negotiating the procedures that would be used for the trial. Agreement among the Allies was difficult because of emerging Cold War rivalries and divergent legal traditions. At one point in the discussions about the structure of the emerging trial, Russian major-general Iona Nikitchenko turned to Jackson, asking, "What is meant in the English by 'cross-examine?'"[9] It was just a foretaste.

Nuremberg was just the first of hundreds of war crimes trials that ultimately prosecuted thousands of defendants. Hitler, Goebbels, and Himmler had all killed themselves earlier; others had gone missing. At Nuremberg, the Allies prosecuted the highest-ranking Nazi leaders they could find— leaders who ran the economy, the military, and the propaganda apparatus. Here was the opportunity for the world to see them up close, to hear them, to try to understand what made them tick.

The trial involved approximately fifteen hundred interpreters, lawyers, interrogators, jailers, and others who were closely monitored by hundreds of journalists, including Rebecca West, Walter Lippmann, and John Dos Passos, as well as visiting movie stars like Rita Hayworth and Marlene Dietrich. Not surprisingly, orchestrating this was a nightmare.[10]

I've been in courtrooms before and know their rituals of who sits where and who speaks when. I have seen how each side tries to spin its version of the truth and have sat through hours of tedious testimony. I can't imagine what it would have been like to sit in that courtroom for a ten-month trial. The reports are clear that at Nuremberg there were long intervals of monotony, punctuated by horrifying testimony and frankly odd behaviors on many peoples' part, no matter where they sat in the courtroom.

There was discord among the judges and prosecuting attorneys. Justice Robert Jackson had voluntarily stepped down from the Supreme Court to be the lead prosecutor; it rankled him to have his pleadings decided on by judges like Francis Biddle, whom he regarded as his junior. Biddle, in turn, scorned Jackson, writing: "Jackson's cross-examination, on the whole, has been futile and weak. . . . Bob doesn't listen to the answers, depends on his notes, always a sign of weakness. He hasn't absorbed his case."[11]

Most observers agreed that Jackson was indeed rusty on his cross-examination skills but enormously eloquent in his prepared statements. His closing statement, for instance, replete with allusions to Shakespeare, still rings loudly today: "[The accused] stand before this Trial as blood-stained Gloucester stood by the body of his slain king. He begged of the widow, as they beg of you: 'Say I slew them not.' And the Queen replied: 'Then say there were not slain. But dead they are . . .' If you were to say of these men that they are not guilty, it would be as true to say that there has been no war, there are no slain, there has been no crime."[12]

Despite his gift for eloquence, Jackson believed that the case would be made on the basis of an abundance of captured Third Reich documents. From Jackson's point of view, documents had advantages over witnesses. Witnesses could be problematic—there might be difficulties locating them, their memories could be hazy, and their motivations impugned. But documents were there in black and white. At Nuremberg, the amount of documentary evidence was breathtaking. It filled six boxcars and sprawled over millions of pages, including a hundred thousand affidavits and potential testimony from more than thirty-five thousand witnesses.[13]

Jackson was correct, but others noted that the trial was important beyond simply convicting the defendants. General William Donovan, head of the Office of Strategic Services (OSS), believed that live testimony was crucial if the trial were to have an impact on the German people and the rest of the world.[14] Without riveting testimony, it was unlikely that the trial would garner attention. Donovan volunteered to assist Jackson with the prosecution, but sadly, their blurred reporting lines and responsibilities fostered distrust.

Donovan was also keenly aware of the rapidly fraying alliance between the Soviet Union and the West. In his view, it was vital for the West to secure an alliance with their former German enemies against the Russians and for the West to acquire the remnants of the Nazis' military capabilities. Although these matters would become very important in the Cold War years, they were irrelevant to Jackson.

Their disagreements became personal: Jackson considered Donovan a shallow social climber who was trying to smear him.[15] Donovan thought that Jackson was naive about the larger picture of foreign relations and world opinion. Such conflicts percolated down to their legal staffs. Who was more important—the document sleuths or the interrogators?

The international competition was both intense and petty. Thomas Dodd, one of the American prosecutors, painted a vivid description of the rivalries in his letters home. "There is terrific jockeying for position. Everyone wants to be in the act. A lot of little people in big uniforms frantically seeking a place in the sun."[16]

The bickering was ever-present. The whiff of fame turned many a level head. On the first day of trial, there was a quarrel among the judges over whose chair was higher or lower. Even at the end, on the day of execution, the pettiness continued. When the court's judgments were read on October 1, 1946, Jackson refused the military's request to sit as official observers with the prosecutor's team. The generals got their revenge weeks later. Remembering Jackson's slight, the military retaliated by refusing to admit one of Jackson's staff members as a witness to the execution.[17]

Even after months of negotiating procedures for the trial, there were conflicting interpretations of jurisprudence among the Allies. The Russians' behavior was troublesome. The Russian Nikitchenko switched jobs in midstream from prosecutor to judge and had different ideas about judicial impartiality. He saw no need for a lengthy trial just to "create a sort of fiction that the judge is a disinterested person. . . . [That] would lead only to delays."[18] As a spokesman for Stalin, he believed in speedy trials.

The Course of the Trial

Warden Burton Andrus fretted about the prisoners' security. He complained bitterly that there were not enough guards, that their training was inadequate and morale was low. At Ashcan, he had worried about a jail breakout or else vigilantes breaking in. At Nuremberg, other problems preoccupied him. His concerns would be borne out.

Suicide was a constant threat. Andrus was hardly a fan of psychiatry and psychology, but he rather liked the blunt-talking Kelley and, despite initial reluctance, followed many of Kelley's recommendations for maintaining the prisoners' morale. Simultaneously, Andrus imposed strict security on the prison. Prisoners and their cells were repeatedly searched; access was tightly controlled, and guards observed all prisoners one-on-one for twenty-four hours a day. The desks and chairs in the cells were flimsily constructed so that they could not be used for harm.

It didn't work. Dr. Leonardo Conti managed to hang himself on October 5, 1945. Conti had been the SS chief of health, and his specialty was mercy killing. He was being held at Nuremberg for a later trial, but he escaped through suicide. It wasn't the last suicide at Nuremberg either. There would be two more, each more spectacular than the last, and Andrus's reputation sank lower with each suicide. He kept tightening security, drilling his staff, and enforcing such harsh discipline on the prisoners that he came to haunt the prisoners in their dreams. Eight of the defendants told their attorneys that they had recurrent nightmares about the warden.[19] There were other problems—scuffles and bickering among the prisoners. Streicher spat on Hans Fritzsche of the propaganda ministry; SS general Ernst Kaltenbrunner had a stroke. This was not going an easy assignment for Andrus.

On October 19, 1945, Warden Andrus delivered the indictments to the prisoners. They were asked to write down their responses. Hermann Göring inscribed, "The victor will always be the judge and the vanquished the accused." Rudolf Hess wrote, "I can't remember." When offered a list of possible lawyers, Julius Streicher said, "Jews, these are all Jew names, and I know the judges are Jews too." Robert Ley, holding his arms out like Christ on the cross, greeted the group by shouting, "Why don't you just line us up against a wall and shoot us?"[20]

At last the trial began on November 20, 1945. After all of the testimony, the prosecution summarized the case beginning on July 26, 1946, and the tribunal adjourned for deliberation. Their judgment was delivered on October 1, 1946 (fig. 8). Two weeks later, the sentences were carried out.

Fig. 8. Judgment day. The court rises as judges enter at the beginning of the session to announce their judgment of the defendants at Nuremberg. (National Archives)

The Defendants' Behavior during the Trial

The trial presented an unusual opportunity for psychological observations in the courtroom, in the jail dining room, and in the prisoners' cells. Some of the defendants' behavior was apparent to all; some was revealed only during psychiatric interviews. It was immediately apparent that the defendants were extraordinarily heterogeneous. Some were very high-ranking; others were indicted almost by accident as prisoners of convenience. Whatever their rank in the Nazi hierarchy, many of them loathed each other. Joachim von Ribbentrop and Hermann Göring continually sparred. On one occasion, Göring tried to strike Ribbentrop with his marshal's baton, shouting, "Shut up, you champagne peddler," while Ribbentrop retorted, "I am still Foreign Minister and my name is *von* Ribbentrop," thereby asserting his nobility.[21]

Under the mounting pressures of the trial, the animosities increased. Göring called witnesses for the prosecution "swine," and Streicher cackled gleefully that they would all hang, even people like Albert Speer, former minister of armaments and war production, who had cooperated with the prosecution. The defendants were in agreement about one thing: Foreign Minister von Ribbentrop's incompetence. Baldur von Schirach, head of the Hitler Youth and Gauleiter (district leader) of Vienna, was delighted to see Ribbentrop revealed as "a phony." Hjalmar Schacht, minister of economics and Reichsbank president, called him a "scatter-brained idiot," and Franz von Papen, Hitler's vice-chancellor, referred to him as a "nitwit."[22] As the Nuremberg interrogator Joseph Maier succinctly summed up, "What a motley crew!"[23]

Most of the defendants shifted blame elsewhere, principally to the dead Hitler and Himmler, who could no longer retaliate against them. Ten months of testimony had repeating themes: it was terrible that all these things happened, but we didn't know, or if we did know, we didn't know the extent of the killing, or if we opposed the killings, Hitler would have ordered us shot, or all we did was fill out the forms. Defendant Fritz Sauckel's response is typical: "I just can't get it through my head how these things were possible.—About the misuse of foreign workers.—I am really not responsible for that. I was like a seamen's agency. If I supply hands for a ship, I am not responsible for any cruelty that may be exercised about ship without my knowledge. I just supplied workers to places like the Krupp works at Hitler's orders. I am not to blame if they were later mistreated."[24]

Göring would have none of that. He viewed such arguments as craven and undignified excuses. It was tantamount to selling your soul to the enemy, and he was determined to dominate the trial and his fellow defendants. Prosecutor Dodd observed: "He is browbeating and threatening them—and particularly those who might admit some guilt. He wants all to hang together—and to prove that Roosevelt was the cause of the war!"[25] After hearing a particularly damning witness for the prosecution, Göring shouted to his fellow defendants: "Dammit, I just wish we could all have the courage to confine our defense to three simple words: Lick my arse."[26]

Göring, who fancied himself the leader of the defendants, told Kelley, "We are sort of like a team, all of us who have been accused, and it is up to us to stick together to accomplish the strongest defense. Naturally, I am the leader, so it is my problem to see that each of us contributes his share."[27]

In the early days of the trial, Göring cracked the whip at lunchtime if he saw anyone wavering. He didn't want any dissension, plea deals, shifting of blame, or acknowledgment of guilt. Speer tattled on him, and Andrus promptly changed the lunch-hour regulations. Strange things pop up in archives. I was working at the National Archives in College Park, Maryland, when I stumbled on the warden's seating chart for lunch (fig. 9). There it was, a map of the tables with seating assignments for each table. You would think this was a formal dinner party, but what was really being "served" was Göring's isolation from the other defendants. He sat alone.[28] In the prisoners' dock that isolation was impossible, with Göring in the front row whispering and commenting sotto voce throughout the trial.

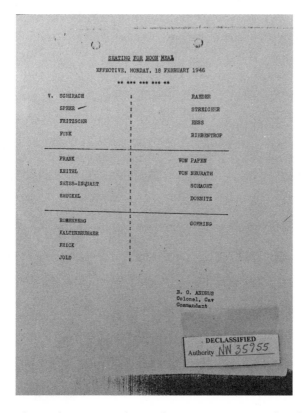

Fig. 9. The warden's seating chart isolating Göring. (National Archives)

During the trial, Hess pretended to be bored and uninterested by ostenta-tiously reading novels or else moaning in pain. He would pose enormous challenges not just for the judges but also for his defense attorneys. Strei-cher was absolutely impossible, antagonizing any sentient being within ear-shot. There is an old saying, "The tongue is enemy to the neck." This proved quite literally true for him.

The Outcome of the Trial

After almost a year of testimony and deliberation, the courtroom went quiet. The observers and participants in the trial were happy to leave the bombed-out city and start writing their memoirs. The participants knew they had lived and worked in a setting of extraordinary historical impor-tance and tensions. Ursula Sherman, a research analyst at subsequent Ger-man war crimes trials, summed it up: "All of us that worked on those things went a little nuts. We used to have temper tantrums. It was one way of letting off steam. The horror kind of crept up on me during the year and after."[29]

Thoughtful observers were troubled by what the trial revealed about hu-man nature. Brady Bryson, one of the Nuremberg attorneys, remarked, "We live in a very dangerous, vicious, wicked world, and this trial hasn't done anything at all to turn off the tap of human energy that nourishes war. . . . [Our] Big Brain. . . . was fatally flawed, because it brought together immense intellectual resources and the commitment to violence."[30]

In large organizations, there are inevitable rivalries and gossip, leaks and memoirs, but there was something else going on at Nuremberg. Sitting in that courtroom day in and day out for ten months, listening to the horrify-ing testimony, viewing the appalling exhibits, and watching the defendants try to excuse their actions—there was something profoundly contaminating about all of this, and it seared the lives of all who were in attendance.[31]

4

War Criminals with Psychiatrists and Psychologists?

Nazism was a socio-cultural disease. . . . I had at Nuremberg the purest known Nazi-virus cultures—22 clay flasks as it were—to study.
—Douglas Kelley, *22 Cells in Nuremberg*, 1947

THE FLIGHT FROM MONDORF-LES-BAINS to Nuremberg was uneventful. Robert Ley, Julius Streicher, and Hermann Göring gaped at the ruins of Nuremberg as they were being transported to their new and decidedly gloomier quarters (fig. 10). No longer were they in a former resort ringed by barbed wire. Now they all were in a very clear *jail* that held the twenty-two Nuremberg defendants and others who were destined for later trials. Ashcan and Dustbin (the British equivalent) had been dumped into Nuremberg. The prison was a large, cold, stone cellblock with three tiers of cells, each measuring about a hundred square feet. The building was musty, and the air had a staleness that one could taste. In the ensuing months, the menacing silence of the cellblock was broken by the sounds of turning keys, marching guards, and Streicher's occasional screams.

Two new characters who figure prominently in this book joined the Ashcan émigrés. Prisoner Rudolf Hess flew in from England, and a new prison staff member arrived, Kelley's soon-to-be nemesis, Gustave Gilbert.

Fig. 10. Nuremberg in ruins. (National Archives)

Rudolf Hess Arrives from England

Deputy Führer Rudolf Hess had been detained in England since 1941. A gangling and shy man, he had *no* interests aside from the Nazi Party. Hess inspired the party faithful, spoke at mass rallies, and helped ratify the Nuremberg laws, which enabled the coming genocide.

On May 10, 1941, Hess stunned the world by stealing a two-engine Messerschmitt and flying to Scotland in the hopes of persuading England to ally with Germany. Hess plummeted out of the sky dressed in a Luftwaffe uniform and landed in a field, where an astonished Scottish farmer discovered him. It was almost a scene out of *Fawlty Towers*, with Hess declaring to the farmer: "I have an important message for the Duke of Hamilton." The farmer didn't know what to do with him. Hess later wrote: "[He] helped me to get into the house; put a rocking chair near the fireplace and offered me tea."[1] Hess was promptly whisked off to the Tower of London and then to a fortified country house, where he stayed for a year. Finally, he was moved to Maindiff Court Military Hospital, where he was confined for three years.

Throughout it all, Hess was under constant medical observation because of back and ankle injuries resulting from his parachute jump as well as repeated suicide attempts, agitation, constant medical complaints, and a very odd and changeable mental status. His psychiatric records from that time are unusually extensive and public because he requested their release so that people in the future would learn that "in some hitherto unknown manner people can be put into a condition which resembles . . . hypnosis, leaving its after-effects . . . a condition in which the persons concerned do everything that has been suggested to them, under the elimination of their own will, presumably without their being conscious of it."[2] Hess's release of information statement gives us a hint of what the psychiatrists were dealing with.

His first doctor, J. Gibson Graham, noted that Hess was intensely suspicious of his food.[3] Hess was also known to suddenly swap plates with his guards, and sometimes, he would eat only if the psychiatrist tasted his food first. Hess worried that perhaps a kitchen worker, "acting for international Jewry," would try to poison him.[4] On the other hand, he also thought that an unknown Jewish conspiracy was poisoning him when he felt *good* after eating. Hess complained that noises in the house or from the neighborhood were part of a plot to stop him from sleeping. Graham concluded: "He showed marked hypochondriacal, paranoid tendencies, apprehension and delusions of persecution. Simple incidents were misinterpreted and given a sinister meaning."[5]

In the course of his British confinement Hess was seen by many psychiatrists. Psychiatrist J. R. Rees was struck by Hess's insomnia, anxiety, depression, suspiciousness, and lack of insight. "[I would diagnose] him as a psychopathic personality of the schizophrenic type . . . [who is] suggestible and liable to hysterical symptom formation."[6] The next psychiatrist, Henry

Dicks, described Hess as a "typical schizophrenic [who] oozed hostility and suspicion."[7] Dicks noted Hess's complaints of impaired concentration, but he had his doubts about their veracity, so he surreptitiously tested Hess's IQ by telling him that the Raven's Progressive Matrices intelligence test was just a game. Hess scored in the top tenth percentile. No problems with concentration here!

Psychiatrist M. K. Johnston reported that Hess hid small pieces of paper in his room and complained that he couldn't concentrate, couldn't remember words, and had memory loss because of brain poison. Hess developed intermittent amnesia for both short-term and long-term memory. He stabbed himself in the chest and then said that Jews had tempted "him to commit suicide because he was the only person who knew of their secret power of hypnosis."[8] Johnston also reported that Hess met with an official from the Swiss embassy to insist that the embassy analyze his table wine for poison.

The doctors continued: "He . . . made a signed declaration . . . of his desire to die as he considers that his abdominal condition is incurable. He wishes his corpse to be dressed in his flying uniform and to be sent to Germany, where on examination 'poison will obviously be found.'"[9]

Sometimes, it appeared that Hess was simulating amnesia. For instance, he couldn't define what "skiing" meant or remember who Shakespeare was—certainly not typical amnesia. At times, he was indifferent to the memory problems; at others, he complained bitterly that he was slipping into a fog. The doctors suggested an Amytal injection to improve his memory, but Hess initially refused, stating, "I do not suffer unless I am reminded. . . . Perhaps it is even a merciful dispensation of fate which makes me forget. If I got back my full memory, I might suffer more."[10] Nonetheless, he did agree to one interview on May 17, 1945, when he was sedated with Amytal and then interviewed by psychiatrist Henry Dicks. The excerpt below gives a flavor of the Amytal interview. Throughout it all, Hess merely complained of his belly pains. He didn't recover his memory in the slightest.

> D. What troubles you?
> Pt. Pains! In my belly! (Severe groans.) Oh if only I were well. Belly-ache (groans). Water! Water! Thirst!

D. You will soon have water. Tell us now what you have forgotten.

Pt. Oh, I don't know. Pain! Thirst!

D. You will tell us now what you have forgotten [sic].

Pt. Water! Pain in my body! A fog . . .

D. Remember your little son's name?

Pt. (whispers) I don't know.

D. Your wife's: Ilse it is.

Pt. I don't know.

D. You remember your good friends, Haushofer . . .

Pt. No. (groans) Bellyache! Oh God!

D. Why this pain?

Pt. . . . (groans).

D. And how you lived in Alexandria as a little boy.

Pt. No.

D. And all the stirring times with Adolf Hitler in Munich.

Pt. No.

D. You were with him in the fortress at Landesberg.

Pt. No.

D. Come, it will help you to tell us all that hurts you.[11]

Hess told the doctors that his body was riddled with disease, and he stuffed his pockets with homeopathic and nature-cure medicines, including an elixir from a Tibetan lamasery.[12] These weren't new symptoms. All his life he had been preoccupied with his health and diet, and he brought his own food to eat even when he dined with Hitler.

After four years of British detention, the psychiatrists concluded that Hess was unstable in three respects: paranoid suspicions that the British were poisoning his food and interfering with his sleep, extensive hypochondriacal preoccupations, and an amnesia that made no medical "sense." Churchill agreed, commenting that "[these] transcripts . . . seem to me to consist of the outpourings of a disordered mind. They are like a conversation with a mentally defective child who has been guilty of murder or arson."[13]

All of this was superimposed on extreme eccentricity. Hess was a devotee of astrology, believed in ghosts, consulted fortunetellers, and said that he flew to Scotland because his mentor had dreamed that Hess was piloting an airplane. At best, he was extremely odd, but was he mad? That determination would have to wait until Nuremberg.

On October 10, 1945, Hess flew home to a very different Germany. Gone were the adulating throngs of Storm Troopers filling the immense plazas of Nuremberg. They had been replaced by ghosts and ruins. He was welcomed to Nuremberg, not by his beloved Führer, but by Warden Burton Andrus. Hess promptly handed Andrus packets of his food and chocolates and demanded that they be analyzed for poison. Throughout his long detention, Hess's memory would come and go. Was there a method to his madness?

Gustave Gilbert Arrives

Because Douglas Kelley spoke little German, a prison officer named John Dolibois translated for him at Mondorf-les-Bains and Nuremberg. Dolibois was an easygoing, likeable interpreter, but he was anxious to move on.[14] He was succeeded on October 23, 1945, by psychologist Lieutenant Gustave Mahler Gilbert, a dour man on a mission (fig. 11).[15] Born in New York to

Fig. 11. Gustave Gilbert (right) with some of the
Nuremberg defendants. (National Archives)

a poor Austrian Jewish émigré family, Gilbert was raised in an orphan-age, attended the City College of New York, and completed his doctorate in psychology at Columbia with a special focus on social psychology. He had studied the Rorschach briefly at Columbia but was not particularly inter-ested in it.[16]

Before his Nuremberg assignment, Gilbert had been working in the army interrogating POWs. His German was superb and proper, and he was de-termined to ferret out those who were responsible for the Nazi war crimes. He regarded the Nuremberg assignment as an opportunity to "write his-tory's most perfectly controlled experiment in social pathology."[17]

Kelley and Gilbert had different strengths and approaches. Kelley viewed his Nuremberg position as yet another interesting assignment, comple-menting his vast clinical and forensic experience. The Nazi prisoners were interesting to him, but they were, after all, just more prisoners. Kelley was, however, intellectually stimulated by the challenge of his job and was trou-bled by the Nazis. *Colonel* Kelley viewed *Lieutenant* Gilbert as his interpreter and assistant, particularly since Gilbert was replacing Dolibois and Kelley outranked him. Gilbert's perspective didn't coincide at all with Kelley's. To him, the Nazi defendants were the devil incarnate, and he viewed his task not as Kelley's interpreter but as an interrogator who criticized the prison-ers for their moral failings.

In addition to his job as interpreter, Gilbert was given an ambiguous assignment by Warden Andrus: he was to be the warden's eyes and ears among the prisoners. Gilbert and the warden had a fraught relationship. Although Gilbert was not insubordinate to Andrus, he conveyed disdain, particularly when Andrus offered his own peculiar ideas about the prison-ers' psyches. The interactions got so bad that Andrus wanted to transfer Gilbert from Nuremberg, but Kelley dissuaded him, while also warning Gilbert to mend fences with the warden.[18]

The ambiguous responsibilities and reporting relationship between Kel-ley and Gilbert also aggravated their interactions. Kelley was a Rorschach expert but spoke little German; Gilbert was fluent in German but was not very knowledgeable about the Rorschach. Kelley was dispassionate and sar-donic; Gilbert was intense and humorless. Kelley was from an affluent, long-established California family; Gilbert was raised in poverty in New York as the child of recent immigrants.

One night over dinner, Kelley and Gilbert talked about the prisoners in their care and decided to write a book based on their observations. As a first step, Kelley suggested that Gilbert take notes about each interview. Gilbert felt that taking notes in the prisoners' presence would inhibit the conversation, so he did the best he could to reconstruct the interactions and gave Kelley a copy of his notes. At that point, he had no reason to suspect Kelley's motivations.

Lobbying for Scientific Study

For many years, I wondered what Kelley and Gilbert were doing at Nuremberg and if there was another explanation for how they got there. Library special collections and archives are like neighborhood estate sales: you never know what you will find. Working in the vaults of the Library of Congress, I chanced upon microfilmed correspondence among academics, intelligence officers, and Nuremberg prosecutors. The documents proposed studying the war criminals' psyches with Rorschach tests.

On June 11, 1945, Dr. John Millet of New York wrote to Justice Jackson on behalf of a group of renowned professors (Alvin Barach, Carl Binger, Richard Brickner, Frank Fremont-Smith, Adolf Meyer, Tracy Putnam, and George Stevenson) who represented a remarkably diverse group of professional societies.[19] In 1945, all of these disparate groups were convinced that the brains of executed Nazi leaders should be studied. It was a decidedly unusual letter. The trial had not yet started, but the academics were already recommending that the prisoners be executed in such a fashion that their brains could be studied post mortem. In addition, the letter specifically requested that the prisoners be tested with the Rorschach.

> Detailed knowledge of the personality of these leaders . . . would be valuable as a guide to those concerned with the reorganization and re-education of Germany. . . . In addition to the psychiatric interviews it would be desirable to make a number of psychological tests such as . . . the Rorschach. . . . If and when the accused has been convicted and sentenced to death, it would be desirable to have a detailed autopsy, especially of the brain. Therefore it is urged that the convicted be shot in the chest, not in the head. [Signed,] John Millet[20]

Millet's letter was followed three days later by a letter from OSS agent Sheldon Glueck to General Donovan, urging that a psychiatric panel of experts be appointed at Nuremberg. "A chief aim of the trial . . . will be to convince posterity of the facts and to interpret those facts and the entire Nazi leadership from the points of view of law, medicine, and sociology. For the first time in history, a thorough scientific study of the types of mentality possessed by German military, political and industrial insiders will be made." Glueck also urged that Rorschach experts be included in the panel.[21]

It may seem peculiar that there was so much interest in testing the defendants with the Rorschach, but in the 1940s the Rorschach test was THE psychological test. The Swiss psychiatrist Hermann Rorschach (1884–1922) observed that patients would project their fantasies and concerns onto a neutral, ambiguous inkblot card. Rorschach also noted that the inkblot task could provide a rough guide to how patients approached tasks cognitively— a brain scan, so to speak, long before such things were technologically possible.[22] Its ability to map what was on a person's mind made it a useful adjunct to psychiatric evaluations at a time when the field focused heavily on the unconscious, and its unstructured nature lent itself to evaluating patients who were noticeably guarded or uncooperative. Thus, its inclusion as a core component in the psychological evaluation of the Nuremberg war criminals was entirely logical.

The correspondence file about the psychological testing is voluminous. Donovan wrote Jackson the very next day supporting Glueck's proposal, and on June 23, Jackson replied to Millet, with cautious support. He agreed that Millet's proposal had merit but worried that psychiatric assessments might be prejudicial to the trial if they were performed before a determination of guilt. "It is not unlikely that [their lawyers] would demand production of [the] reports. The result might easily be that we would be compelled to litigate or discuss . . . questions of the mental condition of the defendants as to which it is conceivable your group would be in disagreement among themselves. . . . Rumors of a most troublesome kind might grow that we were preparing an insanity defense."[23]

Jackson agreed that such assessments might be made after the verdicts were in: "I also think that if the defective mentalities and abnormalities and perversions of these people were scientifically ascertained and laid before the world, it would be helpful in preventing coming generations of Germans from building up a myth that they were supermen." Responding to Millet's request for sparing the defendants' brains, Jackson concluded: "As to your suggestion that a victim be shot in the chest and not in the head, I would say that the general attitude of the Army is that those who are subjected to death sentence as criminals should be hanged rather than shot as the hanging seems to carry with it an implication of dishonor."[24]

On August 16, 1945, Millet wrote back to Jackson volunteering to suggest experts whenever Jackson was ready for them. Jackson replied one month later, thanking Millet for his advice and noting that "to have in a small space in a common jail a little group of men who have been able to exert such an evil influence upon the whole world is a rare experience. [But, he cautioned] they are undergoing interrogations . . . and, as you know, numerous examinations or interrogations are upsetting to them."[25]

In the meantime, circumstances changed, and Jackson realized that he would indeed need psychiatric examinations on some of the defendants— not for the sake of history or science, but because of concerns about their fitness for trial. Thus he wrote Millet on October 12, 1945, requesting specific names of experts. In an interesting aside, Jackson revealed both the urgency of his request as well as his understanding that getting multiple scientific societies to agree on such a list rapidly was not very likely. "If it is not possible for you to suggest these [names] as the official suggestion of the Committee, I would much appreciate your own advice as to names for the reason that I may have to act very suddenly and without opportunity for adequate consultation."[26]

The Urgent Problem: Dealing with Hess

Hess's mental status was the likely precipitant for Jackson's change of course regarding psychological testing. His amnesia and paranoia were becoming such a problem that Douglas Kelley wrote to Warden Andrus suggesting an Amytal interview. Kelley acknowledged that there had been rare fatalities with such interviews but stated that in his experience with over one thousand cases, he had never seen a major adverse effect.[27] Jackson denied Kelley's request because of the small but potential risks from Amytal, although he noted that if Hess had been his family member, he would have been inclined to follow Kelley's suggestion.[28]

Five days later, General Donovan requested that the court appoint a commission to "inquire into his [Hess's] state of mental health as well as his ability to confer with his counsel in the preparation of his defense." In December 1945, the tribunal decided to allow examination of the defendants "by qualified psychiatrists who wish to make purely scientific investigations unconnected with any issue in the trial."[29] By then, however, Kelley and Gilbert had completed their Rorschach studies, so the "authorization" was a moot point.

In June 1946, Millet wrote to Justice Jackson once more to say that there was no need to send over a group of psychiatrists to conduct extensive studies of the prisoners, given Kelley's credentials and observations, but he wondered whether there would be sufficient psychiatrists and psychologists on hand to observe the prisoners between the day of verdict and their presumable execution.[30] One senses that Jackson was becoming exasperated when he replied, reminding Millet that an adequate number of psychiatrists and psychologists were already on hand and that the anticipated period between day of sentencing and day of execution would probably be so brief that if Millet wanted additional experts, they would need to be ready on short notice.

The Alliance between the Intelligence Community and Psychology

I read these various letters with a sense of incredulity. They revealed a surprisingly cordial relationship among psychology, psychiatry, and the intelligence community. In 1945, everyone noted the Nazi regime's fascination and preoccupation with death and killing, fires and flaying—almost as if that was a goal in itself.[31] As a result, there was a sense of common purpose between academe and government that is unimaginable today.

German psychoanalytic émigrés such as Erich Fromm and Frieda Reichmann, as well as social philosophers like Theodor Adorno and Herbert Marcuse, wrote extensively about the Nazi psyche even before the war started. Sociologists such as Talcott Parsons helped with morale efforts, and anthropologists like Margaret Mead and Gregory Bateson were hired to help explain national character (enemy cultures) and to assist with white propaganda (to bolster domestic morale) and black propaganda (to undermine the enemies' morale). Psychoanalytic thinking regarding toilet training and infant swaddling heavily shaped their discourse.[32]

Harvard historian William Langer headed the research and analysis branch of the OSS. This forerunner of the Central Intelligence Agency (CIA) was heavily stocked with psychiatrists and psychologists.[33] Langer's brother Walter was a psychoanalyst who coauthored a classified "Psychological Analysis of Adolf Hitler" with Harvard psychologist Henry Murray, Ernst Kris of the New School for Social Research, and Bertram Lewin of the New York Psychoanalytic Institute.[34] The War Department's special project branch was headed by Murray Bernays, a young lawyer who had married Sigmund Freud's niece. This was clearly not a time when the social sciences stood in opposition to the government. On the contrary, the developing American social sciences and the OSS were so intertwined that it was hardly surprising when the intelligence services expressed interest in testing the Nuremberg prisoners.

Finally, General Donovan had a long track record of interest in psychological analysis throughout the war, and he brought those interests with him when he arrived in Nuremberg. His agency had embraced many sensible psychological goals—analyzing propaganda, supporting morale, inferring the enemy's motivation and goals, establishing screening procedures for new recruits—as well as some less sensible ideas like launching incendiary bats at the enemy's cities or drugging Hitler's vegetable garden to alter his behavior.[35]

The Routine Use of Psychiatry in Prison Settings

In most Western countries prison officials are concerned about the mental health of their detainees, even those on death row. Although the purpose of imprisonment is to detain and punish, the state also provides some medical and mental health care to prisoners; it doesn't want them to escape via illness or suicide.[36] As Warden Andrus put it, "A guy could go nuts sitting in a little cell with what some of these boys have got on their minds."[37]

So, Nuremberg was not particularly unusual for having prison chaplains, morale and welfare officers, and psychiatrists on staff. Even though the detainees were facing likely execution, their well-being was closely monitored. For instance, Kelley had recommended a prison library and exercise time for the prisoners. Andrus initially thought this was coddling them but subsequently agreed with the idea.

The psychiatrists and psychologists were also responsible for ensuring that the prisoners were fit for trial and could cooperate with their defense counsel. For a handful of defendants, this was not an assured thing. The industrialist Gustav Krupp had already been excused from prosecution because of his age and senility. Other prisoners were deeply depressed and had attempted suicide. In fact, Leonardo Conti had already hung himself in the Nuremberg jail.

All were aware that something was wrong with Hess. The tribunal worried that he was starving himself to death because of his suspicions that the Allies were giving him "brain poisons," and his memory problems raised questions of his ability to assist in his own defense. The judges appointed an international panel to assess his fitness for trial.

Kelley and Gilbert had their hands full dealing with the interpersonal frictions between Streicher and the other defendants. Streicher was so, well, creepy that the court appointed a panel to assess his fitness for trial, too. As a result, international experts were also summoned to verify Streicher's fitness for trial. Göring was straightforward from a forensic perspective. In his case, there was no hint of diminished capacity.

Kelley's Special Examinations

Douglas Kelley was one of the few individuals to have completely unfettered access to the prisoners. He and his interpreter, John Dolibois, set about visiting them daily. Dolibois did favors for the Nazis, such as helping them communicate with their wives. The Nazis thus welcomed Dolibois's presence during the psychiatric interviews and testing sessions, and his presence, if anything, facilitated Kelley's interviews. Kelley later claimed to have spent eighty hours with each prisoner, but he may have stretched things a bit. He clearly did spend an enormous amount of time with Göring, but it is hard to believe that he could have spent eighty hours with each of the twenty-two Nuremberg defendants. After all, the defendants arrived in Nuremberg on August 12, 1945, and Kelley left in January 1946.

Kelley's gift of gab helped him with the prisoners. In his writings, he stated that he considered them all desk murderers, buccaneers, and careerists, but in interacting with them, he kept those thoughts to himself and was not judgmental or critical. The prisoners were accustomed to frequent interrogation about what they had done. Kelley's questions, however, were different; he wanted to understand them as people, and the prisoners enjoyed his visits.

In addition to Kelley's formal role in the prison, he had a personal agenda. He would characterize the war criminals' minds by testing their IQ and by administering the most powerful psychological test of the day—the Rorschach.

Gustave Gilbert's Role

Gustave Gilbert entered Nuremberg as Dolibois's replacement in late October 1945, and he could not have been more different. Dolibois wanted out of Nuremberg; he had other aspirations for his final years of military service. On the other hand, Gustave Gilbert desperately wanted in at Nuremberg to study and characterize the depravity of the Nazi leadership. In the beginning, Kelley and Gilbert appeared to work together satisfactorily, but they had an enormously different interpersonal style—Kelley with his easygoing blarney contrasted with Gilbert with his intensity and efficiency. In their writings, one senses profound differences in terms of how the Nazis affected them. Kelley found the Nazis to be "interesting specimens" and relished telling stories about them to the news media. One doesn't get the sense that he lost sleep over his interactions with the Nazis. Gilbert didn't find them interesting in Kelley's dispassionate way but loathed them and told them so. There were other differences as well. Kelley had an enormous amount of clinical experience and expressed sympathy for the many GIs he treated for combat exhaustion. Gilbert was less sympathetic to the troops, describing them years later as "misfit solders."[38]

The men's differences in style and temperament were exemplified in their vacation plans over the Christmas holidays in 1945. Kelley went off on vacation, pure and simple. Gilbert traveled to Dachau to interview concentration camp guards who were awaiting execution.[39]

With these varied styles, they appealed to different prisoners, some liking Kelley's easygoing manner, others appreciating Gilbert's serious formality. Kelley noted that the prisoners were eager to talk: "Seldom have I found psychiatric interviews so easy as were most of these. . . . They talked almost without probing or prompting." He commented that Hess kept his distance but that Göring "was positively jovial over my daily comings and wept unashamedly when I left Nuremberg for the States."[40]

Advising the Prosecution

There was no doctor-patient confidentiality at Nuremberg. Both Kelley and Gilbert advised the prison administration (Warden Andrus) and the prosecution (Justice Jackson) regarding prisoner interactions and some of the defense strategies planned by the defendants' legal teams. They even suggested prosecutorial strategy.

Kelley wrote Donovan telling him that Göring claimed to have a "particular friendship for General Donovan and stated flatly that the general and myself [Kelley] are the only two individuals in the world in whom he really has any confidence." In the same note, Kelley warned Donovan that Baldur von Schirach was now "parroting statements of GOERING to the effect that 'of course in the courtroom we must present a united front.'"[41] Not to be outdone, Gilbert also routinely advised the prosecution. One commentator describes him, rather uncharitably, as "rooting around like a truffle-pig for gobbets of Intelligence."[42]

The Psychological Assessment

Kelley and Gilbert supplemented their interviews with psychological tests. Gilbert modified the Wechsler-Bellevue Intelligence Scale for use in German, and Kelley oversaw the Rorschach administration to characterize the prisoners' thinking and motivation.[43] When Gilbert was unavailable,

Kelley brought along another interpreter. Because the prison cells were so small, they would sit on the prisoners' cots, with the prisoner sandwiched between them.

The IQ scores reveal a range of intelligence from Julius Streicher at 106 all the way to Hjalmar Schacht at 143. The prisoners proudly compared their scores, like American high school students talking about their SATs. After he left Nuremberg, Kelley was interviewed by the *New Yorker* and asked about the prisoners' intelligence. "[I didn't] find any geniuses. Goering, for example, though with an IQ of a hundred and thirty-eight—he's *pretty* good, but no wizard."[44] Kelley's comments about the prisoners' IQs are amusing because, of course, HE was a bona fide genius, certified as such by Lewis Terman himself.[45] Many of the prisoners were enchanted by the Rorschach testing. Göring "expressed regret that the Luftwaffe had not had available such excellent testing techniques."[46]

Kelley and Gilbert shared an office, and they rounded on their prisoners both together and separately. There is no indication that they quarreled about the testing or the translation of the war criminals' responses. For unclear reasons, some of the prisoners completed the Rorschach repeatedly, sometimes with Kelley and sometimes with Gilbert.[47]

With time, Gilbert started to feel that he was doing the lion's share of the work, writing up the notes from their interviews and giving Kelley copies. Both were ambitious men who realized the importance of the topic and how later publication could influence their personal careers. Both have also been accused of exaggerating their assessments of the prisoners for later fame and fortune.[48]

Kelley Departs

On February 6, 1946, Kelley left Nuremberg; he hadn't seen his wife since 1942 and wanted to get home.[49] He was also eager to begin writing his book about the Nazi mind. Psychiatrist Leon Goldensohn succeeded him at Nuremberg.[50]

People had different views about Kelley's departure. Warden Andrus had resented Kelley's self-promoting interviews with the press and maintained that the glare of the limelight had intoxicated him. With his characteristic verve, Kelley was superb in interviews and left reporters with memorable lines, though sometimes their veracity was questionable. He told reporters that he "practically lived with Hess" and that Göring took his pain pills "like peanuts, throwing them in his mouth as he read or talked."[51] Kelley described Göring to the press as "dominant, aggressive, merciless, yet a jovial extrovert capable of occasional tenderness." He reported that Hitler had surrounded himself with "yes-men" and that Göring had responded that "all the no-men are six feet under."[52] This was how to talk to a reporter![53]

On September 6, 1946, Warden Andrus complained to the War Department about Kelley: "[He] left here under more or less of a cloud because it had been suspected that he was giving information to newspaper reporters in violation of security regulations and worse than that in violation of policies expressed by the Tribunal and in disobedience of orders." Andrus was particularly furious about an interview Kelley gave to the London *Sunday Express* on August 25, 1946, and noted ruefully:

> Since Dr. Kelly has been separated from the service I am not familiar with what action can be taken, but I am reporting this in the hope that something can be done. . . . The enclosed article in almost every line violates the policies of International Military Tribunal and constitutes a complete breach of trust. In addition to that, from the words he put into the mouths of the accused, I am satisfied that, for the most part, he is misquoting them.[54]

The *Sunday Express* article's subheadings give a flavor of Kelley's show-and-tell tone that so infuriated Andrus and others: "Hitler's stomach the cause of all the trouble; When Ribbentrop wanted a medal; Why Hitler delayed marriage."

Although Andrus was pleased by Kelley's departure, most of the prisoners were sad to see him go. Indeed, on December 26, 1945, Alfred Rosenberg, former Reich minister of the Occupied Eastern Territories, wrote Kelley: "I regret your departure from Nuremberg, as do the comrades confined with me. I thank you for your humane behavior and also for your attempt to understand our reasons. . . . I wish you luck in your later life."[55] For a while, it appeared that luck would indeed be with Kelley, but his inner demons chased him down.

PART THREE

FACES OF MALICE

5

Defendant Robert Ley: "Bad Brain"

I had the spiritual responsibility for peace of labour, production of the factories, and confidence of the worker to the system of National Socialism. It has been proved that I accomplished my task. . . . Until the 1 May 1945 there was neither a strike nor reports of sabotage. To the contrary, the production of armament showed a steady rise, even among foreign labour. I cannot think of a better vote of confidence.
—Robert Ley, autobiographic statement, 1945

The Nazi foreign labor policy was a policy of mass deportation and mass enslavement . . . of underfeeding and overworking foreign laborers, of subjecting them to every form of degradation, brutality and inhumanity.
—Thomas Dodd, prosecutor, testimony on forced labor at Nuremberg, December 11, 1945

The Choice

EVERY ONE OF THE NUREMBERG defendants was uniquely compelling. It was difficult for me to choose which defendants to discuss in this book, but ultimately I settled on four who were poles apart in terms of their backgrounds and behaviors. We have met them in Chapters 2 and 4, and now it is time to describe each in turn at greater length. What were they like while in power?

What did Kelley and Gilbert make of them in prison? What were their fates in front of the tribunal?

Why these four? Two of them (Rudolf Hess and Julius Streicher) raised so many psychiatric flags that the tribunal formally requested their psychiatric evaluation. Robert Ley killed himself in prison, and after examining his brain, researchers theorized that his malice was driven by brain pathology. Hermann Göring was, quite simply, the principal defendant and highest-ranking Nazi official. I have chosen to present them in the order of their deaths and thus start with Robert Ley, one of the most complex defendants, who is all but forgotten but shouldn't be.

May We Have His Brain?

When Robert Ley hung himself in 1945, he had no way of knowing that he had fulfilled the wishes of multiple American academic societies that had written to Justice Robert Jackson requesting the brains of the war criminals. As noted in Chapter 4, their letter requested: "If and when the accused has been convicted and sentenced to death, it would be desirable to have a detailed autopsy, especially of the brain. Therefore it is urged that the convicted be shot in the chest, not in the head."[1]

Of all the war criminals, only Ley gratified their wish, and his brain was meticulously examined. The rest of the executed war criminals were cremated, taking the secrets of their brains with them.[2]

An old and established medical tradition links malice to brain injury— "bad brains," if you will. It comes as no surprise that this neural explanation was a prominent sentiment at Nuremberg, particularly in the case of Robert Ley. In his instance, there was both a history of major head injury and a certifiably abnormal brain.

Ley's Background

Robert Ley held the benign-sounding position of head of the German Labor Front, which controlled 95 percent of German workers (fig. 12). In that capacity he ordered the murder of union activists who did not support the Nazi Party line and helped set up slave labor factories throughout Germany.

Fig. 12. Robert Ley on his arrest. (Reprinted with permission from the United States Holocaust Memorial Museum, courtesy of Henry Plitt)

He was also indicted for his propaganda activities. He ranted against the Catholic Church and, like many in the party, edited an anti-Semitic newspaper. He wrote: "Degenerate to their very bones, . . . nauseatingly corrupt, and cowardly like all nasty creatures—such is the aristocratic clique which the Jew has sicked on National Socialism. . . . We must exterminate this filth, extirpate it root and branch."[3] On another occasion, he wrote: "Sure the Jew is also a person. . . . But the flea is also an animal—only not a very pleasant one. And since the flea is not a pleasant animal we don't see it as our duty to watch over and protect it, to allow it to flourish so that it can stick and pain and torture us, rather we must render it harmless. And so it is with the Jews."[4]

Ley was born in 1890 into a large but poor farming family in the Rhine Province. As mentioned in Chapter 2, he sustained a major head injury in World War I. The injury left him with a stammer for the rest of his life. Following World War I, he led an erratic life, drinking heavily, but despite this, he returned to university and obtained a PhD magna cum laude in chemistry. He worked briefly for the I.G. Farben chemical corporation but was fired because of his drinking and his Nazi political activities. In later years, he remembered his Farben days and encouraged Hitler to use lethal chemical weapons in the war.

Ley was fanatically loyal to Hitler and regarded the Nazi Party as "our religious order, our home. Without it we cannot live."[5] Hitler was his Messiah, the Jew was his Devil, and World War II was a titanic, apocalyptic struggle of good versus evil. To win that war, Germany needed a harmonious and united country.

Ley was a major propagandist for the party. After the war, the Associated Press noted some of his aphorisms. On war: "War is a blessing of God. . . . It is the expression of the highest and best in manhood." On America: "Hate! Hate! Hate! Every German must hate the gangsters, the murderers, the assassins who [come] from the center of world Jewry and capitalism—the United States of America. . . . In this war there can be no compromise with these half-breed Americans who come across the sea to slay in a war that does not concern them."[6]

He politicked at international labor conferences praising National Socialism as a workers' paradise, but his foreign relations missions were not particularly successful. While attending one international labor meeting, he got more drunk than usual and alienated the Latin American delegations by saying that they looked as though someone "had lured them out of the jungle with bananas."[7]

Dismissed by others in the party as a "laughable bugaboo" and an "eccentric idealist," Ley had a goal of creating a reliable and loyal German workforce.[8] If the workers cooperated, he would do everything in his power to assure their comfort. He was the workers' champion, and he advocated for equal pay for women workers, for mandatory vacation time, and for hiring more workers rather than forcing others to work overtime. He campaigned for better housing, humane working conditions, and for "strength through joy." To support this last goal, he set up a travel agency for workers and provided generous, inexpensive vacation benefits that were wildly popular; 85 percent of German workers used them to take cruises on the Rhine or vacations on the North Sea beaches.[9] Ley even bought a cruise ship for workers, modestly renaming it the *Robert Ley*. He helped establish the Volkswagen as the people's car and championed building with prefabricated materials. According to Ley, a happy worker would be a productive worker, and all of these extensive benefits would be provided under the watchful and protective eye of the Gestapo. Other Nazi leaders were jealous of his expanding power and skeptical of the value of all of these worker benefits. Göring, for instance, sniffed: "The Labor Front should make more strength and less joy."[10]

On the flip side of the coin, Ley was not just a benign futurist but a ferocious fighter for the party. If the workers did not cooperate—if they went on strike, for instance, or opposed the party—they would be "removed." He was quite capable of treachery when it came to controlling the workforce. His ruthlessness was evident early on in dealing with labor leaders who opposed the party. On May Day, 1933, the Nazi Party honored workers with parades and fireworks. The next day, the Nazis pounced, seizing union buildings, arresting union leaders, freezing union bank accounts, and closing union newspapers. Many other instances of Ley's brutality were notable. When the Allies breeched the German borders, Ley and Goebbels created the Werwolf battalions to fight a guerrilla war in Germany against the invaders and carry out sabotage and assassinations, ultimately killing between three and five thousand people.[11]

Ley was a complex man. While living extravagantly, he always remembered growing up in poverty and focused his efforts on improving the morale of the underclass. "There is nothing more degrading and humiliating for someone," he said, "than when he recognizes that he is without value in human society."[12]

He flew into frequent, violent rages, and was even more corrupt than usual for the Nazi leadership. His drinking problems were legendary. In 1937, he drunkenly careened around Munich with the Duke and Duchess of Windsor in tow. As one of his aides later recounted: "He drove the car through the locked gates and then raced up and down at full speed between the barracks, scaring hell out of the workers and nearly running over several. The next day Hitler told Goering to take over the Duke's visit before

Ley killed him."[13] As Ley's limitations became clearer to the Nazi leader-ship, Albert Speer assumed many of his functions.

Ley in Prison

The Americans captured Ley in May 1945. He bristled at being described as a war criminal and complained that it was illegal to apply international laws retroactively. "I don't see how you can make a law after things have been done. Even God first made the Ten Commandments and judged the people by them afterward."[14] While awaiting trial in Nuremberg, he told Kelley and Gilbert, "Stand us against a wall and shoot us, well and good, you are victors. But why should I be brought before a Tribunal like a c-c-c-[criminal]. . . . I can't even get the word out!"[15] Writing his lawyer, he continued in the same vein: "I understand that the victor thinks he has to exterminate and destroy his hated opponents. I am not defending myself against being shot or killed. I am defending myself, and with every right, against being branded as a criminal and against a procedure without any legal foundation based on pure caprice. . . . I am a German and a National Socialist but I am no criminal."[16]

In his prison interrogations, Ley was surprisingly open and insightful when he talked about the Nazi defeat. On September 1, 1945, he said: "I wish to say at this time that . . . one thing broke us—not only externally but within ourselves. . . . We had the belief that the will of the human being was omnipotent and that we did not need the compassion of Heaven. The catastrophe [that is, defeat] taught us different."[17]

Ley's interrogations revealed a curious mélange of remorse, insight, and astonishing misjudgment. He reported that in his cell he had been talk-ing about the war with his dead wife and thought that the Jews would par-don him if only he could talk with Zionist leader Chaim Weizmann. He wanted to form a committee of anti-Semites and Jews and, getting carried away with the idea, wanted to establish a non-anti-Semitic Nazi Party in the United States.[18]

Interrogations of Ley were difficult because he was hard to understand, not just because of his stammer, but also because he was so excitable and uninhibited. The interpreter John Dolibois noted that Ley would jump up off his chair, wave his arms, pace, and shout at least three times during each interview.[19] Kelley commented that Ley "was totally unable to carry on a coherent conversation" without starting a ranting speech. "He would stand, then pace the floor, throw out his arms, gesticulate more and more violently and begin to shout."[20]

An interrogator at Nuremberg asked Ley about how the Nazi Party was organized, and Ley went off on a tangent, describing his mystical ideas about the nature of the state and the importance of blood, race, being, energy, and power. I quote excerpts from his response because there is something not quite right about the flow of associations, something that the Ashcan observers had noted months earlier.

> The higher a people is placed, the more needs it has. Naturally it has various needs, like the needs of labor, traffic, and culture organizations. Many organizational positions are required. The important thing at first is to find out the basic substance of the nation; the feeling of the national—the blood, the race, the being, and the historical background of the nation. Comparing it with the laws of energy it is just like one big field of power. One has to recognize these powers ones self, and one can recognize them better when one has lived through the procedure and being of the people. The state is a concept that was founded by the people in order to satisfy their needs. And the people always looked upon the state as its partner, as its party.[21]

One week later, Ley was questioned about his accomplishments. In the transcript below he omits describing how, as he put it, he "discharged" the original trade unions and their leaders. In actuality, they were destroyed and murdered.

> We have of course discharged the functions of the trade union, but at the same time we have added the following: Strength through Joy, leisure time, and recreation to a very large extent, generous health projects with plant physicians and so forth, then also a vast specialized educational program, a program for increasing over all efficiency with model plants, general recommendations to be followed in factories in which millions of workmen participated, housing projects on a vast scale, and a public education program for millions of people. . . . I endeavored to make the fate of both the German workman as well as the workman of foreign origin as pleasant as

possible . . . I regret very much that this ideal organization will not be introduced in other countries for the benefit of their people.[22]

Ley received his indictment in October 1945, and somehow it came as
a shock. He didn't mind being treated as an enemy but was humiliated
to be considered a criminal. Although he had been imprisoned since May
and repeatedly interrogated, he apparently denied the implications of the
interrogations until he was formally indicted. When he was offered a list
of attorneys who might represent him before the tribunal, he replied, "If at
all possible, I would like to have a Jewish person as my defense counsel."[23]

He would be dead in two weeks, and not at the hands of the tribunal.
On October 25, 1945, he rigged a noose out of strips of towels and stuffed
his mouth with his underpants to muffle any sounds of moaning. He then
patiently tied the other end of the strip of towels to a sink pipe, sat down on
the toilet, leaned forward, and strangled himself. The guard realized too late
that Ley was not just sitting on the toilet seat. Warden Andrus commented
later, "What a way to die—strangled with his own loin cloth on his own
dung heap."[24] Andrus's sardonic comment aside, this was not a promising
beginning of the trial, and Andrus knew it. He increased the number of
guards and announced that his jail was now suicide-proof. The Greeks have
a word for that: *hubris.*

Ley left multiple suicide notes. In one, he went out of his way to say that
he was not mistreated in prison. In another, he expressed remorse and guilt
for his activities during the war:

> I can't stand the shame any more. . . . I have been one of the responsible
> men. I was with Hitler in the good days, during the fulfillment of our plans
> and hopes, and I want to be with him in the black days. God led me in what-
> ever I did. . . . We have forsaken God, and therefore we were forsaken by
> God. Anti-Semitism distorted our outlook, and we made grave errors. It is
> hard to admit mistakes, but the whole existence of our people is in question.
> We Nazis must have the courage to rid ourselves of anti-Semitism. We have
> to declare to the youth that it was a mistake.[25]

The other prisoners could not have cared less about the news of Ley's
suicide. Prison physician Rene H. Juchli reported to General Donovan

that Ley's fellow prisoners regarded him "as a fantastic dreamer with his dreams as confused as his talks" and felt that "[his] death should have occurred fifteen years sooner." Reich economics minister Hjalmar Schacht added caustically that he "only regretted the delay of the incident." Göring was "thoroughly disgusted," and Streicher was "ashamed to be locked up with such a weakling." Hitler Youth leader Baldur von Schirach thought that Ley's death was cowardly as well as unfair to the rest of them in that Ley would no longer be able to help with their defense.[26] Empathy, for this group, was in short supply, but there was certainly an abundance of nastiness. This paucity of empathy would be a key point in the emerging arguments concerning psychopathology in the Nazi leaders.

Kelley's and Gilbert's Assessment

Given Gilbert's arrival on October 23 and Ley's suicide just two days later, Gilbert made few observations of Ley. Kelley, however, knew Ley from his Ashcan days as well as Ley's early days in Nuremberg. He had observed Ley daily for six weeks and wrote his summary of Ley to the commanding officer of the Internal Security Detachment at Nuremberg just days before Ley killed himself. Reading Kelley's notes, one recognizes the familiar cadence of a mental status examination.

> Normal psychomotor reactions and normal attitudes and behavior. Mood is normal, but affect is extremely labile. Ley is easily excited and demonstrates marked emotional instability. Content is normal although euphoric trends are present. Sensorum is intact. Insight is good and judgment fair. Rorschach examination reveals emotional instability and evidence of frontal lobe damage manifested by color and shading responses, confused form and inadequate construction of responses. . . . [He is] one of the most potentially suicidal prisoners due to his extreme instability secondary to his old head injury. . . . [Ley is] competent.[27]

Commenting on Ley's Rorschach response, Kelley noted: "The over-all picture of Robert Ley's Rorschach record is definitely that of an individual suffering from damage to his frontal lobes."[28] Elsewhere, Kelley reported that Ley's "inhibitory centers . . . had ceased to function."[29]

The details of the Rorschach responses are arresting. Ley was easily de-railed. Here is Kelley's verbatim description: "In Card IV, he saw a 'funny bear, fur spread out,' and in the inquiry he stated: 'You can see the head and teeth with terrific legs. It has shadows and peculiar arms. It is alive and represent[s] Bolshevism overrunning Europe.' Once started on this point, there was a short intermission until we could get Dr. Ley off the subject of Bolshevism and back to the subject of Rorschach cards."[30]

Kelley was struck most of all by Ley's emotional instability, which he at-tributed to frontal lobe damage. Ley had grandiose dreams of immigrat-ing to the United States to solve America's labor difficulties. In the month before he killed himself, Ley wrote to "Sir Henry Ford" asking for a job, reasoning that since both he and Ford were in the automobile business and both were anti-Semites, they would be natural partners.[31]

Regarding Ley's suicide, Kelley wrote sardonically in 1946, "Since Ley kindly made his brain available for postmortem examination, we were pre-sented with the rare chance to verify our clinical and Rorschach findings."[32]

Ley's Brain

Ley's death presented an opportunity to literally get one's hands on a Nazi leader's brain; at least, that is the way the popular press portrayed it. Indeed, his brain was the *only* Nuremberg brain available for scrutiny. The brain was removed from Ley's body a few hours after his suicide and was shipped to the Armed Forces Institute of Pathology in Washington, DC. Eminent neuropathologist Webb Haymaker examined the brain. His initial report, recorded in pencil on yellow lined paper noted brain atrophy, suggested by widened folds (sulci) on the brain's surface and thickened. membranes (meninges) on the brain's surface, which could have resulted from a long-ago head injury. He commented: "We are dealing with a case of confirmed degenerative atrophy of the frontal lobes. . . . The appearance is that of a longstanding degeneration, or 'chronic encephalopathy,' the etiology of which is unknown."[33]

Haymaker explained that the frontal lobes were "the seat of our inhibi-tions—the real control center that keeps most people from committing acts of violence. It's this part that enables us to have sympathy with our fellow man."[34] Microscopic examination of Ley's brain revealed "chronic encephalopathy of sufficient duration and degree to have impaired Dr. Ley's mental and emotional faculty and could well account for his alleged aberrations in conduct and feelings."[35]

When this news got out, the *Sarasota Herald Tribune* quoted Major General Turk, surgeon general of the army, as saying that the changes "were sufficient to account for the unusual behavior [of Ley]." Not to be outdone, *Life* magazine ran a story showing Haymaker dissecting Ley's brain. The AP headline from the *Washington Times Herald* stated simply, "Ley's Brain Was Warped." The *Washington Post* was more restrained: "Nazi Ley's Brain Found Diseased."

A photograph of Ley's left cerebral hemisphere is reproduced here (fig. 13). It does demonstrate slight frontotemporal atrophy with widened sulci, or folds. There is no evidence of contusion, but the membrane that surrounds the brain is fibrotic and thickened. Severe alcoholism with malnutrition typically alters the mammillary bodies in the brain. Haymaker would certainly have looked for this, and we must infer that there was no abnormality, given his silence on the matter.

Kelley felt that Ley's frontal lobe damage probably resulted from the World War I head injury, noting that Ley had been unconscious for several hours afterward. In addition, Ley had sustained a second head injury in an automobile accident in 1930. Following yet another extended period of unconsciousness, the car accident worsened his stammer and also left him with severe tinnitus.[36] Kelley commented: "To overcome . . . [his stammer], he turned to liquor. He found that if he drank a lot, the impediment became less noticeable."[37] The neuropathologists, observing bilateral frontal lobe changes, disagreed with Kelley's assessment that the frontal lobe changes reflected traumatic injury. Instead, they were inclined to attribute the encephalopathy to alcohol abuse.[38]

There is an important postscript to the story on Ley's brain. It turns out that Haymaker asked a colleague for a second opinion on the neuropathology. Dr. Nathan Malamud of the Langley Porter Neuropsychiatric Institute in San Francisco examined the tissue with Nissl and van Gieson stains and wrote back on March 31, 1947: "As I warned you beforehand, I am not

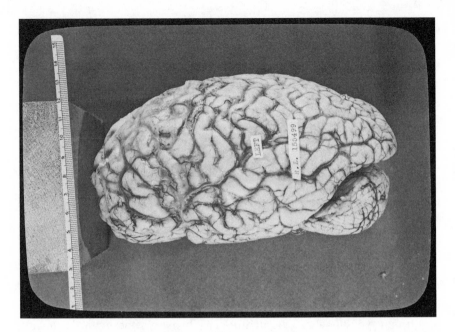

Fig. 13. Robert Ley's left cerebral hemisphere. (Courtesy of Douglas Kelley)

impressed with any definite pathology in this case, at least such as would lead one to suspect a clinical organic condition. The findings are . . . difficult to evaluate because of post-mortem or fixation artefact, but if real, the changes are not too significant. . . . The histological picture is that of a chronic diffuse encephalopathy of non-specific type, even if one allows for artefacts of fixation and paraffin embedding."[39]

The microscopic examination supports Malamud's interpretation (fig. 14). It is an unremarkable slide that shows some fixation artifact but no evidence of syphilis (no microglial hyperplasia, perivascular plasma cell cuffing, or neuronal dropout) or evidence of Alzheimer's disease (no plaques or tangles) or of Pick's disease (no intraneuronal inclusion bodies). If there was malice here, it was not discernable on the slide.

With Malamud's second opinion in hand, Haymaker wrote to Kelley on December 15, 1947, "I have gone over the case very carefully and found changes, but they were of a lesser scope than we had at first believed. Personally, I think maybe we had better let the whole thing lie buried, as the degree of change could be subject to a difference of opinion."[40]

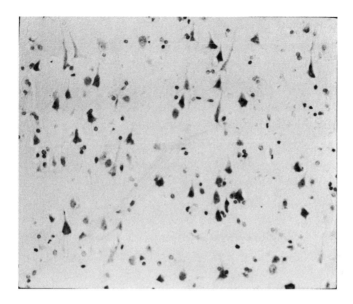

Fig. 14. Microscopic view of Robert Ley's brain. (Courtesy of Douglas Kelley)

As is typical with press reports about medical discoveries, no effort was made to correct the historical record. As far as readers of the Associated Press were concerned, Robert Ley's behavior had been definitively traced to his bad brain. "Bad brain or not," Ley was not a "monster" in the Frankenstein sense. Indeed, he was one of the few Nuremberg defendants to express remorse over his actions.

A Perspective from the Twenty-First Century

Of all the Nazi war criminals, Ley would definitely have been evaluated differently in the twenty-first century. After all, his neuropsychiatric presentation posed many questions. He suffered from two major head injuries and a prolonged loss of consciousness, and for a while, he had total aphasia. For the rest of his life, he was described as having a profound stammer, but one wonders in retrospect if this was an expressive aphasia. The accidents left him with impulsivity and erratic behavior, no doubt aggravated by his legendary alcoholism.

Today, we would document his impulsivity and map its extent with psychological testing. But we wouldn't stop there because memory and judgment would also have to be assessed. Most assuredly, we would obtain neural imaging to map the extent of his brain injury. These evaluations would be absolutely routine. If we had a brain biopsy, we would perform newer staining techniques (immunohistochemistry). Had Ley come to trial, all of these assessments would be sitting on his lawyer's desk, and the court would have to struggle to weigh their relevance.

6

Defendant Hermann Göring:
"Amiable Psychopath"

Goering is a supreme egotist and a consummate liar but a charming rascal.

    —Thomas Dodd, Nuremberg prosecutor, March 18, 1946

They don't have to show films and read documents to prove that we rearmed for war.—Of course, we rearmed!—Why, I rearmed Germany until we bristled!—I'm only sorry we didn't rearm still more.—Of course, I considered your treaties . . . so much toilet paper.—Of course, I wanted to make Germany great! If it could be done peacefully, all well and good, if not, that was fine too!

    —Hermann Göring to Gustave Gilbert, December 11, 1945

Interrogating Göring

GÖRING AND LEY WERE STRIKINGLY DIFFERENT. If Ley regarded his indictment as a devastating humiliation, Göring had contempt for the whole trial and looked forward to going down fighting. Even their suicides were different. Ley's was driven by guilt and remorse. Göring's was motivated by his desire to humiliate the Allies and die a martyr's death.

In his prime, Hermann Göring was president of the Reichstag, founder of the Gestapo, commander in chief of the Luftwaffe, and creator of the first concentration camps. He cultivated a jovial persona, but behind that was a three-dimensional complexity that was at once attractive and repellant.

Göring was larger than life—a dissolute man with a taste for luxury and larceny. Compared to others in the Nazi hierarchy, he was personable and expansive, eccentric and amusing. Seeing himself as a latter-day Caesar, Göring loved dressing up in costumes, wearing expensive brooches, and giving extraordinary parties at his mansion, Carinhall, where he kept pet lions and had a miniature airplane that could drop bombs on his model railroad. After regaling his guests with this unusual entertainment, he would escort them into another room to watch cowboy and Indian movies, which he adored.

Although Göring was massively corrupt and plundered art from everywhere, he had a soft spot for animals and was proud to be chief forester of Germany, promulgating rules to ensure that animals were treated humanely. But there was always that other side of Göring. After enacting antivivisection laws in Prussia, he threatened that anyone who violated those laws would face "severe penalties . . . [and risked] being thrown in a concentration camp."[1] Retribution always prowled behind his facade of caring.

For Göring, racism and anti-Semitism were secondary concerns. When asked why he had appointed as his deputy Field Marshal Erhard Milch, who had some Jewish ancestry, Göring replied, "In Germany, a Jew is whoever I say is a Jew."[2] Years later, he arranged for the rescue and emigration of two Jewish sisters who had saved his life in 1923 when he was badly wounded in the Munich Putsch. Göring thus presented an interesting mix of brutality and tenderness. Writing his wife from prison:

> To see your beloved handwriting, to know that your dear hands have rested on this very paper. . . . Sometimes I think my heart will break with love and longing for you. That would be a beautiful death. My dear wife, I am so sincerely thankful to you for all the happiness that you always gave me; for your love and for everything. . . . I can tell you endlessly what you and Edda [his daughter] mean to me and how my thoughts keep centering on you. I hold you in passionate embrace and kiss your dear sweet face.[3]

These tender feelings, however, did not extend beyond family and animals. He did after all convene the Wannsee Conference, which designed the Final Solution.[4]

In interrogations, Göring, aka "the fat man," was hard to pin down. Intelligence officer Dolibois captured Göring's complexity: "He's been described as everything from the devil incarnate to a silly fat eunuch. . . . He was an able, shrewd manager, brilliant and brave, ruthless and grasping. At times he turned on his charm and it was almost a pleasure to be with him. At other times he was simply a pain in the ass. But every hour spent with him was interesting."[5]

Many of our richest sources about Göring are stored in the National Archives in College Park, Maryland. I was working there one morning in a large room filled with humming and whirling microfilm machines and their quiet, scholarly acolytes. I chanced upon a cache of transcripts containing Göring's interrogations as well as a surprising interrogation of Göring's younger brother Albert. I had never even heard of Albert, but his story is remarkable. He had opposed the Nazi Party and went out of his way to rescue Jews, in one case joining Jewish women who were forced to their knees to scrub the streets with acid. Hermann always bailed him out when he got into trouble with the authorities. On September 25, 1946, Albert was interrogated:

> QUESTION: What did your brother say when you told him about the terrible things that were being done to the Jews?
> ANSWER: Well, his reaction was always that these things were exaggerated, because he had exact reports on them. He said for me not to mix into affairs of state, and affairs of history, because I had no political knowledge whatever. His very words: "You are a political idiot!" . . . Hermann always called me the black sheep of the family for rescuing Jews and opposing the Nazi party.[6]

Göring was incensed by the premise of the Nuremberg Trial and regarded the Allies as hypocrites, pointing out that the British had invented concentration camps in the Boer War, the Russians had massacred Polish officers in Katyn Forest and millions of their own people, and the Americans had slaughtered American Indians. When Göring heard that the Americans had dropped the atom bomb on Hiroshima, he commented, "Aha, *now* who are the war criminals?"[7]

Colonel John Amen interrogated Göring extensively, and the transcript provides an unusual glimpse of Göring's view of personal responsibility. On September 6, 1945, Amen asked Göring about the bombing of Rotterdam.

QUESTION: Did you personally order the bombing of Rotterdam?
ANSWER: Yes, but I did not personally order the bombing of Rotterdam but of the place where the fighting took place. We had dropped parachutists there and they were surrounded and they were fighting there. That was why the place was bombed. I wish to say the entire bombardment of Rotterdam was done by 36 planes, and if the people of Rotterdam hadn't been such cowards, they could have extinguished the fires. Nobody from the people or fire brigades from Rotterdam made any attempt to extinguish the flames and that is why the fire spread so much and demolished all those houses, which were old. The fire then spread throughout the houses and . . . blocks and the situation got worse. And even after the fight was over, nobody attempted to extinguish it. The whole bombing only lasted five minutes."[8]

This interchange is arresting for a number of reasons. Göring had a phenomenal memory for details. Even though the bombing had occurred five years earlier, he remembered every detail of the bombing sites and pointed them out to Amen on a large, detailed map of Rotterdam. Göring's repeated efforts to shift blame are particularly striking. He didn't order the bombing of Rotterdam but only "the place where the fighting took place" (that is, Rotterdam). Further, only thirty-six planes had bombed the city, and at that, the bombing was very brief. Moreover, the buildings were old firetraps, and it was the people of Rotterdam's fault that the place burned down because they were cowards and didn't try hard enough to put out the fire.

Amen's efforts to trap Göring were inevitable flops. Göring parried each leading question with a rebuttal that had its own edge to it. On September 7, 1945, Amen hoped to snare Göring into admitting that he had ordered reprisals:

QUESTION: Don't you remember giving out a statement . . . to the effect that if the British killed any of your aviators, that you were going to kill ten for every one that the British killed?
ANSWER: No; I never said that.
QUESTION: That is what the documents show.
ANSWER: I would like to see the documents.
QUESTION: I know you would, and maybe you will eventually, but I am trying to see if you don't remember about it first. . . .

ANSWER: Does that mean that this document contains an order, which I gave to that effect in writing?
QUESTION: I am not answering the questions; you are answering the questions. . . .
ANSWER: Well, the Colonel has the documents to ask me from and I have nothing to rely upon but my recollection.[9]

Göring could be surprisingly candid. When questioned about the Nazis' use of slave labor, he stated, "They served to help in the economic war. We used this labor for security reasons. So they could not be active in their own country and work against us."[10] In an interview with Leon Goldensohn, the psychiatrist who succeeded Kelley, Göring commented on the proceedings: "Frankly, it is my intention to make this trial a mockery. I feel that a foreign country has no right to try the government of a sovereign state." Göring went on to criticize the structure of the trial and even the tribunal's selection of defendants. "I have desisted from making any critical remarks about my co-defendants. Yet they are a mixed-up, unrepresentative group. Some of them are so unimportant, I have never even heard of them," referring to Hans Fritzsche, Walther Funk, and Wilhelm Keitel, whom he viewed as small fish compared to himself.[11]

In one wide-ranging interview, Göring discussed genocide, guilt, good, and evil:

Even if one has no compunction about exterminating a race, common sense dictates that in our civilization this is barbaric and would be subject to so much criticism from abroad and within, that it would be condemned as the greatest criminal act in history. Understand that I am not a moralist, although I have my chivalric code. If I really felt that the killing of Jews meant . . . winning of the war, I would not be too bothered by it. But it was meaningless and did nobody any good whatever except to give Germany a bad name. . . . I don't believe in the Bible or in a lot of things which religious people think. But I revere women and I think it unsportsmanlike to kill children. That is the main thing that bothers me about the extermination of the Jews. . . . For myself I feel quite free of responsibility for the mass murders. . . . I heard rumours of mass killings of Jews, but I could do nothing about it and I knew that it was useless to investigate these rumours and to find out about them accurately, . . . but I was busy with other things, and if I had found out what was going on regarding the mass murders, it would simply have made me feel bad and I could do very little to prevent it anyway.[12]

"Unsportsmanlike to kill children"? Göring uses "children" as if they were syntactically equivalent to squirrels or crows. This is hardly a ringing endorsement of his capacity for empathy. Nor did it help him to state that he didn't follow up on the rumors of mass killings "because it would simply have made me feel bad."

Above all else, Göring was a chameleon with many personas. Nuremberg interrogator Joseph Maier astutely observed: "To the French, he was patronizing and scornful. To us [the Americans], he was the hearty, freebooting buccaneer he thought might appeal to presumably naïve Americans succored on Hollywood films. To the cold, skilled British, he was quiet and respectful, anxiously attempting a gentlemanliness he thought might appeal. . . . [With the Russians Göring would] wince and cringe slightly. He knew of no pose that would intrigue a Russian. He was frightened to death of every Russian he saw."[13]

Göring on Trial

Göring saw himself as captain of the team and spokesman for all of the prisoners, and he believed that he deserved special treatment. In response to an order from Warden Andrus that the prisoners had to clean their own cells every Friday, Göring became so incensed that he developed arrhythmias. In this one instance, Warden Andrus gave in to Göring by assigning a prison employee to clean his cell, but Andrus loathed Göring, commenting that "Goering began the extroverted, flamboyant play-acting that was to go on throughout the trial. He lounged with one fat arm spread out behind his thin neighbor, Hess, the other elbow hanging over the edge of the dock. Then he would loll forward, elbows on the barrier of the wooden dock in front of him, a grin spreading across his huge face."[14]

Göring turned his efforts toward organizing a consistent defense for all the defendants, and he fumed when other prisoners took an independent path or admitted responsibility. "Schweinhundt und verraeter [pigdog and traitor]," he hissed at SS general Erich von dem Bach-Zelewski, who was testifying for the prosecution about antipartisan activities on the Eastern Front.[15] Not quite done, he continued: "Dirty, bloody, treacherous swine! That filthy skunk! . . . Selling his soul to save his stinking neck!"[16] He couldn't stop himself, and with jowls aquiver, he jeered at his fellow defendants, calling them "chicken-hearted little boys."[17]

In contrast to the other war criminals on trial, Göring offered no apologies or excuses during his courtroom testimony (fig. 15). Instead, he dominated the court with his patient and condescending "admission" that nasty things happen during a war and no one's hands are clean.

Göring had no illusions about the eventual verdict. He was indignant that he would be hung rather than shot, but he also viewed his execution as a

Fig. 15. Hermann Göring on the witness stand. (National Archives)

path to martyrdom. "I know I shall hang. I am ready. But I am determined to go down in German history as a great man. . . . In fifty or sixty years there will be statues of Hermann Göring all over Germany. Little statues, maybe, but one in every German home."[18]

Jackson versus Göring

In March 1946, Göring gave the performance of his lifetime, testifying extemporaneously for an entire week, giving his account of the war, his role in it, and its justification, and demonstrating a masterful recollection of details. It caught people by surprise; they mistook his corpulence for mediocrity. Janet Flanner, writing for the *New Yorker,* observed: "The Reichsmarschall made Machiavelli's Prince look like a dull apologist; Goering was decidedly more amoral, and funnier. . . . Behind his fancy tailoring, his fat, and his medals he had one of the best brains of a period in history when good brains were rare. . . . It was the complicated narrative of a brain without a conscience."[19]

Göring and Justice Jackson were locked in a duel of wits. At first, Jackson appeared to be winning, and the other defendants watched from the box like a Greek chorus, cheering and moaning as the cross-examination continued.[20] They were not necessarily rooting for Göring; there was too much jealousy for that. Rather, they enjoyed the blood sport of the testimony. Defendant Hjalmar Schacht noted with satisfaction, "The fat one is sure taking a beating so far."[21]

The first round went to Jackson, but it was a temporary victory that was quickly reversed. War correspondent Harold Burson commented succinctly: "Goering made mincemeat out of [Jackson]."[22] Jackson had grown accustomed to the other defendants, whose response to questioning was typically something like: "Oh, those things were terrible, but I knew nothing about them and had no power to stop it." Göring did not apologize and indeed counterattacked, saying in essence: "Of course we did that. We were at war, stupid. You've done such things as well." Jackson, unprepared for Göring's bold stance, was flummoxed, stammering in rage.

Göring picked apart everything Jackson asked and turned it on its head. Fluent in English, Göring complained that the consecutive translation was inaccurate and demanded time to be able to respond to questions. Jackson tried to cut Göring off and was incensed when the judges supported Göring's right to give long-winded replies. The excerpts below give a sense of Jackson's difficulties and his mounting frustration:

JACKSON: And yet, because of the Fueher system, as I understand you, you could give no warning to the German people; you could bring no pressure . . . to prevent that step and you could not even resign to protect your own place in history.
GOERING: There are several questions at once. I should like to answer the first one. . . .
JACKSON: . . . I repeat the question.
Did Seyss-Inquart become Chancellor of Austria with an understanding that he would call in the German troops and surrender Austria to Germany, or did you lead him to believe that he could continue an independent Austria?
GOERING: Excuse me, but that is a number of questions which I cannot answer simply with "yes" or "no."
If you ask me, "Did Seyss-Inquart become Chancellor according to Hitler's wishes and yours?"—yes.
If you then ask me, "Did he become Chancellor with the understanding that he should send a telegram for troops to march in?"—I say, "No," because at the time of the Chancellorship there was no question of his sending us a telegram.
If you ask me, thirdly, "Did he become Chancellor on the understanding that he would be able to maintain an independent Austria?"—then I have to say again that the final turn of events was not clear in the Fuehrer's mind on that evening.[23]

There were many interchanges like this, and most observers gave the match to Göring, who bragged to his lawyer, "Jackson is not up to me."[24] When Göring completed his testimony, he savored his triumph. "Don't forget I had the best legal brains of England, American, Russia, and France arrayed against me with their whole legal machine—and there I was, alone!"[25]

The Assessments of Kelley and Gilbert

Whereas Kelley was sardonic and tended to avoid jargon, Gilbert was judgmental, and his later writings tended to be doctrinaire. Both agreed that Göring was venal, corrupt, and brutal. Gilbert noted: "Goering tried to give the impression of a jovial realist who had played for big stakes and lost, and was taking it all like a good sport. . . . He had abundant rationalizations for the conduct of the war, his alleged ignorance of the atrocities, the 'guilt' of the Allies, and a ready humor which was always calculated to give the impression that such an amiable character could have meant no harm. . . . [He had] a pathological egotism."[26] But that was the extent of their consensus. Gilbert saw Göring as a monster and a contemptible bully with a cowardly core. In contrast, Kelley admired Göring for being the rogue that he was and, furthermore, asserted that the world was filled with such people. "There are undoubtedly certain individuals who would willingly climb over the corpses of one half of the people of the United States, if by so doing, they could thereby be given control of the other half."[27] To Gilbert, this admiration for a "rogue" was not just errant nonsense; it was an *anathema*.

Göring and Kelley hit it off well; indeed, some felt that Kelley was too close to Göring.[28] Kelley encouraged Göring's storytelling, and Göring felt that in Kelley he had an appreciative audience who could do him an occasional favor. Kelley describes his interactions with Göring as follows: "As a prisoner and as a patient, Goering was one of the easiest to get along with and to interview. Each day when I came to his cell on my rounds, he would jump up from his chair, greet me with a broad smile and outstretched hand, 'Good morning, Doctor. I am so glad you have come to see me. Please sit down, Doctor. Sit here.' Then he would ease his own great body—he still weighed about 200 pounds when the trial began—down beside me, ready to answer my questions."[29]

Göring asked Kelley's assistance in contacting his wife and daughter, and Kelley carried a letter to them from Göring. "Today I can send you a letter direct: Major Kelley, the doctor who is treating me and who has my fullest confidence is bringing it to you. You can also talk to him freely. . . . You can send me an answer through Major Kelley, and you will understand how I long for it."[30]

Göring was so grateful that he offered Kelley one of his enormous, bejeweled rings, but Kelley declined. "Well, here is something just as good," Göring said, and gave Kelley an autographed photograph of himself.[31]

Deeply concerned about the well-being of his daughter, Edda, Göring worried what would become of her if both he and his wife died. He turned to the one person he trusted—Kelley—and asked him to adopt Edda if she were orphaned.[32] Kelley's response is unknown. However, from today's vantage point, we would stir uncomfortably, wondering about the boundary issues between psychiatrist and patient. Göring clearly liked Kelley and even wept when Kelley left Nuremberg.[33]

Kelley described Göring as "charming (when he chose to be charming)," highly intelligent, imaginative, and humorous, while also brutal and having a complete disregard of human life.[34] Although Kelley was close to Göring, he still saw Göring's dark side: "He was an individual who one moment could be the life of the party and a friend to all and the next could, without compunction, order all his companions to their deaths."[35] He continued: "[Göring's] personality is that of an aggressive narcissistic individual . . . [who] is dominated by his fixation on himself. . . . He is filled with enthusiasm about everything he undertakes but has little or no interests in the affairs of others."[36]

Given Göring's addiction, obesity, and uncertain cardiac status, Kelley worried that he might not survive the trial. When Göring surrendered, he weighed in at 280 pounds and had various cardiac symptoms. Kelley claimed that he had helped Göring lose weight by appealing to his narcissism, telling him that he "would make a better appearance in court should he lose some weight."[37] Kelley also took credit for curing Göring of his opiate addiction by gradually tapering the dose of pills and appealing to his narcissism as a way of coping with the drug withdrawal. "Goering was very proud of his physical prowess and his ability to withstand pain. Consequently, it was simple to suggest to him that while weaker men like Ribbentrop (whom he loathed) would perhaps require doses of medicine should they ever be withdrawn from a drug habit he, Goering, being strong and forceful would require nothing. Goering agreed . . . and cooperated wholeheartedly."[38]

Kelley reported that Göring's Rorschach showed "a person of considerable intellectual endowment, highly imaginative, given to an expansive, aggressive, phantasy life, with strong ambition and drive to quickly subjugate the world as he finds it to his own pattern of thinking."[39] In another document Kelley said that Göring's Rorschach "demonstrates normal basic personality" but added that his thought content "reveals marked egocentricity and powerful emotional drives." Once again, Kelley concluded: "This man is competent and demonstrates no evidence of psychopathology. He is able to face trial."[40] Elsewhere, Kelley commented: "[He] is in excellent physical condition and is considerably sobered by the recent testimony, is still carrying the general feeling of keen spirit for the Group. . . . Goering faces his fate in a philosophical fashion. Expects to hang and is no psychiatric problem. There is little expectancy that he will break at any point and as the evidence piles up, he will probably harden his personality to face it. He will undoubtedly carry through without trouble."[41]

Gilbert seemed more aware of Göring's viciousness than Kelley (or possibly, Göring revealed this side of himself to Gilbert rather than Kelley). Referring to a transcription of one of Göring's speeches in 1934, Gilbert quoted the record and offered up his own rather stilted interpretation:

> GOERING: I am not here to exercise justice, but to wipe out and exterminate!
> GILBERT: If the frustrated masses had regressed to the aggressive-submissive modes of behavior of their authoritarian culture, clamoring for strong-arm leadership, Goering was not one to disappoint them.[42]

Gilbert's writings were sometimes harsh and doctrinaire, filled with labored and condemnatory jargon. "Like the typical psychopath, Goering never outgrew the uninhibited action out of these infantile ego-drives."[43] In another instance Gilbert primly commented on Göring's relationship with his wife, who was distressed by his blind loyalty to Hitler. When Gilbert mentioned this to Göring, he brushed it off, saying in essence that it wasn't a woman's affair to meddle in such things. Gilbert's interpretation staggers under the weight of his censure and verbiage: "Goering's medieval egotistical sense of values is complete down to the 'chivalrous' attitude toward women, which conceals its narcissistic purpose behind a façade of condescending protective indulgence and allows no womanly humanitarian values to interfere with that purpose."[44]

Gilbert was at his best when he lingered near the prisoners, eavesdropping and summarizing their interchanges. One would have to be Machiavellian indeed to surpass Göring's view of war.

Why, of course, the *people* don't want war. Why would some poor slob on a farm want to risk his life in a war when the best that he can get out of it is to come back to his farm in one piece. Naturally, the common people don't want war. . . . That is understood. But, after all, it is the *leaders* of the country who determine the policy and it is always a simple matter to drag the people along. . . . The people can always be brought to do the bidding of the leaders. That is easy. All you have to do is tell them that they are being attacked and denounce the pacifists for lack of patriotism and exposing the country to danger. It works the same way in any country.[45]

Despite his irony and intellect, you could not miss Göring's streak of sheer nastiness. Because Gilbert often hovered nearby—in the lunchroom, in the prisoners' cells in the evening, or at the courtroom—we can hear some of these unscripted moments. In court one day, defendant Schacht was trying to portray himself as anti-Nazi and Jackson was just starting to make mincemeat out of him when Gilbert overheard Göring whispering to Hess, "Put on your earphones; this is going to be good!"[46]

Gilbert considered Göring "an egotistical extrovert and adventurer; a cunning and cynical realist who regards power politics as a game of self-ish interests and history as a show in which the clever and the strong (like himself) play the hero's role."[47] Gilbert also noted something that Kelley had failed to document. Göring was an excellent "splitter" and fomented quarrels left and right. He "was maligning the psychologist to the psychiatrist, the Catholic chaplain to the Protestant chaplain and vice versa, both chaplains to the psychologist and psychiatrist, and vice versa, while fawning on each in turn."[48]

When Gilbert asked Göring to complete the Rorschach, he wasn't aware that Kelley had already tested him. As Göring saw the cards emerging from Gilbert's briefcase, he commented, "Oh those crazy cards again."[49] Gilbert was humorlessly disappointed that Kelley had been there ahead of him but conceded: "The two Rorschach records are substantially the same, except for some signs of increased depression and morbid anxiety on the retest."[50]

Kelley claimed that Göring's Rorschach showed considerable intellectual endowment. Gilbert disagreed, claiming that the Rorschach revealed "the qualitative mediocrity of his intellect . . . superficial and pedestrian

realism, rather than brilliantly creative intelligence."[51] This interpretation
may reflect Gilbert's bias because elsewhere Gilbert reported that Göring
scored in the gifted range on intelligence.

Gilbert's most famous Rorschach observation stemmed from a small gesture Göring made while viewing one of the cards.

> He literally tries to "brush off" the (blood) spots on card III and figuratively
> gives the morbid and sadistic second response on that card the brush-off
> in the inquiry. . . . It seems to betray the basic consciousness of guilt and
> the need to escape it, in spite of the outward bravado. . . . Lady Macbeth's
> nightmare was hardly more obvious in betraying her anxiety to rub out the
> "damned spot." . . . [He] was a coward who shirked his responsibilities when
> he could have done something about it.

A few days after being sentenced to death, Göring asked Gilbert what the
Rorschach tests revealed, and Gilbert replied:

> Frankly, they showed that while you have an active, aggressive mind, you
> lack the guts to really face responsibility. You betrayed yourself with a little
> gesture on the ink-blot test . . . [by flicking at a red spot on one of the cards].
> You thought you could wipe away the blood with a little gesture. You've been
> doing the same thing all through the trial. . . . You did the same thing during
> the war too, drugging the atrocities out of your mind. You didn't have the
> courage to face it. . . . You are a moral coward.[52]

This was quite an interpretation, but I think it reveals Gilbert's difficulties in navigating his various roles at the trial. Gilbert, no longer the interpreter nor the prison psychologist, could now become the avenger. Gilbert
noted gleefully that Göring was offended by his comment to the extent that
he filed a complaint about Gilbert with his defense counsel.[53] It speaks
volumes about how Gilbert viewed his role with the prisoners. In an interview with a reporter, Gilbert made quite clear his attitude about the war
criminals: "Hermann Goering's front of bravery is all baloney. They're all
cowards, every one of them, including Goering. They're all trembling in
their cells right now. The front they put up in court was all bravado. They
don't find death as easy to take as it was to dish out."[54]

One senses that Gilbert is on firmer ground with his overall description of Göring, a description based not so much on the Rorschach record but on Gilbert's prolonged observations.

[Göring is an] aggressive psychopath with an insatiable lust for power, titles, wealth, food, . . . and ostentatious display, ready to murder, steal, or stage frame-ups to gain his ends; the camouflage of the amiable extrovert and humorist. . . . His behavior at the trial was a reproduction in miniature of the character he portrayed in history: amiable showmanship on the courtroom stage, with a display of bravado, loyalty, innocence and patriotism, while giving vent to his coarser qualities backstage.[55]

Gilbert sums up Göring as "a ruthlessly aggressive personality camouflaged by disarming amiability when it suited his purpose."[56] Years later, he described Göring elegantly and succinctly as an "Amiable Psychopath."[57]

Göring's End

After Göring's sentencing, there were hints of trouble. Lieutenant Colonel William H. Dunn, one of the psychiatrists who had succeeded Kelley, continued his rounds on the prisoners as they awaited their execution. Göring, he warned, "will face his sentence bolstered by his egocentricity, bravado, and showmanship. Goering will seize any opportunity to go out fighting."[58] One hour before Göring was to be hanged, he quietly killed himself with cyanide. He had said all along that he would not let the Allies hang him— that such an end would be beneath his dignity. In his suicide note, Göring wrote: "I would have allowed myself to be executed by a firing squad. But the German Reichsmarschall should not die on the gallows. . . . Therefore I choose the manner of death of the great Hannibal. . . . [I knew] that I would be sentenced to death, because I viewed the entire trial as a political stunt of the victors . . . [but] I expected that I would be granted the right to die like a soldier. Before God, my people and my conscience, I consider myself not guilty of the crimes of which an enemy court has convicted me."[59]

In a letter to his wife, Göring added: "My one and only sweetheart, after serious consideration and sincere prayer to the Lord, I have decided to take my own life, lest I be executed in so terrible a fashion by my enemies. . . . My life came to an end when I bade you farewell for the last time. . . . My last heartbeats are for our great and eternal love."[60]

A small pool of reporters was to observe the executions. Correspondent Kingsbury Smith broke the news that Göring had evaded execution. "Hermann Goering did not lead the last Nazi parade today—the one to the gallows. He lay dead in his cell by his own hand and Joachim von Ribbentrop took his place at the head of the march into eternity."[61]

Colonel Andrus had to announce the suicide to the world. When Kelley heard the news, he commented: "His suicide, shrouded in mystery and emphasizing the impotency of the American guards, was a skillful, even brilliant, finishing touch, completing the edifice for Germans to admire in time to come."[62] Gilbert called it differently: "Goering died as he had lived, a psychopath trying to make a mockery of all human values and to distract attention from his guilt by a dramatic gesture."[63]

How Göring obtained the cyanide is still a mystery, although by the end of the war cyanide was *everywhere* in Germany and suicide rates were skyrocketing.[64] When the Berlin Philharmonic performed Richard Wagner's opera *Götterdämmerung* (Twilight of the gods) in April 1945, Hitler Youth stood at the exits handing out cyanide capsules to anyone who preferred to die rather than surrender to the Red Army at the gates.[65]

While the prisoners and their cells were searched repeatedly and contraband was confiscated, those searches were not as extensive in the rooms where prisoners' property was stored. Although visitors and lawyers were searched, they may not have been searched carefully by the dwindling numbers of soldiers who had limited training as jail guards. Some of the guards became attached to their wards, particularly when they were famous and charming, like Göring. At least two guards have emerged as the possible cyanide carriers. One guard, Herbert Lee Stivers, claimed that his German girlfriend asked him to carry "medicine" to Göring in his last days.[66] Another suspect, prison guard Jack "Tex" Wheelis, was also regarded as being overly friendly with Göring and retrieved various items for him from the prison storage room.

Even the OSS was suspected of aiding in Göring's suicide. They were grateful for his information on German resources and knew that it would be helpful in the looming Cold War struggle with Russia. Allowing Göring a more honorable death was an acceptable tradeoff. Ned Putzell, aide to OSS chief Donovan, claimed that he had given Göring the cyanide because "Donovan secretly decided, with the agreement of the British contingent, to let him die by cyanide. Goering had been very co-operative with us and he genuinely did seem deserving of some sort of mercy. . . . He was glad to have it. It was better than being hanged."[67]

Last, Douglas Kelley himself came under suspicion, particularly after his own similar death years later. Many observers had noted his close relationship with Göring and wondered if he could have smuggled the cyanide in to Göring. Decades later, it is unlikely we will find out who gave Göring the cyanide, but his suicide was a major body blow to Warden Andrus. His adversary had outwitted him, and the press was quick to assign blame. *Time* magazine seethed: "How could it happen? It happened because the Army had placed in charge of the prison a pompous, unimaginative . . . officer who wasn't up to his job. Colonel Burton C. Andrus loved that job. Every morning his plump little figure, looking like an inflated pouter pigeon, moved majestically into court."[68]

Years later, Andrus rebutted *Time* by saying, "My weight was 160 lb, height 5 ft 10 in, chest 44 in, waist 36 in. . . . A plump pouter pigeon?"[69] He didn't bother to reply to the rest. But even on his deathbed in 1977, Andrus was haunted by Göring, calling out in confusion: "Goering's just committed suicide. I must inform the Council."[70]

Defendant Julius Streicher: "Bad Man"

In that initial hour of religious instruction I realized for the first time in my life that the character of the Jew was abominable and detestable.

—Julius Streicher, August 3, 1945

Lt. Col. Griffith-Jones: And do you think to call them "blood-suckers," "a nation of blood-suckers and extortioners"—do you think that's preaching hatred?
Streicher: That is a statement, the expression of a conviction which can be proved on the basis of historical facts.

—Nuremberg trial transcript, April 29, 1946

Our goal was not to inform, but to egg on, to fire up, to urge on. The organ that we founded should in a sense act as a whip to wake the dilatory sleeper from his slumber and to drive him forward to restless action.

—Joseph Goebbels, 1938

On Trial at Nuremberg, Again

SO FAR, WE HAVE MET REMORSEFUL Robert Ley, in many ways a futurist for workers' rights, and Hermann Göring, defiant and charismatic. Neither were stick-figure-thin demons but very complicated amalgams of vision and malice. For sheer nastiness, unalloyed with any saving graces, we need to turn to Julius Streicher.

It wasn't Streicher's first time in the Nuremberg courts; over the years he had been on trial many times for slander, corruption, sadism, and rape.[1] He bragged to Gilbert that he had been tried "12 or 13 times. I've had lots of trials. That's old stuff."[2] He also had experience with the Nuremberg prison itself, having been imprisoned there before the war for a sex crime.[3] He told Kelley he slept well in jail because of his "clean conscience."[4]

Sex and violence were his abiding interests. He was so obsessed with sex that he questioned children about their sexual activities and told them about his nightly wet dreams.[5] He enjoyed beating people and found that he could work off his tensions by whipping prisoners.[6] In the prime of his power, after yet another session with his riding whip, Streicher acknowledged the sexual frisson: "Now I am relieved. I needed that again!"[7]

Streicher was proud of his prison record. At the peak of his power under the Nazi regime, he ordered that a plaque be mounted on his former cell, honoring his former residence. The cell, he bragged, had even become a pilgrimage site for visiting Nazis.[8] However, his prior jail experience did not make it any easier for him when he was imprisoned by the International Military Tribunal. Although he looked brutally tough, the stress of the situation weighed on Streicher. He repeatedly woke the Nuremberg cellblock screaming in the gloom of the night and he developed cardiac arrhythmias.[9] Throughout it all, he tried to maintain his morale by exercising in the nude in his cell, thereby disgusting his guards.

Multiple observers commented on Streicher's unusual physical appearance (fig. 16). British Major Airey Neave noted that Streicher was "like an ape exposing himself in a cage at the zoo," or like a subject in "an indecent sixteenth century woodcut . . . [who looked like] a mediaeval torturer bared to the waist, pitiless and enjoying the smell of burning flesh."[10] The reporter Joel Sayre added his description:

Although only about five feet six inches in height, he weighs around 190 . . . and his thick, underslung body is a seemingly inexhaustible storage battery of Nordic vigor. His head is shaped like an egg, . . . and the only thing on it is a pair of bushy eyebrows and a mustache, which . . . is practically a replica

Fig. 16. Julius Streicher. (National Archives)

of the . . . Fuhrer's. . . . Perhaps the most arresting feature of his face is his eyes—their blue areas blazing, their whites apparently stitched on with red thread. Beneath his chin hang dewlaps like those of a prize mastiff.[11]

Rebecca West described him on a deeper level, noting: "Streicher is pitiable, because it is plainly the community and not he who was guilty of his sins. He is a dirty old man of the sort that gives trouble in parks and a sane Germany would have sent him to an asylum long ago."[12]

As the interrogators soon learned, it wasn't just his appearance that was peculiar. His *behavior* itself was wildly counterproductive. During his prison interrogations, Streicher was strikingly argumentative and unrepentant.[13] In one interrogation he insisted on his innocence and that of the Nazi

Party, stating: "Whatever happened here was the result of a superhuman being [Hitler]."

Streicher was a gifted rabble-rouser whose speeches and writings inflamed audiences. His devoted readers sent him letters about the evil machinations of Jews, and he gleefully recirculated them in the anti-Semitic tabloid weekly *Der Stürmer* (The attacker). For instance, a patient in a mental hospital wrote that Jewish doctors were drugging him with opium to drive him mad and conspiring with his fellow patients to keep him up at night by pretending to be ghosts.[14] Streicher filled the pages of *Der Stürmer* with such stories and worse—tales of Jewish ritual murders, sexual depravity, and proofs that the Jews were responsible for Germany's massive unemployment and ruinous inflation, that they had swarmed in from the east and taken over the best businesses and land. *Der Stürmer* reported that Jewish doctors were poisoning their patients and that, even when the Jews appeared to be doing good deeds, it was for sinister motives.

During his interrogation and trial, the Allies rapidly zeroed in on various articles Streicher had published.

> *Q.* Did you approve the article . . . where he used the word "exterminate"?
>
> *A.* "Exterminate" and "destroy" are two different words in the German language. At the moment I am speaking about destruction. This word "destruction" was used by the Fuehrer. . . . In the German language, when I say that somebody's life should be taken, I would use either "killed" or "murdered," but I think "kill" would be right expression. Extermination can result by sterilization. . . . The word "extermination" does not necessarily mean killing.[15]

That clarification could hardly help his case. He wasn't necessarily advocating *killing* prisoners, perhaps just sterilizing them.

On October 20, 1945, the defendants were formally indicted. When Streicher received his indictment, he said: "This so-called indictment is *reine Wurst*—pure baloney—they must have their victims. I am suspicious of such international justice. International Jewry is a better description."[16]

The International Military Tribunal offered a list of possible defense attorneys, but Streicher refused to choose one because, to him, all the names on the list sounded Jewish and he wanted an anti-Semite as his defense counsel. In a decision that was so emblematic of the man, he settled on Dr. Hans Marx, a former Nazi Party member. The other defendants carefully reviewed the list, thought about the implications, and tried to make a judicious selection.[17]

Streicher saw "Jews" everywhere. He was sure, for instance, that Justice Jackson's real name was "Jacobson" and that Eisenhower was Jewish.[18] He distrusted Gilbert because he felt that all psychiatrists and psychologists were Jews; he had his doubts about Kelley as well.[19] Whatever his political views, Marx had an extremely difficult client to defend.

Streicher kept digging his own grave, and his behavior was both so damaging to his case and so peculiar that the court requested a psychiatric examination by outside experts. The Russians, usually so utterly convinced of the defendants' guilt, actually initiated the request because Streicher told them that he was really a Zionist at heart. As a result of this startling confession, the Russians had certain doubts as to his mental stability.[20] And Streicher's attorney had so many problems dealing with his client that he also requested a psychiatric examination.

Three psychiatrists were summoned from Russia, France, and the United States. In contrast to the extensive psychiatric reports filed on Hess, the experts' findings about Streicher were succinctly definitive: "Defendant Julius Streicher is sane. Defendant Julius Streicher is fit to appear before the Tribunal and to present his defense. It being the unanimous conclusion of the examiners that Julius Streicher is sane, he is for that reason capable of understanding the nature and quality of his acts during the period of time covered by the Indictment."[21]

The case against Streicher was presented on January 10, 1946. Although his day in court was relatively brief, the legal issues in his case were unique. He was too despicable even for the Nazis, who forbade him from making speeches in autumn 1939 and placed him under house arrest starting in 1940. It was thus difficult for the tribunal to prove that he had conspired to start the war or commit war crimes. Instead, the tribunal accused him of zealously fulminating race hatred so long and so effectively that this constituted crimes against humanity.

The prosecution relied on Streicher's writings and speeches as evidence of his incitements to violence. The historical record was *very* ample on that point. Streicher had written, after all:

One single cohabitation of a Jew with an Aryan woman is sufficient to poison her blood forever. Together with the "alien albumen" she has absorbed the alien soul. Never again will she be able to bear purely Aryan children, even when married to an Aryan. They will all be bastards, with a dual soul and a body of a mixed breed. Their children, too, will be crossbreeds: that means ugly people of unsteady character and with a tendency to illnesses. Now we know why the Jew uses every artifice of seduction in order to ravish German girls at as early an age as possible: why the Jewish doctor rapes his female patients while they are under anesthesia. . . . He wants the German girl and German woman to absorb the alien sperm of the Jew.[22]

Elsewhere, Streicher advocated the death penalty for Jews who committed race pollution and urged Germany to invade Russia to rid the world of all Jews and communists: "They must be utterly exterminated. Then the world will see that the end of the Jews is also the end of Bolshevism."[23]

Streicher presented his defense on April 26, 1946, and was cross-examined by the prosecution on April 29. Seeking to draw him out, the prosecution asked whether he thought he had promoted race hatred by writing that Jews were "a nation of bloodsuckers and extortionists." Streicher's response: "It is not preaching hatred. It is just a statement of facts."[24]

His pugnaciousness made a bad impression on the tribunal and even his fellow defendants regarded him as contemptible. During Streicher's testimony, Göring whispered to Hess, "Well, at least we did one good thing: getting that prick [Streicher] kicked out of office."[25] Another defendant told Gilbert, "Well, they've put the rope around his neck after all; at least our end of the dock thinks so."[26]

On his one day of testimony, Streicher got into a loud argument with his attorney. He was furious that Marx wouldn't introduce "proof" of the existence of ritual murder. Instead, his attorney argued that, because Streicher was so widely disliked by the Nazi Party leadership and had been out of office since autumn 1939, he could hardly incite anyone effectively. This strategy, truthful though it was, so humiliated and incensed Streicher that he adamantly denied that he had been stripped of power. He became increasingly belligerent in response to his attorney's questions and shouted out that Marx was doing a bad job and was not presenting the defense in the way Streicher wanted. In response, the justices threatened to have Streicher evicted from the courtroom unless he quieted down; Justice Jackson even tried to get him cited for contempt. As the old adage goes, "The tongue is the enemy of the neck."

In his defense Streicher argued, "Show me one person who said he had killed Jews because of reading my paper." He claimed that he did not know of the killings and couldn't be blamed for them. "I never wrote, 'Burn Jewish homes down; beat them to death.' Never once did such an incitement appear in *Der Stürmer*."[27] Additionally, he claimed that his goal was merely to get the Jews to a homeland of their own, outside of Germany (ergo, his Zionism). In his closing arguments, Jackson ridiculed Streicher's testimony: "A Gauleiter of Franconia whose occupation was to pour forth filthy writings about the Jews, but who had *no idea* that anybody would read them."[28]

The Assessments of Gilbert and Kelley

Gilbert describes Streicher as rigid, insensitive, and obsessive: "He considers the Bible pornographic literature and has no use even for Christ because he was a Jew."[29] Streicher was a master at offending everyone he came into contact with. Even after his longtime house arrest for offending Göring by asserting that Göring couldn't have fathered a child, Streicher couldn't help himself and salaciously repeated the allegation (again!) to Gilbert at Nuremberg.[30]

The following interchange between Gilbert and Streicher gives a sense of their interactions.

> GILBERT TO STREICHER: "Why did you have to print all that sexual filth about the Jews?"
> STREICHER: "Why it's all in the Talmud. The Jews are a circumcised race. Didn't Joseph commit race pollution with Pharaoh's daughter? . . . [The judges] are crucifying me now. I can tell. Three of the judges are Jews."

G: "How can you tell?"

STREICHER: "I can recognize blood. Three of them get uncomfortable when I look at them. I can tell. I've been studying race for 20 years."[31]

Gilbert wrote about Streicher in his diary: "A quarter of an hour with this perverted mind is about all one can stand at one time, and his line never varies: World Jewry and circumcision serve as the channels for projecting his own lascivious thoughts and aggressions into a pornographic anti-Semitism."[32]

Gilbert asked Streicher how he could recognize Jews. Since this topic was a favorite of Streicher's, he jumped right in, but his answer was a tad unusual—the Jewish behind. "The Jewish behind is not like a Gentile behind. The Jewish behind is so feminine—so soft and feminine—and you can tell from the way it wobbles when they walk."[33]

Gilbert tested Streicher's IQ and noted that it took Streicher a whole minute to do a simple mathematics problem ("how much change he would get from fifty pfennings if he bought seven two-pfennig stamps").[34] Gilbert felt that Streicher had no true psychiatric diagnosis but had an abnormal paranoid personality. Gilbert concluded: "There is neither sadism nor shame in his attitude; just a cool, apathetic obsessive quality."[35]

After hearing the prosecution's summation on July 26, 1946, a considerably subdued Streicher confided to Gilbert that he was ready to help the Jews now. "I'm ready to join and help them in their fight. . . . The Jews will dominate the world. And I would be happy to help lead them to victory."[36]

Kelley also made extensive observations of Streicher. He regarded Streicher as a paranoid, anti-Semitic fanatic who "had a systemized series of beliefs . . . which were founded purely on his own emotions and prejudices and not on known facts. . . . In other matters he was essentially rational."[37] Kelley was intrigued by Streicher and remarked, "He was a man who lives, and succeeds, by emotion almost exclusively. To have seen Julius Streicher lounging on his cot, a bald, paunchy, loose-skinned man in cast-off GI work clothes, one would have found it hard to believe that this creature had once held thousands of 'sensible' Germans spellbound."[38]

Streicher saw himself as a hero who was being sacrificed by Jews. He told Kelley: "The entire history of the world has proved that the bearers of truth and understanding are always a minority. I am one of that small group. The knowledge of belonging among the pioneers of the truth gives me the inner strength to survive all hardships of these trying times."[39]

Kelley wrote a brief summary of Streicher on December 13, 1945. He described Streicher's mental status exam as normal, but under "thought content," Kelley scrawled: "Reveals fixed belief in Jewish persecution secondary to self suggestion for many years." He then added his typical boilerplate sentence for all of the war criminals: "This man is competent and demonstrates no evidence of psychopathology. He is able to face trial."[40]

In contrast to this laconic summary, Kelley had a lot to say about Streicher's Rorschach and concluded that it revealed a normal personality with strong extratensive features (responses shaped primarily by emotion and impulsivity).[41] Streicher's stress tolerance (measured by a combination of movement and color responses) was surprisingly high, but his other responses suggested that he was under significant amounts of stress (as inferred by an overrepresentation of shading responses). In terms of inkblot content, Streicher reported many anatomical responses (skeletons, anatomical specimen, hip bone, blood, preserved meniscus). Such responses are traditionally viewed as markers of depression.[42] He was after all in prison and facing trial as a war criminal, a situation where one would expect stress and depression responses.

In a January 5, 1946, prison document, Kelley wrote:

> Streicher represents an extremely earthy type of individual who, unable to gain recognition of the world, has become fixed with an idea. This belief has become, in time, an almost true monomania. There seems little doubt that he actually believes it, and this belief will undoubtedly carry him through the trial. He is of only moderate intelligence and his only accomplishment is measured in the firmness of his almost delusional belief. He is obviously quite sane as his ideas while false and odd cannot be classed as true delusions. They are, of course, false beliefs but he has sought to prove them for so long that he at least actually has converted himself.[43]

A later Nuremberg psychiatrist wrote: "Streicher impresses me as an old psychopathic personality with sexual and other conflicts, whose inadequacy found expression in an obsessive preoccupation which for the past twenty years had filled the narrow stream of his life."[44]

A Perspective from the Twenty-First Century (with a Nod to Cicero)

All the observers commented on Streicher's "paranoia," a term that ranges from a variant of personality style all the way to psychosis. Few evaluators felt that Streicher was psychotic; rather, his suspiciousness, violence, and sexual depravity seemed to reflect a lifelong pattern of behavior. Repugnant beliefs and actions reflect moral failings but not necessarily psychiatric disorders. Yet Streicher's suspicious preoccupations do raise some troubling questions. Are rigidly held and distasteful political views instances of psychiatric disorder? That question becomes particularly challenging when such views are widely held in a culture. Contemporary psychiatrists and psychologists exclude such culturally held beliefs as a basis for a psychiatric diagnosis. We cannot "treat" a culture even if its beliefs are grounded in error or incite violence.

Streicher is arresting because his behavior was off-scale even for the Nazis. He was not just another violent corrupt, ideologically committed, anti-Semitic Nazi. Instead, for Streicher, anti-Semitism was more central to his being. It was his North Star, so to speak—a beacon that guided his actions.

Autobiographies intrigue me—not just their content or style, but because they reveal how individuals sift through and select the features of their life that they wish to emphasize. While waiting in jail in October 1945, Streicher wrote two autobiographical statements. The longer text, two and a half typed, single-spaced pages, devotes 60 percent of the space to his beliefs that the Jews were dangerous.[45] He also composed a short handwritten letter in response to Kelley's request:

> To Major Kelley
> I have been born on 12 February 1885. I had three brothers and three sisters. I am the fifth of the children. I am a writer. I used to be Gauleiter in Franken.
> "He caused the east wind to set forth in heaven; and by His power He brought on the south wind."
> I feel physically healthy.
> Julius Streicher[46]

The letter starts with a formulaic statement about Streicher's family and then claims his identity as an author and a party leader. But the embedded quotation from Psalms 78:26 is unusual and seems out of context. One could read it as a statement of humility, fatalism, or grandiosity. In any event, it suggests "something" other than his habitual paranoia.

But Streicher was unusual in other respects as well. His relationships with his fellow Nazis were characterized by continual arguments and remarkably poor judgment. The man could not stop himself and his malicious gossiping about Göring almost got himself killed—only to be rescued by a sentence of house arrest for the duration of the war.

Then, there were all those sex crimes.

Streicher's behavior was certainly facilitated by National Socialism, but something else was going on as well. He would probably meet criteria for a personality disorder. Personality denotes the enduring pattern of an individual's life, his or her climate, so to speak. We all have bad weather in our lives, bouts of cloudy, stormy times that can in some instances be severe. But personality is our individual *climate,* and in Streicher's case, his climate was aberrant—marked by corruption, suspiciousness, violence, and sexual assault.

Personality patterns have always been a hazy area in psychiatry. We all know people who are belligerent, distrustful, compulsive, or morose. Others are mercurial, "odd," or infatuated with themselves, and many people manifest a fluctuating mixture of all of these traits. When these ways of relating to the world become glaring and inflexible, they constitute full-fledged disorders. More often than not, these disorders are shape-shifters with unclear contours.

Personality disorders are diverse. Many patients suffer profoundly from their personality disorders; some of them make others around them suffer. Many are repulsive individuals. Others are capable of being quite charming. If one had a long list of adjectives for describing Streicher, I do not think anyone would describe him as "charming."

My house is strewn with books. One night, when I couldn't sleep well, I picked up Cicero's *Tusculan Disputations* and was startled to come across his description of personality patterns run amok. From the perspective of 45 BCE, Cicero commented that people are troubled by "all kinds of depravity and perversity": "There are more disorders of the mind than of the body, and they are of a more dangerous nature. . . . The mind, when disordered, . . . can neither bear nor endure anything, and is under the perpetual influence of desires." These "depravities," Cicero noted, are deep-seated and driven by societal forces. "[When] the multitude, who declare unanimously for what is wrong, then are we altogether overwhelmed." You would think he was writing about Streicher under National Socialism.[47]

But perhaps I am skirting a central issue. If Streicher, against all odds, had straggled into the office of a psychiatrist or psychologist, he would probably have been diagnosed as having some form of personality disorder—a long, entrenched pattern of distorted relations with others and disrupted sense of identity. In any context other than a therapist's office, he would be regarded, quite simply, as "bad seed"—argumentative, violent, corrupt, suspicious, depraved. In Chapter 12 we shall consider whether individuals like Streicher reveal a different perspective on the nature of malice.

The Execution

It was policy. Before each man was hanged, he was asked his name. Streicher refused and, in his last act of defiance, shouted out, "Heil Hitler! You know my name very well!" The hangman wrestled the noose over his head, and Streicher's last words were "Purim Feast, 1946," a surprisingly astute reference to the biblical Book of Esther and its recounting of Haman's execution by hanging. He went on to scream, "The Bolsheviks will hang *you* one day!"[48]

The observers reported that it was a messy execution. Streicher struggled on the gallows, and when the trap was opened, he went down kicking and it was not a straight drop. Streicher's dying moans were heard for quite some time. In a final, ironic twist, his ashes were placed in an urn under the name of Abraham Goldberg until they could be scattered.[49]

8

Defendant Rudolf Hess: "So Plainly Mad"

Hess was noticeable because he was so plainly mad: so plainly mad that it seemed shameful that he should be tried. His skin was ashen, and he had that odd faculty, peculiar to lunatics, of falling into strained positions which no normal person could maintain for more than a few minutes, and staying fixed in contortion for hours. . . . He looked as if his mind had no surface, as if every part of it had been blasted away except the depth where the nightmares live.

—Rebecca West, "Greenhouse with Cyclamens I," 1946

Diagrammatically, if one considers the street as sanity and the sidewalk as insanity, then Hess spent the greater part of his time on the curb.

—Douglas Kelley, *22 Cells in Nuremberg*, 1947

An Enigma

IN CONTRAST TO STREICHER'S sheer nastiness, the cadaverous bushy-eyebrowed Hess posed enormous problems in psychiatric assessment (fig. 17). Compared to Göring's corrupt and extraverted hedonism, Hess was, well, "different"—he was an introvert who was rigidly honest and shy but fanatically loyal to Hitler (Gilbert describes his "doglike devotion to his master").[1] Hess complained intermittently of amnesia and constantly of aches and

Fig. 17. Rudolf Hess reading in his cell. (National Archives)

pains, and was convinced that the Allies were trying to poison him because they were hypnotically controlled by Jews. He would rock back and forth moaning about abdominal pain, but this behavior could stop instantly if he was distracted. He seemed hollow and adopted bizarre postures throughout the trial. A courtroom observer remarked that he "was gaunt, and just not 'with it.' . . . I'm no psychiatrist or psychoanalyst, but he looked to me like a man who had completely withdrawn from life and the developments around him."[2]

Medical observers shared this view. An editorial in the *Lancet* concluded that Hess's "main probable diagnosis would appear to be paranoid schizophrenia," complicated by additional problems of hysterical amnesia, malingering, and negativism.[3] On the other hand, some observers felt that Hess was primarily a skilled malingerer who hoodwinked countless experts.

The British Experience before Nuremberg

Hess had been imprisoned with Hitler in the 1920s and helped him write *Mein Kampf.* Subsequently, Hess led the Nazi Party and oversaw its activities in education, religion, and labor as well as its outreach to international pro-Nazi bunds. Despite his unusual appearance and persona, he was a popular speaker in the early Nuremberg rallies, filling his speeches with mystic sentimentality and appeals for self-sacrifice. Hitler, he often said, "is fulfilling a divine mission to German destiny." His other recurring theme was a militaristic cry for "guns before butter." As deputy Führer, he helped plan the invasions of Austria and Czechoslovakia.

As the war dragged on, Hess's influence waned because of his eccentricities and because of jealousies within Hitler's inner circle. Hess tried to forestall a second front to the war—the approaching Nazi invasion of Russia—with a bizarre and grandiose scheme. He secretly flew to England in hopes of persuading the British to align with Germany against Russia. The British didn't know what to do with him, and a shocked Hitler furiously stripped Hess of his party membership and proclaimed him "unsound."

The British soon got a taste of this "unsoundness," as we read in Chapter 4. The British psychiatrists suspected that Hess was schizophrenic, noting: "He was convinced he was surrounded by secret service agents who would accomplish his death by driving him to commit suicide, committing a murder staged to look like suicide, or administering poison in his food."[4]

Amnesia in Nuremberg

Hess has one of the best-documented psychiatric histories of any political figure. His mental status changed repeatedly throughout his imprisonment, alternating between paranoia, amnesia, and preoccupations with his health. When he arrived in Nuremberg, one question dominated the court: Was he faking it?

Dissembling mental illness is an ancient stratagem for prisoners. The Old Testament recounts that David simulated insanity to protect himself from the king of Gath by scribbling on the gateposts and drooling into his beard (1 Sam. 21:12–15).[5] Throughout history defendants have pretended to be insane to avoid punishment. Was Hess just another instance of this? John Amen, head of the American army interrogations unit, thought so, as did many others. The following extracts give an idea of Amen's interrogation. Whatever the source of his memory problems, Hess was a clever man.

> AMEN: "When did you get the idea of losing your memory? When did you think it would be a smart thing?"
> HESS: "You imagine I think it would be a good idea to lose my memory to deceive you?"
> AMEN: "If you didn't remember your crimes, that would make it tougher for us, wouldn't it? . . . You say you can't remember your wife's name, yet the British told us you wrote to her all the time."
> HESS: "Ah, yes, I received letters from her, so I copied the name from the envelope."[6]

Subsequent interrogations continued in the same vein—Amen always trying to trick Hess, Hess shrewdly claiming amnesia and somehow or other always putting a "spin" on his response. If this were a soccer match, Amen would have lost.

> Q. What was your last official position?
> A. Unfortunately, this already comes into a period which I cannot re-member any more. . . . The doctor has told me that this is a frequent occurrence, especially in time of war, but that there is some chance that my memory will return. There are many cases where I cannot even remember what happened ten or fourteen days ago. . . . Yester-day, I was told by a doctor . . . that it happens sometimes that people don't even know their own names any more, and he said that possibly by a shock it would suddenly all return again. This is terrible for me, and everything depends on it for me because I will have to defend myself in the process which is going to come soon. There is nobody to defend myself if I cannot do it myself.
> Q. You mean that you cannot even remember what your last official position was in Germany?
> A. No; I have no idea. It is just like a fog.
> Q. But you don't know what the proceeding is for?
> A. I have no idea. I don't even know whether I was told what I am accused of. I know that it is a political trial.
> Q. Do you know who Jews are?

A. Yes; they are people—a race.

Q. You didn't like them very well, did you?

A. The Jews, no.

Q. So you had some laws passed about the Jews, didn't you?

A. If you tell me, I have to believe it, but I don't know it.[7]

The interrogation continued the following day:

Q. How is your memory today?

A. The same, it hasn't altered any. I don't feel very well just now. I just had a cramp in my intestines.

Q. When did you get this idea of losing your memory?

A. I don't know. It is a fact that I don't have it now.

Q. I say, when did you get the idea that it would the smart thing to lose it?

A. I don't quite understand that. You mean to say . . . that I thought it might be a good idea to lose my memory and then deceive you like that?

Q. Yes. That is just what I mean.

A. Well, I can only say that that is not true.

Q. Well, it might be very helpful in connection with the coming proceedings, might it not?

A. . . . I don't see the benefit I could derive from losing my memory there.

Q. Oh, no, but, for instance, when you directed the murder of various people, which you did.

A. I did that?

Q. Yes, so the witnesses say.

A. You mean that because I can't remember it, the witnesses are less creditable?

Q. Oh, somewhat.

A. Or, do you mean because I am lying?

Q. To make people feel sorry for you also.[8]

Colonel Amen served Hess with his formal indictment in October 1945 and then returned two weeks later, accompanied by Kelley. On this occasion, Hess denied even recognizing Amen despite his many previous interrogations. This was going to be a hard struggle.

When Hess arrived at Nuremberg, he passed Göring in the corridor and promptly said, "Heil Hitler," giving the Nazi salute. Yet he claimed later that he didn't know Göring.[9] He told Warden Andrus that he needed his chocolates from Ashcan as part of his defense to show that the British were poisoning him. It was Andrus's opinion that Hess was "a total fake."[10] If Hess had amnesia, he asked Kelley, how is it that he could remember how to speak English? Andrus was obsessed with crashing through Hess's memory loss. He showed Hess movies of early Nuremberg rallies, but Hess claimed he still didn't remember. "I must have been there because obviously I was there. But . . . I don't remember."[11]

The interrogators tried to jog Hess's memory by bringing in his wife, his former secretaries, and his old professor. Hess didn't remember any of them. Warden Andrus felt that this proved Hess's homosexuality. After all, he and Hitler had shared a cell in Landsberg Prison years before, and Hess could remember Hitler's name but not his wife's. In a note to Kelley, Andrus confided: "We think that the only reason he remembers Hitler is because of abnormal sex relations with him. A homosexual naturally would tend to remember a man with whom he had abnormal sex relations, instead of his wife with whom he had normal sex relations. We think that abnormality [homosexuality] might possibly be affecting memory."[12]

Andrus may have been a fine warden, but when it came to interrogation techniques, he had all the subtlety of a Mack truck. He suggested that Kelley could trap Hess by telling him, "You have all the other Doctors fooled; but you're not fooling me. Since you and I are the only ones wise to the fact that your memory hasn't gone bad, I want to ask you something. If you get out of this trial all right, and I think you have a very good chance if I don't tell what I know, will you testify against the other prisoners? If you will not do this then I will expose you."[13]

In the courtroom, Hess was seated next to Göring. Early in the trial, Hess whispered to Göring: "You'll see, this apparition will vanish, and you will be Fuhrer of Germany within a month." Göring told Gilbert that with that statement he was SURE that Hess was crazy.[14] The redoubtable Colonel Amen interrogated Göring about Hess on October 9, 1945.

> Q. Did you think that Hess was telling the truth?
> A. Yes, absolutely. He is completely changed . . . , but he gives me the impression that he is completely crazy.

> *Q.* You say he seemed to be crazy before he went off on this flight?
> *A.* I wouldn't say outright crazy, but he was not quite normal then, and he was very exalted, so to speak, very exuberant.
> *Q.* Was he any worse at the time when he flew over to England than he had been before?
> *A.* . . . In spite of the high position, he had relatively little to do after the outbreak of the war, and his ambition to do things . . . may have caused his attitude. It was his wish all the time to do something . . . decisive, and this made him very, very nervous. Then he probably also felt that his next subordinate, Bormann, was talking to the Fuehrer and not telling him about it, and that may have added to it. Then he got the idea that he had to do something decisive, that he had to fly to England and bring about peace; in other words, to do something to compensate for this relative inactivity, which was forced upon him.[15]

Göring told Kelley that Hess was always odd and told another psychiatrist that Hess had been "slightly off balance for as long as I can recall."[16] Throughout it all, Hess kept to himself, goose-stepping across the jail's courtyard during his daily exercise.[17] He was suspicious and uncooperative, and he kept a fastidious diary reminding himself to avoid all sleeping pills and eggs and to be very cautious about whatever he ate.[18]

Meanwhile, Justice Jackson finally agreed with Wild Bill Donovan that the court testimony had to become more riveting. The trial could not be just an endless dispute over documents, but it needed real testimony about the Nazi crimes themselves. As an initial step, the court viewed a film about the concentration camps. Gilbert and Kelley stood on either side of the dock to observe the defendants' responses. Here was a chance to see if Hess remembered anything. He was described as glaring at the screen and showing sustained interest, but he made no comment.[19] When asked about Nazi crimes against humanity, Hess angrily rejected any responsibility and accused his British doctors of being the "real abusers and torturers."[20]

The Court's Response to the International Experts

The court was troubled by Hess's behavior and called in an international team of seven physicians to examine him. The group included psychiatrists, neurologists, internists, and psychoanalysts, as well as Winston Churchill's personal doctor, who happened to be president of the Royal College of Physicians. The *Journal of the American Medical Association* noted approvingly in an article of March 23, 1946, that because of how this case was being handled, "the role of the psychiatrist in the trial of the leading Axis war criminals has attained historical significance."[21] Historical significance certainly, but unanimity—hardly. The Russian doctors did not think Hess was schizophrenic and saw nothing in his behavior that should mitigate a sentence, preferably death. The British documented Hess's paranoia but felt that he could understand the proceedings and that ultimately he had a "psychopathic personality." The Americans and French argued that Hess was not legally insane and that his amnesia reflected a mix of hysteria and malingering.[22] Finally, the examining committee hammered out a consensus: "Our examination revealed that Hess is not insane, has no disorder of consciousness, understands the nature of the proceedings against him. . . . A part of the memory loss is simulated. . . . It is probable that this type of response was originally developed consciously as a protective measure during a period of stress; that it has become habitual and has therefore become unconscious in part."[23]

The experts based their opinion on their personal examinations of Hess, but they were also very influenced by Hess's peculiar behavior in court. He ostentatiously paid no attention to the proceedings, took his earphones off and instead read novels during some of the testimony. The experts saw this behavior as decidedly unusual and pointed out that a patient with true amnesia would have followed the testimony with interest. "He therefore has a *selective* amnesia, hysterical in type. . . . He has no brain disease as such and his capacity for thinking is basically intact." The conclusion was thus that Hess was not insane "in the strict sense of the word."[24]

THAT was the kernel of the experts' reports—Hess could follow the proceedings, knew that he was on trial, but, by virtue of his memory problems, might not be able to assist in his defense very well. What an interesting, nuanced summary! Hess's defense attorney argued predictably that if he could not assist in his own defense, he should not be tried. The prosecution countered that there was no evidence for a neurological origin of Hess's memory problems and that, whether his amnesia was malingering or unconscious in nature, the trial should proceed. Curiously, the Russian experts predicted that Hess might snap out of his amnesia during the trial. "Such behavior often terminates when the hysterical person is faced with an unavoidable necessity of conducting himself correctly. Therefore the amnesia of Hess may end upon his being brought to trial."[25]

Justice Jackson argued that since Hess had refused all treatments suggested for his amnesia, he was responsible for the consequences of his impaired ability to assist in his own defense. "He is in the volunteer class with his amnesia. In England, as the reports show, he is reported to have made the statement that his earlier amnesia was simulated. He came out of this state during a period in England, then went back to it. It is now highly selective. That is to say, you can't be sure what Hess will remember and what he will not remember. His amnesia is not of the type which is a complete blotting out of the personality, of the type that would be fatal to his defense."[26]

In her observations on the trial, the novelist Rebecca West summed up Jackson's point more eloquently: "Sanity is to some extent a matter of choice, a surrender to certain stimuli and a rejection of others."[27]

In this swirl of courtroom arguments, the judges were leaning toward excusing Hess from needing to be in the courtroom. A hearing was held on November 30, 1945, to decide the matter (fig. 18). Just before the session, Gilbert told Hess that he might be considered incompetent and excused from the proceedings. The court returned to session, and Hess's lawyer had begun to summarize the arguments for dismissing Hess on psychiatric grounds when Hess suddenly stood up and shouted that he had made up the amnesia:

> In order to anticipate any possibility of my being declared incapable of pleading, . . . I would like to give the following declaration . . . . Henceforth my memory will again respond to the outside world. The reasons for simulating loss of memory were of a tactical nature. Only my ability to concentrate is, in fact, somewhat reduced. But my capacity to follow the trial, to defend myself, to put questions to witnesses, or to answer questions myself is not affected thereby.[28]

Kelley thought that Gilbert's "suggestion undoubtedly upset [Hess] considerably, since he felt that to be denied a trial would indicate mental infe-

Fig. 18. Gustave Gilbert confronting Rudolf Hess with the news. By happenstance, a US Army photographer captured the precise moment when Gilbert (third from left and facing camera) informed Hess (standing in suit) and his attorney that Hess would not be able to appear in his own defense and therefore would be the only defendant not to take the stand. (National Archives)

riority and he felt that he must stand trial with his companions. . . . [His behavior reveals] his hysterical nature and his desire to thrust himself into the limelight, fatal as it might be."[29]

Gilbert commented: "He gave his declaration of malingering in Court, apparently as a face-saving device. In later conversations he admitted to me that he had not been malingering and that he knew he had lost his memory twice in England."[30]

Kelley interviewed Hess the evening after his surprise announcement and found him elated over his testimony, proud over fooling everyone, but, all the same, complaining that his memory wasn't quite right. Kelley regarded Hess's courtroom statement as a "typical dramatic, hysterical gesture," commenting that people who have recovered from mental illness will downplay their former symptoms "to protect their ego."

Hᴇss: How did I do? Good, wasn't I? I really surprised everybody, don't you think?

Kᴇʟʟᴇʏ: I shook my head and said I didn't think "everybody."

H: Then I didn't fool you by pretending amnesia? I was afraid you had caught on. You spent so much time with me.

K: I asked Hess if he remembered some movies that had been shown earlier of the top Nazis. . . . At the time he claimed he could not recognize the men. . . .

H: Yes, I remember. . . . I thought you knew I was pretending. All the time you looked only at my hands. It made me very nervous to know you had learned my secret.[31]

Hess explained that he started having memory problems in England, and when he realized that his interrogation sessions were shorter when he said that he couldn't remember, he decided to exaggerate his complaints of amnesia. The next day, Kelley found Hess increasingly preoccupied with delusional beliefs about poisoned food. Over the next two weeks Hess was suspicious and increasingly distant. He started admitting that some of his memory problems were very real.

Gilbert, ever lurking around the prisoners' dock and lunchroom, captured snippets of the others' opinions of Hess and his quixotic attempt to make peace with England: "Such stupidity . . . such childish naiveté. . . . It is disgraceful—it shows what irresponsible people ruled Germany."[32] Hess's confession and behavior shocked the prisoners. Streicher said: "If you ask me, I think Hess' behavior was a shame. It reflects on the dignity of the German people."[33] There were other opinions regarding the origins of his problems. Göring thought that Hess's oddness was caused by excessive masturbation. Noted Göring, "In strictest confidence, Hess couldn't satisfy his wife."[34] Göring went on:

You know, Hess isn't normal—He may have recovered his memory, all right, but he is still suffering from a persecution complex. For instance, he makes remarks about a machine having been put under his cell to drive him insane with the noise of the motor. I told him I hear the same motor under my cell. He keeps coming out with remarks like that.—I can't remember them all, but you might expect things like this: if the coffee is too hot, they are trying to burn him; if it is too cold, they are trying to upset him. He didn't actually say that, but that is the kind of thing he comes out with.[35]

With all of this swirling around, the court decided to accept Hess at his word, and he was allowed to continue attending the trial. Paradoxically, Hess's testimony clouded the picture further. As one of the Nuremberg attorneys described it, "[Hess's] statement kept him in the lawsuit, and convinced us lawyers that he really was not very sound of mind, because he was out of the case and he'd talked himself back into it."[36] He was "about to get off" on an insanity defense; only a crazy person would stand up under such circumstances and announce that he had made it all up![37] Such considerations may have saved Hess from execution; instead, he was sentenced to life imprisonment. All of this is confusing enough in the twenty-first century, but experts lacked a common psychiatric vocabulary in Nuremberg in 1945 and 1946. The court was troubled about how to proceed and did not know whether it should even allow Hess to testify. Kelley advised trying Hess and then seeking a psychiatric opinion about whether a death sentence "was justifiable for someone in Hess's state of mind."[38]

Hess's Postscript to the Trial

After the trial was concluded, on November 16, 1946, Hess wrote a long, meandering letter from prison to Sir Oswald Mosley, head of the British Union of Fascists. Mosley, who had been married secretly in Goebbels's Berlin house, was a longtime ardent fascist who spent time in Mussolini's company. He spent most of the war either in prison or under house arrest because of his political views. What on earth could Hess have hoped to achieve by writing to Mosley? In the National Archives, I found the typescript letter with Hess's handwritten edits in the margins. It is hard to convey just how peculiar this wandering document is. I think it supports the case for Hess's extensive paranoia and disorganization. He had nothing to gain from the letter; after all, he had already been sentenced to life imprisonment.

The letter begins: "To be transmitted in the most secret way to Sir Oswald Mosley in London, a VERY high gratification will be granted later on." Hess continues: "The following is the first part of the intended but never spoken 'final word.' In the spring of 1942 I suffered from an obstruction of my intestine. The doctor gave me laxatives, however they did not produce any relief. . . . Later, when I again drank cocoa the stomach obstruction reoccurs." Hess details his bowel complaints for many pages, and the letter goes downhill from there:

> [There was] unexplainable behavior of some people who were around me in England. These people were replaced from time to time. Some of those . . . with me had a strange appearance in their eyes during the first days. They were glassy, dreamy eyes. . . . The appearance of their eyes did not come to just my attention alone, since the doctor, Dr. Johnston, who was with me in the spring of 1942 noticed them also. . . . Doctor Johnsten [sic] did not real-ize that he himself had the same eyes the first time he visited me. But now comes the important part: In one of the reports of the previously mentioned proceedings—specifically the Moscow proceedings—it states that the defen-dants had unusual eyes; they were glassy, absent, dreamy eyes.[39]

These passages do not read like the intellectually sharp Hess who had du-eled so well with his interrogator. Pages later, Hess repeated to Mosley ex-cerpts from his closing statement to the Nuremberg Court: "It was granted to me for many years of my life to serve under the greatest son Adolph Hit-ler which my people have brought forth in its thousand-year history. Even if I could, I would not blot out this period of my existence. I am happy to [be] a loyal follower of the Fuehrer. I regret nothing."[40]

Kelley's Assessment

Kelley saw Hess daily and wrote a report to Justice Jackson on Octo-ber 16, 1945, noting that Hess seemed somewhat depressed but was com-petent and not particularly suspicious. Hess had unusual memory prob-lems, however—he couldn't remember his birthdate or any facts of his early life. Kelley requested authorization to administer an Amytal interview. The request was denied.

Kelley worried that Hess was not eating enough, and Hess told him: "If they don't hang me I can get fat then, when I am home; but if they do hang me what difference will it make if I take medicine or more food than I care to?"[41] Over the course of the trial, Hess felt that his stomach cramps improved and attributed the improvement "to the homeopathic effect of the minute doses of poison which 'have been placed in my food.'"[42] Both Kelley

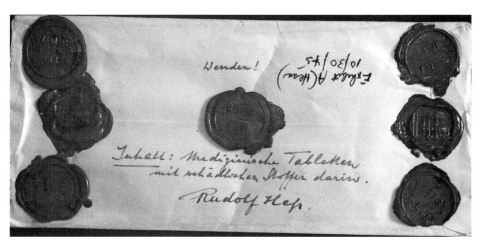

Fig. 19. Rudolf Hess's sealed envelope containing spots of his marmalade, which, he was convinced, contained brain poison. (Douglas Kelley personal papers, photo by author)

and Gilbert described how Hess continued to save samples of his food, placing bits of marmalade on blotter paper so that he could seal them up with red wax and send them to be analyzed for brain poison (fig. 19).[43] He told Kelley that he couldn't get these ideas out of his mind and that he couldn't control them. "Even now, at times these ideas come over me. I will look at a piece of bread . . . and suddenly I feel sure that it has been poisoned. I try to talk myself out of this belief, but usually solve the problem by simply putting the food away."[44]

Despite Hess's above-average intelligence, Kelley noted his inconsistent memory symptoms and was certain that they represented both malingering and hysteria (or what would today be called dissociation). One of Hess's former secretaries tried to help him reclaim his memory by giving him an old photograph to look at, but Hess waved it away, saying, "I do not want any help." Kelley noted: "It was obvious to all present that he did not want to run any risk of giving himself away."[45]

Kelley commented that Hess's memory switched off and on, sometimes volitionally and sometimes when he was under great emotional pressure. Hess later told him that much of his amnesia had been real and that his boast in court had been false. He continued that although his mind was improving, it was "still weak and my brain tires easily." To support his assertion that Hess was not always malingering, Kelley noted that the amnesia was not providing any gain: it interfered with his defense and handicapped his lawyer. It did not "get him off" the case but actually thrust him back into it. In January 1946, Kelley wrote:

> His flight to England was a grandiose gesture . . . which when unsuccessful, resulted in the development of a severe paranoid reaction with delusions of persecution by the British. He also developed some partial amnesia and as the amnesia became deeper, the paranoid reactions vanished. After his second suicidal attempt, the amnesia cleared and the paranoid reactions returned. These reactions again vanished with the development of the amnesia which was present on his arrival [at Nuremberg]. His dramatic statement in court was a hysterical theatrical reaction. . . . Careful examination made here shows that Hess still has some true areas of amnesia. He admits that, at times, he is unable to remember certain events and that this process has occurred off and on for many years. His paranoid reactions . . . are in the area between conscious and unconscious. He has enough insight to realize that the idea that the food may be poisoned is not rational. On the other hand, these ideas do recur. . . . He may also develop a recurrence of his amnesia and it is extremely likely that he will produce some hysterical gesture before he is finally disposed of.[46]

Kelley bemoaned Hess's aloofness: "On my departure he was the only prisoner who failed to thank me for my interest in his welfare. This is typical of Hess' personality—a paranoid and suspicious individual with gross hysterical manifestations who failed in the most spectacular effort of his life. . . . He considers himself to be the only standard-bearer left of the Nazi Party, and will continue true to his adolescent ideals to the end—provided of course that his basic instability does not precipitate another psychotic episode."[47]

Kelley's prison chart note on Hess was more restrained; it concluded that Hess had "no evidence of psychopathology." In this brief note dated December 13, 1945, one recognizes the familiar cadence of a contemporary psychiatric examination. Hess was frequently aloof and at times not cooperative. His psychomotor reactions were slowed and mood was described as flat. Kelley noted "marked hysterical trends and mild paranoid reaction . . . ideas of being poisoned, similar to those he manifested in England." At the time of this assessment, his memory was intact, but Kelley added a cautionary clause "at present."[48]

The term "mild paranoid reaction" is a relic of diagnostic language in the 1940s. Until DSM II appeared in 1968, all psychiatric disorders were called "reactions," reflecting a belief that they were not so much entities as they were responses to the environment. The term "mild" also gives us pause. Kelley is clearly distinguishing Hess from flagrantly paranoid patients who may be found in emergency rooms or psychiatric hospitals. However, the fact that Kelley used "paranoid" at all indicates that he thought Hess was more than just "suspicious." But what did he mean by "hysterical"? This is trickier. In 1945, hysteria would have meant something like flamboyantly overexpressive or theatrically dramatic.

In other writings, Kelley gave a radically different assessment, calling Hess "insane, . . . an introverted, shy, withdrawn personality who, suspicious of everything about him, projected upon his environment concepts developing within himself." He went on to describe Hess as "emotionally juvenile, the only prisoner who failed to recognize the reality of his situation, . . . to admit the total defeat of Nazism. . . . [He was a] paranoid and childish individual, with gross hysterical manifestations, who had always failed in whatever he attempted. . . . Later, as he realizes that he will not hang, he may relax and appear to recover. . . . However, Hess will continue to live always in the borderlands of insanity." In typical Kelley fashion, he concluded: "Diagrammatically, if one considers the street as sanity and the sidewalk as insanity, then Hess spent the greater part of his time on the curb."[49]

Gilbert's Assessment

Gilbert was more successful than Kelley in relating to Hess, but Gilbert acknowledged that Hess "was so negativistic, secretive, and amnesiac, that very little information could be obtained from him directly."[50] Gilbert gave him a copy of his indictment and Hess returned it after writing, "I can't remember—Rudolf Hess."[51] Gilbert described Hess's apathetic absentmindedness but thought that his forgetting had a theatrical quality and that

Hess was "deliberately suppressing a recollection that flickered through his clouded mind."[52]

Gilbert was a careful methodologist who documented Hess's memory with repeated testing sessions from December 1945 to June 1946 (fig. 20). Gilbert was scientific in his approach, repeatedly asking Hess about his memory of various events in his life. For instance, he asked whether Hess could remember his childhood or his membership in the Nazi Party. After certain pivotal events in the trial, Gilbert asked if Hess remembered the testimony. He also tested his memory with digit span calculations.

In December 1945, Hess had normal recall of life events and superior memory in the digit span test. Thereafter, his memory faded. He couldn't remember childhood events, joining the Nazi Party, or his flight to England. He couldn't remember ongoing testimony at the trial. Sometimes, Hess described his amnesia to Gilbert as a pretense; at other times, he stated that his thinking and ability to concentrate were clearing up.[53]

Hess continued worrying about his food. He attributed his headaches, diarrhea, and confusion to poisoned crackers, and he asked all sorts of people to sample his crackers—Kelley, Gilbert, even his fellow prisoners. Would they get the same reactions, or was this batch of crackers "safe"? His fellow prisoners had reached their own conclusions. Schacht said succinctly, "By the way, Hess is crazy."[54] Gilbert patiently ate one of Hess's biscuits, telling him calmly, "Well, I'll let you know if the crackers give me a headache or any ill effects."[55]

Gilbert struggled to understand Hess intellectually and emotionally. He also tried to give Hess various face-saving ways of surmounting his amnesia, suggesting that if he rested or perhaps kept a diary, his ability to concentrate would improve and his memory would follow. It was a shrewd clinical intervention, but it's not clear that it helped. Hess's complaints shifted from amnesia to difficulties concentrating and then to his recurring abdominal pains. Hess was pretty sure that SOMEBODY was doing this to him, perhaps Colonel Andrus? Most of the other prisoners had somatic problems, including stomach aches, headaches, palpitations, and insomnia—all pretty much what one would expect in a stressful situation—but with Hess, these preoccupations were all-consuming.

Examination date

Event	Dec. 1	Dec. 16	Jan. 20	Feb. 24	Mar. 2	Mar. 17	Apr. 6	May 11	June 2
Childhood	+	+							
Nazi Party	+	+	±						
Flight to England	+	+	±						
Trial: Psychiatric examination	+	±							
Witness General Lahousen (Dec. 1)		+							
Witness von dem Bach-Szilewski (Jan. 7)				+					
Witness General von Paulus (Feb. 12)				+					
Göring's defense (Mar. 8–22)									
Hess's own defense (Mar. 25–26)									
Approximate recollection span	Life	Life	2 months	2 weeks	2 weeks	2 days	1 day	1 day	½ day
Digit span (total forward and backward)	12	15	9		7	7		8	7

Fig. 20. Gilbert's memory chart on Hess. *Key:* + is normal recollection (allowing for normal forgetting); ± is incomplete recollection (absence of essential details); gray shading is slight recollection (barely identifying event); black is no recollection whatever; white cells indicate data missing. (Adapted with permission from J. R. Rees, *The Case of Rudolf Hess: A Problem in Diagnosis and Forensic Psychiatry* [New York: W. W. Norton, 1948], with thanks to Charles Gilbert for authorizing the adaptation)

The Rorschachs

Kelley noted Hess's response to Rorschach card II (see Chapter 10) as "two men talking about a crime, blood is on their minds." Kelley had administered thousands of Rorschach tests, and he noted that the blood response was not terribly rare. However, Hess then went off on a tangent and "became preoccupied with the bloody thoughts . . . [which were] a projection of his bloody memories."[56] Hess reported bizarre elements on other card responses, which Kelley viewed as demonstrating anxiety and abnormal thinking. He summarized the Rorschach in one brief sentence— "Indicates basic hysterical personality without evidence of psychosis"—and concluded, "This man is competent and demonstratives no evidence of Psychopathology."[57] He commented that Hess's suspicious responses to the Rorschach were not so extensive as to suggest an active paranoid process but that a psychotic episode could develop in the future.[58]

"Hess suffers from a true psycho-neurosis, primarily of the hysterical type which is engrafted upon a basic paranoid personality," Kelley wrote. "In other words, . . . Hess is an introverted, shy, withdrawn personality who basically is suspicious of his environment and projects upon his surroundings concepts developing within himself." He continued that Hess's Rorschach revealed some bizarre responses, such as "marked shock reactions to the color and shade cards, tension during the test, the crude use of color and shade and some shifting in the form quality." Kelley felt that Hess "was suffering from an hysterical amnesic reaction, but it was equally obvious that a large portion of his total amnesia was deliberately assumed."[59]

Gilbert noted that Hess was very guarded and offered minimal responses to the Rorschach cards. Typically, people report seeing two or three different things on each of the ten cards. Hess reported just fifteen responses to the whole deck. Gilbert noted "the lifelessness of the figures seen, showing lack of empathy and inner life; . . . [and] emotional instability shown in the poor colour control, breaking out into the hysterical 'blood' response." In contrast to a typical Rorschach, where people will report that at least some blots have movement (for example, seeing a flying bat), Hess's reports were devoid of movement and vitality.[60]

Gilbert also noted cryptically that he readministered the Rorschach to Hess, but it did not show "any improvement in the limited cognitive and creative-ideational capacities upon re-test."[61] He concluded that Hess showed "severely constricted affect and lack of emotional contact characteristic of the schizoid personality."

Evaluating Hess in the Twenty-First Century

Hess mystified observers in 1945. Most courtroom spectators thought that he was insane. Gilbert and Kelley, as well as the international experts, noted a host of maladies but felt that he was competent to stand trial. Everyone agreed that Hess had poor reality testing. His grandiose flight to Scotland was bizarre in the extreme. How could the deputy Führer have concluded that he could make an unauthorized and spontaneous peace treaty? Everyone also granted that Hess was exaggerating his symptoms, although the extent of that exaggeration was debatable. If he were evaluated today, could we do any better? We can answer this question using clinical tools available in routine practice as well as research probes that are not yet routinely employed.

Routine practice has come a long way in specifying diagnostic criteria, but in Nuremberg, there were no widely agreed-upon criteria for determining what were hallmark signs of various psychiatric disorders. Indeed, the ideology of the time emphasized the continuity of human experience—that symptoms blended into each other like pigments in a watercolor wash. Since 1980, when DSM III was published, psychiatrists and psychologists have used increasingly precise diagnostic guidelines for recognizing psychiatric disorders, but there are still two enormous problems.

Far more often than we would like, people's problems blur at the edges. I am, I suppose, a DSM "mandarin," having been involved in writing the current DSM 5, but even I have to admit that our criteria are merely guidelines. So-called textbook cases are not all that common. Instead, patients commonly straddle two or more diagnoses, and we must rely on clinical judgment to diagnose and treat them.

The other problem—assuming truthfulness—is even more problematic. Doctors assume that patients are telling the truth, yet patients forget,

dissemble, and distort their history and symptoms. This is a problem for
all medical specialties, but psychiatry is particularly vulnerable to distorted
history because we have so few physical findings or laboratory tests to
guide diagnostic decision-making. Especially in forensic contexts, we have
a higher index of suspicion that the patient is not being candid, but by and
large we rely on the patient's report and the doctor's judgment about the veracity of the symptoms. David Rosenhan and colleagues famously demonstrated that if healthy normal control subjects came to a psychiatric hospital
falsely reporting that they had once heard atypical auditory hallucinations,
the doctors would admit the patients and try to help them.[62] In other words,
the default assumption is that patients are telling the truth as they see it
unless there is good reason to doubt them. Why else would someone go to
the time, expense, and trouble of seeing us? In forensic settings, however,
lying is "the rule." Twenty to 30 percent of violent criminal defendants will
claim that they don't remember their crime, but we have helpful tools for
characterizing the nature of their amnesia.

From a clinical perspective, we could probably "fit" Hess into a number
of diagnostic categories, but it might take some pushing and shoving to
make them precise. He could certainly be diagnosed as malingering. Alternatively, he could be viewed as having a dissociative disorder, a somatic
symptom disorder, schizophrenia, or a delusional disorder. We would probably do a better job than the psychiatrists of 1945 because we would specify
exactly which criteria Hess manifested. But the fact is, Hess probably suffered from multiple psychiatric disorders. As Shakespeare put it: "When
sorrows come they come not single spies / But in battalions."[63]

Even if doctors had been more precise in flagging each of Hess's symptoms, we would be puzzled today by his waxing and waning paranoia. In
today's experience, when a patient like Hess reports an uptick of delusions,
the first thing we suspect is that the patient has stopped taking his or her
medication. Seventy years ago, when there were no medications for treating schizophrenia, doctors were accustomed to the recurring onset and off-
set of psychotic symptoms, but today, we are less familiar with the clinical
course of patients who have never taken antipsychotic drugs.

Researchers have a somewhat easier time with this because there are
some research probes that can help confirm a diagnosis of schizophre-

nia (for example, genetic markers and measuring the neural response to startle).[64] However, these remain research tools and are not incorporated in clinical practice. There are also many types of lie detector devices. But detecting lies with polygraphs, event-related potentials, brain imaging, or pupillary response is only marginally useful because of false positives and negatives.

Cognitive testing is one area where researchers have made enormous strides since 1945. Confronted with Hess today, a forensic neuropsychologist would certainly be able to identify whether he was exaggerating his symptoms.[65] However, once the exaggeration was noted, it would be difficult to distinguish between dissociation and malingering. That distinction is made by inferring motivation and intentionality—never an easy task.[66] Sadly, I'm not so sure that today's clinicians and researchers would do much better at diagnosing Hess than our colleagues who saw him from 1941 to 1946.

The End

There are some who believe that the Allies treated Hess unfairly, and as a result, he "faked everything," hoodwinking both the psychiatrists and the court.[67] He had flown to Scotland on a mission for peace and had been locked up and never given an opportunity to meet with the proper authorities. He pretended to have amnesia because it got him out of interrogation. He saved samples of his food, wrapped in paper and sealing wax, because it gave him something to do. He worried that his food was being poisoned, but it must be allowed that the intelligence community did in fact have considerable interest in drugs and mind control.[68] I don't think that such arguments stand up to his consistently abnormal behavior, which extended over years, spanning events before, during, and even after the trial.

In 1946, the experts were clear in stating that Hess did not fit one clear diagnostic category. He was obsessed about his health and would have been diagnosed as having hypochondriasis or somatization disorder in DSM IV or as having somatic symptom disorder in DSM 5. He also manifested spotty and inconsistent memory loss. Some of this amnesia appeared outside of his volitional control and would be viewed today as dissociative amnesia.

At other times, the amnesia appeared to be willfully exaggerated in order to limit his interrogation; this would be an instance of malingering (not a psychiatric disorder at all). Last, he was a deeply suspicious man, convinced that he was being poisoned. All his life, he had had peculiar ideas about food, contamination, and additives. Today, I suspect that most psychiatrists would diagnose him as having paranoid schizophrenia.

In his final statement to the court on August 31, 1946, Hess gave a long and rambling statement complaining that he was surrounded by people with glassy strange eyes and recalling that in the Moscow show trials, the defendants also had "glazed and dreamy eyes." After twenty minutes of this, the judges said that this had gone on long enough and that he should conclude. Hess pulled himself together, no longer talked about glassy eyes, and instead stated: "I was permitted to work for many years of my life under the greatest son whom my people has brought forth in its thousand-year history. . . . I do not regret anything."[69] The judges must been struck by this curious testimony that juxtaposed paranoid delusions about glassy eyes with defiant loyalty to Hitler.

Rebecca West described the day of sentencing: "The darkened mind of Hess passed through some dreadful crisis. He ran his hands over his brows again and again as if he were trying to brush away cobwebs, but the blackness covered him. All humanity left his face; it became an agonized muzzle. He began to swing backwards and forwards on his seat with the regularity of a pendulum. . . . He was taken away soon, but it was as if the door of hell had swung ajar."[70]

The tribunal sentenced Hess to lifetime imprisonment in Spandau Prison in Berlin. He was sent there together with six other war criminals, but from 1966 on, he was the sole prisoner in this large, forbidding structure. He continued being deeply suspicious and complained of stomach pains, wailing into the night and refusing to see his wife and son for many years. On August 17, 1987, at age ninety-three, Rudolf Hess hanged himself in Spandau. It was an ironic and troubling end to a man who had dodged hanging at Nuremberg forty-one years previously. Spandau Prison was demolished lest it become a neo-Nazi shrine. In its place stands a modern shopping center.

PART FOUR

CODA TO NUREMBERG: RORSCHACHS AND RECRIMINATIONS

9

Douglas Kelley and Gustave Gilbert:
A Collaboration from Hell

Insanity is no explanation for the Nazis. They were simply creatures of their environment, as all humans are; and they were also—
to a greater degree than most humans are—the makers of their
environment.
                    —Douglas Kelley, 22 Cells in Nuremberg, 1947

What kind of animal species is it that organizes and executes sense-
less, coldblooded, systematic slaughter of endless numbers of its
own members . . . ?
    —Gustave Gilbert, "The Mentality of SS Murderous Robots," 1963

The Early Partnership

I WONDERED WHAT HAPPENED to Kelley and Gilbert after completing their
duties at Nuremberg. What does it do to someone who encounters malice so
close up? Kelley and Gilbert sat, day in and day out, cheek by jowl, with the
war criminals. Sitting on a small cot with Streicher and his ilk sandwiched
between the two of them brought them uncomfortably close to repellant
behavior, and it appears that a little of that malice rubbed off on them.

The dank odor of the place, the pressure-cooker environment, and the
ever-present rubble of warfare on the streets offered them no respite. Most

of us would be on edge in such circumstances. If we had a close friend or loved one with us, we would get through it, perhaps somewhat the worse for wear. Alas, Kelley and Gilbert had only each other, and they weren't exactly close friends.

They weren't even good collaborators. I always tell my trainees: "Be careful in your choice of collaborators." A good collaboration is like a good marriage; a bad one, well, is as bad as a bad marriage can be—filled with stalking and years of lawyers. Kelley and Gilbert's collaboration fell more in the latter category. Thrown together by circumstance and convenience, their roles and responsibilities were unclearly defined, and their worldviews differed profoundly. They shared little in common: brilliance, strong personal ambition and a deep interest in understanding the Nazi leaders.

Kelley's strengths were his easygoing garrulousness, which attracted people as diverse as war criminals and newspaper reporters. Gilbert's strengths were his seriousness and attention to detail. They both devoted considerable time to the prisoners, amassing a wealth of notes, observations, and Rorschach results. Kelley got there first, reporting to Ashcan on August 4, 1945, and leaving Nuremberg in January 1946. Gilbert had a longer duty, from October 23, 1945, to October 1946. Predictably, their timelines were a source of rivalry: "I got there first" versus "I was there longer."

Their collaboration on a book about Nuremberg was a poorly kept secret. Kelley loved talking with reporters, and even quiet Gilbert disclosed to a *Pravda* correspondent that they were writing a book. All this leaked back to Warden Andrus, who was not at all pleased.

The Rupture

Kelley left Nuremberg, taking all his notes and, Gilbert claimed, HIS notes as well. According to Gilbert, Kelley said that he was no longer interested in their book project on the Nazi prisoners and instead planned on writing a book about racial prejudice.[1] In reality, Kelley was already trying to negotiate a book contract about the Nuremberg work.[2] A couple of weeks after his departure, Kelley wrote Gilbert from the United States asking for copies of more interviews and transcripts from the trial. Gilbert declined.[3]

When Kelley left Nuremberg, he embarked on a flurry of ill-advised interviews with the press. He loved being the center of attention and told extravagant stories about Nuremberg that were big hits in the tabloids. In August 1946 he gave an interview to Howard Whitman at the *Sunday Express* entitled, "What Goering and Company Talk about in Their Cells."[4] As if this wasn't provocative enough, Whitman placed an even longer version of the Kelley interview weeks later in *Collier's,* with the headline "Squeal, Nazi, Squeal."[5]

The Nuremberg court personnel were not amused. Sir Geoffrey Lawrence, presiding judge of the Nuremberg Tribunal, complained to Warden Andrus, who in turn filed a written complaint, which I came across in Andrus's papers at the US Army Military History Institute in Carlisle, Pennsylvania.[6] Kelley had left the army months before and Andrus was under no illusion that anything could be done about Kelley's indiscretions, but one senses that Andrus, ever correct and punctilious, wrote his complaint "for the record."

It wasn't all tabloid fluff. In a series of articles, Kelley started to reveal his unique perspective on the war criminals. He presented a preliminary paper on the Nazi Rorschachs at a meeting in New York in April 1946, which he subsequently published in the *Rorschach Research Exchange.* The paper offers a preliminary sketch of his ideas: "[The Nazis were] essentially sane, . . . [and they] knew precisely what they were doing during their years of ruthless domination. . . . We must also realize that such personalities exist in this country and there are undoubtedly certain individuals who would willingly climb over the corpses of one half of the people of the United States, if by so doing, they could thereby be given control of the other half."[7]

In a subsequent interview in the *New Yorker,* Kelley continued in the same vein: "With the exception of Dr. Ley, there wasn't an insane Joe in the crowd. . . . I've never met twenty-one people who considered themselves so pure and lily white."[8] The *New Yorker* article offered a wonderful overview of Kelley's thoughts and a glimpse of how astonishingly gifted he was at characterizing people: "[Göring is] a buccaneer. . . . In the old days, he would have had a fine house ashore, loved his wife and children, held great parties, slipped away during the evening to sink a ship and every living soul on board, and then returned to the party and had the time of his life."

Regarding Göring's drug withdrawal at Ashcan, Kelley noted that "he complained of pains in his legs and thighs. I told him he was acting the way Ribbentrop would act, and he never complained again." His description of Hess was vivid: "[Hess is a] delayed adolescent, the kind of fellow who would attend marshmallow roasts and campfires, and watch parades with his mouth open."

Meanwhile, back in Nuremberg, Gilbert stewed. Kelley was stealing the limelight.

The War of the Books

In between his many press interviews and speeches, Kelley wrote *22 Cells in Nuremberg* and entered negotiations on a book contract with Simon and Schuster. Meanwhile, Gilbert, back at Nuremberg, was writing his own book, *Nuremberg Diary*, and began negotiating a contract with Farrar, Straus and Giroux. Kelley was ahead in the book race with his short book. Gilbert's book would be longer than Kelley's, but it was still incomplete.[9] The publishers knew of the competition and urged both authors to write quickly, but ultimately the competing manuscripts would blight each other's prospects.

Simon and Schuster declined Kelley's book, but a small publishing house, Greenberg, published the book in 1947. It met with mixed reviews. One reviewer wrote, "I found it so interesting that I could scarcely skip a page. . . . One of the major appeals is the non-technical language." Continuing insightfully, he said, "While I compliment the book on its admirable objectivity for students of human nature and the social sciences, I believe this same objectivity could be easily misunderstood by the general public as a too sympathetic account of the Nazi mentality."[10] Other reviewers were less sympathetic and were offended by Kelley's breezy style. A prominent psychoanalyst confided to publisher Greenberg: "I find it such trash that frankly I regret that you are publishing it. It is not even good reporting, much less good psychiatry."[11] Style aside, the book deeply angered readers by suggesting that "the Nazi revolution . . . was not the fabrication of warped minds out of the wards of a psychopathic hospital, but the creation of ordinary men, not unlike many with whom we brush elbows every day . . . in the United States."[12]

Eventually, Gilbert published *The Nuremberg Diary*.[13] Predictably, the two books had different styles, and given the antagonism between the two men, they (and their followers) emphasized their differences rather than their many similarities. It is striking that neither of these classic books discussed the Rorschachs, other than in passing. Instead, the books are filled with the authors' observations and recollected conversations with the war criminals as well as the authors' assertions about the meaning of these interactions.

Kelley's book was small and contained no references or footnotes. Kelley was very clear that he was writing a book for the popular reader, not the professional. The cover notes are punchy and provocative: "What kind of men were the Nazi overlords? How did they get that way?—And could it happen again? A Rogue's gallery of the arch criminals of all time by the official United States psychiatrist who examined them and learned their most intimate secrets."

Kelley trumpeted his credentials, noting that he served as the Nuremberg psychiatrist for five months and interviewed the prisoners daily. He mentioned Gilbert, acknowledging him for adapting the intelligence tests, and noted that Gilbert "was assigned to my office as an interpreter and, at my direction, made records of many of the conversations which I had with these prisoners and which are reported in this book." Kelley noted that although most of the defendants spoke "fairly good English" sometimes he relied upon an interpreter "to prevent misunderstandings." This was all fairly polite, but it also was marking the territory for Kelley and relegating Gilbert to the role of his assistant.[14]

In his book (also lacking in notes or references), Gilbert thanked Kelley, "prison psychiatrist for the first two months, for facilitating my assignment to the Nuremberg jail with free access to all the prisoners."[15] The clause "for the first two months" was certainly not necessary, but it was a way for Gilbert to circumscribe Kelley's role and emphasize his brief tenure at Nuremberg. So, who knew most—Kelley with his experience in Ashcan and Nuremberg from August 1945 to January 1946 or Gilbert with his Nuremberg experience from October 1945 to October 1946?

The battle of the books shifted to Europe. Kelley's editor at Greenberg wrote him that they had the advantage by being first to publish in the United States but that, regrettably, Gilbert had beat them to the audience in England.[16]

What Did They Really Say?

Kelley and Gilbert agreed that the defendants, perhaps with the exception of Hess, were neither legally insane nor psychotic. If the defendants weren't psychotic, what *were* they? Were they mentally ill at all, and what, by the way, did Kelley and Gilbert mean by "mental illness"?

The irony was that Gilbert, whose training was in social psychology, diagnosed the defendants as narcissistic psychopaths whose lives were deformed by a diseased German culture. Kelley, the expert in psychopathology and forensic psychiatry, saw things from a social psychological perspective and viewed the defendants as basically ordinary people who were creatures of their environment, influenced by mendacity and bureaucracy. He compounded this assertion by saying that one could find such people anywhere. In 1947, many viewed this claim as a lancinating insult.

Kelley and Gilbert also differed massively in style and tone—Kelley, ever sardonic and dispassionate, as compared to Gilbert, humorless and intense. The selected quotations below highlight their differences.

> KELLEY: "Nazism is a socio-cultural disease. I had at Nuremberg the purest known Nazi-virus cultures—22 flasks as it were—to study. . . . Strong, dominant, aggressive egocentric personalities, . . . [with] their lack of conscience, are not rare. They can be found anywhere in the country—behind big desks deciding big affairs."[17]

> GILBERT: "[They were] ruthlessly aggressive, [had] emotional insensitivity, [and presented with] a front of utter amiability."[18]

What Is in the Nature of a Disorder?

In 1947, how did psychiatry and psychology define mental illness? Gilbert espoused the prevailing view: the Nazis were distinctly "other." Basing his understanding on the burgeoning literature describing psychopathy, Gilbert concluded that psychopaths were so profoundly different in their worldview that they wore a "mask of sanity" (see Chapter 12). Kelley's view, by contrast, was profoundly out of sync with 1947, but it anticipated the developing field of social psychology, which noted that under the wrong conditions, decent people could make appalling life choices (see Chapter 11).

Kelley and Gilbert fundamentally disagreed about the nature of diagnosis. Gilbert felt that the Nazis represented a unique *category* of psychopathology. Kelley saw nothing distinctly different about the Nazis but saw their behavior as one end of a *continuum* of behavior. Edmund Burke, the great British statesman, framed the contrast between categories and continuums vividly in a different context: "Though no man can draw a stroke between the confines of day and night, yet light and darkness are upon the whole tolerably distinguishable."[19] That is, day fades into night gradually; nonetheless, the two are distinctive. Gilbert, in essence, focused on day versus night, but Kelley considered the zones in between—dawn and twilight—more interesting to study.[20]

What is served by labeling the Nazi leaders' behavior as a psychiatric disorder (for example, Gilbert's "narcissistic psychopaths") or as an example of profound moral failing (Kelley's view)? In reality, these are not alternatives but rather separate questions (see Chapter 12). Psychiatric disorders are largely characterized by thoughts, feelings, and behaviors that are distressing and impairing, but are all repugnant behaviors "disorders"?

Legal systems are finally beginning to tease the issue apart into two separate questions: "Is a disorder present?" *and* "Is the individual responsible for his or her actions?" As a thought experiment, consider the following four court scenarios, which play out frequently in theme and variation in contemporary courthouses:

1. A psychotic individual in the thrall of delusions and hallucinations may never be brought to trial because he or she is unable to understand the trial or assist in the defense.

2. A patient whose paranoid schizophrenia is in remission may receive a lesser sentence if the crime was committed under the influence of hallucinations.

3. A person who committed a crime under the influence of amphetamine-induced delusions would probably receive a stiffer sentence because there was an element of volition in choosing to use drugs in the first place.

4. Courts would likely impose the most severe sentence on an individual with a personality disorder who has a long history of impulsive violence and shallow interpersonal sensitivity.

These four examples demonstrate the range and diversity of psychiatric disorders and how they may influence our society's judgments of the perpetrator's responsibility. Unfortunately, such nuances did not appear in the acrimonious arguments between Kelley and Gilbert about the nature of the Nazis' diagnoses. Kelley, ever sensitive to the range of suffering in mental illness, saw little to be gained by including "narcissistic psychopaths" in the same boat as patients with depression or schizophrenia. Indeed, he devoted considerable energy after Nuremberg in helping government agencies to weed out impulsive and aggressive individuals from government service. To Kelley, psychopaths were not mentally ill; rather, they were merely *unsuitable* for government service. To Gilbert, psychopaths bore the mark of Cain.

Molly Harrower, the Would-Be Mediator

But how did Kelley and Gilbert use the Rorschach tests to back up their suppositions? Oddly, neither of them extensively discussed the Rorschachs in their books. Kelley wanted confirmation by other Rorschach experts before he would release his Rorschachs, and Gilbert recognized that he was on intellectual thin ice in providing a scholarly analysis of the Rorschachs.

Kelley and Gilbert trusted only one person in common, Molly Harrower, a Rorschach scholar who had been raised in South Africa and was active in the arts as a dancer, painter, and poet (fig. 21). She eventually settled in the United States and obtained her doctorate in psychology, completed a postdoctorate at Rockefeller University, and then moved to the Montreal Neurological Institute to work with the eminent neurosurgeon Wilder Penfield on the brain and emotion. When World War II started, she began to

Fig. 21. Molly Harrower in her later years. (Courtesy
of University of Florida Digital Collection)

use the Rorschach to screen military recruits, thereby acquiring massive
datasets of Rorschach responses from many types of subjects. Her congeni-
ality helped her persuade fractious groups to work together for the common
good. She even persuaded Kelley and Gilbert to agree provisionally to bury
the hatchet. It was an agreement stitched together with very thin thread.

In 1947, Harrower began planning for an international mental health
congress in London, where she hoped to have the Nuremberg Rorschachs
available for review and discussion. Having been appointed editor of a new

series of books to be published by Charles Thomas, Harrower was in a position to disseminate the Rorschach findings both at the meeting and in print.

Meanwhile, Kelley and Gilbert were squabbling and accusing each other of having purloined each other's notes. It was a serious business and frankly hard to adjudicate. If Kelley performed the interviews and Gilbert translated and then later summarized the interviews, whose "property" was it? Kelley described the complexity of the situation to his publisher:

> Since both of us were present at these interviews—actually I think they only include three or four conversations[—]it would seem to be reasonable that both of us should use them. If Gilbert, however, wants to put up a squawk, there is no doubt whatsoever that the conversations were mine and his official position was exclusively that of interpreter-secretary. I have been very careful in our book to avoid the use of the intelligence findings which Gilbert did himself, although at my direct order. Consequently, I have no fear of any problems arising from their side although we are clearly in a position to put the screws on them if we want.[21]

Both planned follow-up books that would focus on the Rorschachs and were determined to get there first. Kelley threatened to sue Gilbert if he used Kelley's Rorschach materials. Harrower pieced together a reasonable but doomed-to-fail compromise by suggesting that they collaborate on one book in which each would have his own chapters discussing his own Rorschach findings with commentary from independent Rorschach experts supplementing the chapters. In the meantime, she worried about Gilbert, writing a colleague in October 1947 to share her concerns that Gilbert was so affected by the conflicts with Kelley that it was adversely affecting him personally and his work.[22]

For a (very) short while, it looked as if the compromise would work, but as it started to unravel, Harrower chronicled the failure in a series of letters now buried in the archives.[23] The intellectual division of territory was not that controversial. Kelley and Gilbert could agree about who would write each chapter, but Gilbert started sniping that he doubted Kelley's truthfulness and suspected that Kelley had doctored his records. Then Gilbert insisted on being first author and relegating Kelley to a status of "with the assistance of Goldensohn and Kelley."[24] Not "Kelley" even as a third author but "with the assistance of" to denote his clearly peripheral status. To make matters worse, Gilbert decided he did not want Rorschach experts commenting on his contributions and referred to them in his correspondence with Molly as "the experts" (in quotation marks), implying that he questioned their expertise. He was also reluctant to acknowledge the "experts" as coauthors on the monograph.

Nonetheless, Harrower and Gilbert identified the Rorschach experts and drafted a letter. Molly gave Gilbert her letterhead and he sent out the invitation letters on her behalf, but he set the deadline date for an impractically short interval. After receiving the Rorschachs, almost *all* of the experts declined.[25] Imagine if you received a letter on behalf of Molly Harrower, gracious and world renowned, asking if you would look at the protocols that might address the most troubling question of the day—the mind of the Nazi war criminals. Imagine if she invited you to discuss your findings and offered to publish them in a book series she was editing. How could you turn her down? Maybe some experts would have schedule difficulties, but almost all declined.

Perhaps they were offended by the short deadline. However, Harrower offered two other explanations. By then, everyone in the field knew of the acrimony between Kelley and Gilbert and did not want to get mired down in a dispute that threatened lawsuits. Kelley wrote to Harrower:

> I am determined, through our Board of Trustees and Legal Advisors to bring an injunction and suit about Gilbert if this material appears. I have simply turned the whole thing en masse over to our legal staff. They point out that permanent prevention of such unethical publication will be difficult since the material is not copywrited, but they feel that an injunction would blast the whole thing into the public eye with sufficient publicity to require that the ethics committee of the American Psychiatric Association . . . hold a formal hearing. . . . The publisher obviously does not realize he is publishing stolen goods.[26]

In addition to the threats of legal action, Harrower thought that there was another reason why colleagues had declined to comment on the Rorschach tests: the experts felt an odd sense of unease.

> We expected the Rorschach . . . would reveal an idiosyncratic psychopathology, a uniform personality structure of a particularly repellent kind. We espoused a concept of evil which dealt in black and white, sheep and goats. . . . Our concept of evil was such that it must be a tangible scoreable element in psychological tests.[27]

> [The records] did not show what we expected to see, and what the pressure of public opinion demanded that we see—that these men were demented creatures, as different from normal people as a scorpion is different from a puppy.[28]

For all of these reasons, the experts were "too busy" to participate in the project.

For a short time, there seemed to be a grudging truce between Kelley and Gilbert. Then the nastiness resumed. In September 1947, Kelley wrote disparagingly about Gilbert: "He continually startles me by his apparent neglect of basic ethics. . . . And it is this sort of thing that makes me wonder whether we can get together."[29] Gilbert fired back with multiple letters, raging that he wouldn't stand for any more of Kelley's nonsense and disparaging Kelley's work as "pathetic."[30]

After this fusillade, Kelley and Gilbert again threatened each other with legal action should either publish material about the Rorschachs, even though this meant that their work would be held hostage by their quarrels. In a flurry of letters, Gilbert indicated how impatient he was to get the work in print and how furious he was that the process had stalled. After peppering Harrower and her publisher, Charles Thomas, with questions about how soon his second book might appear, he then committed a major scholarly faux pas by submitting virtually the same manuscript to another publisher, W. W. Norton, without informing Harrower or her publisher. How was this discovered? Before publishing the book W. W. Norton wanted an expert to read the manuscript and advise whether to publish Gilbert's work. The blind reviewer was Molly Harrower—it was an uncomfortable coincidence![31]

Harrower was incensed. This was her thanks for being a peacemaker. The letters went back and forth—Harrower, Gilbert, W. W. Norton, Charles

C. Thomas—and ultimately both publishers declined to publish Gilbert's book. When Gilbert eventually published his second book *Psychology of Dictatorship* with Ronald Press, he again omitted the Rorschach data, possibly because of Kelley's legal threats but also perhaps because of his own lack of expertise with the Rorschachs.[32] As Eric Zillmer and coauthors summarized shrewdly, it was as if "Gilbert found himself in the possession of a large cache of foreign money but did not know how to exchange it."[33]

Many people had been bruised by the time this fight burned itself out. One of the proposed Rorschach experts wrote Harrower in January 1948, commenting, "Regarding the Kelley-Gilbert controversy—you must recall that psychologists are human beings. In fact that is the whole problem namely, that human beings are human beings. I am fortunate in having a slight reserve of philosophical attitude. I think it may have something to do with my survival."[34]

Decades later, referring to other vitriolic arguments concerning Holocaust research, historian Ian Kershaw observed, "It often seemed . . . that emotionality, from whatever its motives, had overtaken rationality. Given the subject matter, that was understandable but still regrettable."[35]

Kelley's Later Years

When Kelley left Europe in 1946, he settled initially at Bowman Gray Medical School (now Wake Forest School of Medicine), where he lectured widely on his Nuremberg experience and gave many press interviews. Finally, an opportunity emerged for him to return to California as professor of criminology at Berkeley. He moved into an elegant home on the outskirts of Berkeley and filled his study with memorabilia from Nuremberg—photographs, packets of food that Hess had saved as evidence of poisoning, letters from Göring, slides of Robert Ley's brain, and transcripts.

Kelley flourished at Berkeley. His forensic work mushroomed, and he helped police departments and the Atomic Energy Commission in personnel selection, relying on the Rorschach as a key tool.[36] He directed a TV show on science for KQED. He was a psychiatric consultant to Hollywood on *Rebel without a Cause*. He wrote an astonishingly large number of book reviews and still had time for magic, becoming vice president of the Society for American Magicians.

In short, the man was a dynamo, but it was clear that his wheels were spinning too rapidly. Lewis Terman wrote to Kelley, gently cautioning him to slow down: "I am amazed by the number of activities you are engaged in and can't help but wonder, whether it is too many for your long-range professional good."[37] Kelley's drinking increased, as did his irritability. Years later, his son commented, "He was a cross between a sponge and a rampaging bull. He was a Renaissance man on speed."[38]

Sadly, it all ended on January 1, 1958. Kelley had gotten enraged with his wife, ran upstairs to his study and returned to the living room, where he killed himself in front of his parents, his wife, and his children. The suicide was a devastating end to a brilliant troubled man, but what also stood out was his mode of suicide—cyanide.

Everyone was quick to note the link to Nuremberg and Göring. These two individuals, so close, had chosen the same end—suicide with cyanide. Dark questions and speculations were raised as to where Kelley got the cyanide. The *San Francisco Chronicle* reported that Kelley's poison "was brought back from the war criminal trials."[39] The *New York Times* took the matter further, stating that the cyanide was "one of several capsules Dr. Kelley had brought home from Nuremberg. The capsules had been discovered on Hermann Göring."[40] And Molly Harrower went even further, asserting that Göring had given Kelley the pill when Kelley visited him in jail.[41] None of this was proven, but one fact was clear: at the age of forty-five, this brilliant, complex man's life was over.

People were disinclined to look through his files or trouble his family. The files were there, but they were out of sight, moldering in cartons and forgotten. It required considerable sleuthing to unearth them. Some files were sent to the archives section at the University of California, Santa Cruz, although there was no logical reason why they wound up there. Kelley's family kept other files, and they are documented in Jack El-Hai's excellent book about Kelley and Göring.[42] Molly Harrower had yet other files that are now archived in the University of Akron, and Columbia University houses the files of Kelley's publisher, Greenberg.

Gilbert's Later Years

Gustave Gilbert left Nuremberg in 1946, moving to Princeton University and then to Michigan State before eventually returning to New York, where he was a longtime faculty member and chair of psychology at Long Island University. His lectures about Nuremberg were described by his students as riveting, but others have been less charitable, suggesting that some of his observations did not add up and were self-serving, puffing himself up at the expense of Kelley.[43]

In 1961, Gilbert's expertise with the Nazis was tapped yet again. He testified in Jerusalem at the Adolf Eichmann trial. The court requested his testimony because years before, he had interviewed the commandant of Auschwitz, who had disclosed Eichmann's crucial role in orchestrating the mass killings. In addition, the prosecutor requested Gilbert's expert opinion about the psychology of the murderers. To Gilbert's chagrin, the judge ruled that the latter question was irrelevant to Eichmann's guilt, and that aspect of Gilbert's testimony was disallowed.[44]

And the Rorschachs Moldered

Meanwhile, the Rorschachs rested in file cabinets. They slept like Rip van Winkle while the world went on. Finally, decades after they were administered, Gilbert's Rorschachs were published in 1975 by Florence Miale and Michael Selzer in their book *The Nuremberg Mind*. They make one of the nastier ad hominem arguments I have ever seen, dismissing Kelley's Rorschach interpretations as "manifestly erroneous. . . . It is possible that the nature of his own death may throw light on his idiosyncratic perception of the Nazi leaders." With this gratuitous swipe at the dead, Gilbert's records were then revealed.[45]

Kelley's Rorschachs, however, were still missing. Zillmer and coauthors recount the captivating saga of how Kelley's records were repeatedly lost and then eventually found in 1992.[46] Kelley had entrusted his records to Rorschach expert Samuel Beck, but with the acrimony between Kelley and Gilbert and Kelley's unexpected death, Beck was hesitant to bring them to light. Years later, just as Beck had begun to write about them, he died as well. These Rorschachs were cursed! They were eventually deposited at the Institute for Psychoanalysis in Chicago but remained unexamined and were even slated to be removed (that is, discarded). Through remarkable serendipity and perseverance, Reneau Kennedy rescued them from obscurity in 1992.[47]

What started out in 1945 as a contentious collaboration between Kelley and Gilbert and then as an unseemly rush to publication led to a fifty-year sequestration. The Beck archive contained all of the Gilbert Rorschach records as well as six of the seven lost Kelley Rorschachs.[48] One can only imagine Molly Harrower's feelings when these Rorschachs, last seen in 1947, emerged from the dust and cobwebs. Kelley was long gone; Gilbert was gone. There was finally no obstacle to studying the Nuremberg Rorschachs. But what would they reveal?

A Message in the Rorschachs?

The principle to be kept in mind is to know what we see rather than to see what we know.

—A. J. Heschel, *The Prophets*, 1962

Now, wouldn't you be happier if I had been able to show you that all of these perpetrators were crazy?

—Raul Hilberg, "The Significance of the Holocaust," 1980

Scoring the Rorschach

In 1945, Dr. John Millet and his colleagues urged using the Rorschach to study the Nazi leaders' malice. Finally, both Kelley's and Gilbert's protocols were located and could be studied. There were, however, problems. It's not so much that the tests had moldered on fragile paper or that the ink had flaked off but rather that psychiatry had moved on and found such tests to be less meaningful.

When I was a resident at Massachusetts General Hospital, we studied the Rorschach test. It was a curious exercise because the test was so removed from our day-to-day interactions with patients and also because it seemed so "musty," a relic from an earlier time. In 1945, in Nuremberg, it was "cutting edge," but deciphering this ambiguous and slippery test has never been easy. Biblical scholar Abraham Heschel cautioned against being blinded by preconceptions in interpreting Scripture. His warning was eerily relevant to the challenges of interpreting the Nuremberg Rorschachs.

Before delving into the Nuremberg Rorschachs, it would be helpful to see how one scores the test. There are ten Rorschach cards, and it is the composite response to all the cards that counts. Card II is illustrated here (fig. 22). Please study the card. The standard Rorschach questions are, "What do you see in the card? What did you see in the card that made you say that?" Alternatively, and since this is certainly NOT formal Rorschach testing, What leaps out at you? What intrigues you about it? What do you see

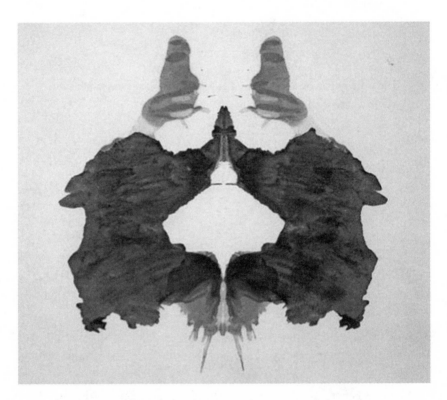

Fig. 22. Rorschach Card II. Write your responses below. What might this mean? What parts of the card made you say that?

_____

_____

_____

_____

(photo: https://commons.wikimedia.org/wiki/File%3ARorschach_blot_02.jpg)

in the inkblot? Do you see things that disturb you or conversely amuse you? As you think about it, are you responding to the whole blot or just a part of it—the black parts, the gray parts, the red parts, or the white parts? Write down your responses before reading further.

There are two fundamentally different ways of interpreting Rorschach responses. One approach focuses on the content or themes that the patient reports, and the other examines technical aspects of how those themes are identified. It is not so important to learn the various codes used in interpreting the Rorschachs as it is to get a sense of what Rorschach experts do and the hazards of their craft.

There are shorthand conventions, which allow the tester to summarize rapidly how an individual responds to a card. It's a code. The letter W, for instance, is shorthand for the fact that the individual used the whole blot in describing the card. Other symbols denote whether the person responds to a large detail (D) or small detail (d) on the card. The testing process generally requires about an hour.

People who report relatively more W responses are more likely to take in the total sense of the blot and better able to integrate complex data. Some individuals respond to the blot by attending particularly to the shading or texture of the blot. Shading responses (Y) are more common in subjects who are anxious or depressed. There is no reason for this association; it suffices that in thousands and thousands of records, certain types of responses are more likely in the context of different clinical settings.

Some of the Rorschach cards include color, and responses based on color suggest that emotional factors strongly influence the subject's perceptions. Blots are also scored when the person perceives movement (M) in the blot. High M responders, for instance, are more likely to be creative and intelligent. The blots are also scored in terms of their form quality—that is, how well the blot description matches up with the shape of the blot. Poor form scores are found more commonly in psychotic patients.

The rater pays attention to the content of the description. Are these popular interpretations (P)? Psychotic patients have fewer P responses, depressed patients have fewer human responses, and people with larger numbers of plant and nature responses tend to be more isolated interpersonally. It is a very complicated code with shorthand symbols and an enormous clinical "memory" for what the codes imply. Recall that it is the composite score across all the cards that counts.

All of these features are complicated enough, but Rorschach experts also use some esoteric terminology to describe the test findings. To those familiar with the Rorschach, these specialized terms are shorthand ways of communicating complex matters. To others, they are mere shibboleths.[1]

Skilled testers attend to all of these variables and more. In the 1970s John Exner systematized the scoring of Rorschach records. As a result, there is good inter-rater reliability in scoring the responses as to form, shading, color, movement, and other factors, but reliability is lower when clinicians decide what the various codes mean in terms of a patient's personality.[2] Over the years, as more and more tests were administered and evaluated, norms developed to help categorize the responses. However, there is no clean cut-off that allows one to state confidently, "This patient is in group X." It is true that after thousands and thousands of testing sessions, we can recognize an unusual response. But that assessment depends on the context of the testing. Who knows what is an unusual response in a jailed cabinet minister facing a death sentence?

Another problem with Rorschach scoring is that information about the patient can bias the tester. A referral note will typically say something like "Please evaluate this forty-three-year-old woman who complains of persistent abdominal pain." Furthermore, the interaction between tester and patient, although meticulously prescribed, does give the tester some information about the patient other than what is revealed by the patient's inkblot response. In a clinical context, this is all to the good. In a scientific context, however, knowledge of the patient's identity interferes with objectivity. This issue of blinded evaluation came to haunt the Rorschach data from Nuremberg. If you knew that the inkblot record was Göring's, how could you possibly interpret it objectively?

The War Criminals' Responses to One Rorschach Card

The Nuremberg war criminals each saw the same Card II (as well as the other nine Rorschach cards). This chapter presents their responses to that specific card as well as Kelley's and Gilbert's commentaries. When all ten cards were analyzed, a furious debate began about what they actually revealed.

Both Kelley and Gilbert tested Hermann Göring. According to Kelley, Göring reported: "Two dancing men. A fantastic dance. Two men, here are their heads, their hands together, like whirling dervishes. Here are their bodies, their feet." Kelley commented, "These figures are seen extremely well; colors are not used except that they can be part of the costume of the men."[3]

Gilbert's notes are similar, that Göring laughed and said: "Those are the two dancing figures, very clear, shoulder here and face there, clapping hands [cuts off bottom part with hand, including red]. Top red is head and hat; face is partly white."[4]

Gilbert entrusted his Rorschach records to Miale and Selzer, who had a field day with Göring's response, asserting that the "two dancing figures" reflected Göring's attempt to hide his depression—that is, it was a hypomanic defense. This is plausible, but then they conjectured that because Göring saw the face in both the blot and the white space, "[it] strongly suggests the emptiness of his being," and furthermore, his reporting the hat as red "indicates an emotional preoccupation with status."[5]

Only Kelley examined Robert Ley. He recorded his numerous responses to the card (the words in brackets are Kelley's):

A butterfly. There are colors here. That's funny. It is a funny butterfly. [The whole picture is used and he states that it is a form of a butterfly but the colors are important. The colors actually struck him first.] [An additional response, spontaneous at this point is lamp. This is the center white space form only]. Black and red and white. [He repeats this several times and then moving the card near and far, states the colors look different when you consider the distance. At this point, he brought card close to him and went over the description of the butterfly again.] A stork, or goose would be better. It looks like it was tipped over with its legs pulled in. It seems unique. This top is red. [Form is vague—no movement except perhaps tension.] It is alive. Jaws of the butterfly. [These are the top red details which he described previously as the mouth of the butterfly].[6]

I think that this is one of the more intriguing Rorschach responses. Ley perseverates, moves the card back and forth, repeats "black and red and white," and discloses unusual and unsettling form responses ("jaws of the butterfly"). Something is clearly wrong.

As with Ley, only Kelley tested Julius Streicher. According to him, Streicher proffered two interpretations of the card, both rich in pictorial details as one might expect, given that Streicher was an amateur painter, but there was also a peculiar preoccupation with themes of revolution. Kelley wrote:

> He looks the card over; discusses it, stating that it is pretty. Waves it about his head and finally states that it is two women in the French Revolutionary times with Jacobean caps. He states that they have red socks and caps and are dancing. He then gives dates of Revolution as 1789 and is about to go into a discussion on the French Revolution in general when he is again attracted by the card. Red wine glass on a porcelain platter. Center red and center space detail. In the inquiry he sees an additional white space response, Two Dutch shoes. Upper white space details. He sees glass as red but form is not important. Color is factor for white platter.[7]

When Kelley and Gilbert tested Rudolf Hess, they recorded similar observations. Kelley wrote (again with his own words in brackets): "Also microscopic cross-section, parts of an insect with blood spots. The shape of the cross-section of the leg of a fly with red blood spots; space in the middle is the marrow, although I don't know if the leg of an insect has marrow. A mask. Mask of an island savage, like Fiji Islanders, though I don't know them; the opening is for the mouth; it is devilish, that is why the eyes and beard are red. [testing the limits] Can see female figures."[8]

Gilbert reported Hess saying: "Also microscopic cross section; parts of an insect with blood spots; a mask."[9]

Certainly by content alone, Hess's response was troubling—there are lots of frankly disturbing images and anatomical references, which are commonly interpreted as depressive equivalents. Miale and Selzer regarded his color responses as "the remnants of a violent, excitable, unrelated emotionality, which is still intense but is split off from contact with anything real." They were also struck that he didn't perceive the usual clown figures but described instead a savage, devilish mask and then said, "I don't know them." Miale and Selzer interpreted this as his psychopathic rejection of responsibility. Perhaps they have read too much into his remarks, but I certainly agree that Hess's Rorschachs have an ominous quality.[10]

I have provided these verbatim responses and interpretations because they give a sense of the technique and the formidable challenges of its interpretation. Two starkly differing conclusions about these Rorschachs would emerge decades after they were administered.

Miale and Selzer's Interpretations of the Rorschachs

Florence Miale was an acknowledged Rorschach expert and Michael Selzer was a political scientist with an abiding interest in psychohistory. Their book, *The Nuremberg Mind*, seemed to be an angry shout from the heart against any cultural relativism, any assertion that fell short of concluding that the Nazis were monsters who were profoundly "other."[11] The idea that any one of us could become a Nazi, given a particular set of circumstances, was abhorrent to them. The authors were very clear in stating their beliefs on the book's dedication page by quoting from Deuteronomy: "Remember what Amalek did to you." Richard Rubinstein observed in his book review: "Of all the verses in Scripture, Miale and Selzer chose for their dedication this call for an unremitting, holy war. They could not have spelled out more clearly the nature of their enterprise, which bears no relation to the science of psychology."[12] In other words, to Miale and Selzer, the Nazis were Amalek—cursed beyond redemption and profoundly "other."

Miale and Selzer were none too keen on the scientific method as a way of interpreting Rorschach tests. Although they acknowledged that there were many ways of examining perception, they did not believe that it was useful "to play statistical games with . . . [the Rorschachs].[13] Somewhat less argumentatively, they acknowledged that the Rorschach test cannot be validated because its interpretation depends so much on the evaluator's skill.

In their analyses, Miale and Selzer favored discussion of content themes in the ink blots over the rich and carefully documented Exner approach, with its quantitation of form, texture, movement, and so on. The problem is that their assertions are untestable, and their reasoning strikes one as inconsistent and post hoc. For example, on the one hand, Miale and Selzer claimed that the many comments about texture and fur indicated the war criminals' tendency to "manipulate and hoodwink others, rather than for the establishment of real relationships." However, only two paragraphs later, they maintained that many of the records showed "no response to the furry qualities of the cards at all . . . [which] indicate the destruction rather than the transformation of the subjects' instinctual life." They were unshakable in their core belief: "The Nazis were not psychologically normal or healthy individuals."[14]

Harrower's Critique

Harrower followed Miale and Selzer's work with great interest, especially since Florence Miale was a respected Rorschach colleague. Harrower was grateful that Gilbert's Rorschachs were *finally* published, but when she was asked to comment on Miale and Selzer's work, she was unhappy to witness a flare-up of the old acrimonious fight. She regarded their book as yet another salvo in Gilbert's long-running battle with Kelley, even though Kelley had died twenty years previously.[15]

Personalities aside, Harrower felt an increasing sense of discomfort with Miale and Selzer's observations, which closely reflected Gilbert's views that the Rorschachs proved the war criminals were depressed psychopaths. She was skeptical. How could there be consistent test results among such dissimilar subjects? Based on their life stories alone, Harrower doubted their conclusions.

The other and even more compelling reason for Harrower's skepticism was her concern about bias. If you knew whose record was being scored, wouldn't you be influenced and "read into" the card your own preconceptions? From a clinical perspective, knowing the patient's clinical background enriches the analysis to the Rorschach record, but from a research perspective, it would be vastly more convincing to score the records without knowing the patient's identity.

Harrower devised an ingenious design to address this problem.[16] Above all else, one needed a comparison group. Harrower had access to countless pools of Rorschachs because of her many years of testing. Her records were breathtakingly diverse, including fifteen hundred Unitarian ministers, hundreds of medical students, and hundreds upon hundreds of juvenile offenders, criminals in Sing-Sing, psychology students, nurses, and business executives, as well as sixteen hundred patients from her own clinical practice. All of these groups included patients who spanned a wide range of psychological functioning.

Psychologists Gerry Borofsky and Don Brand employed a Venn diagram to portray the problem of selecting a comparison group (fig. 23). The Nuremberg war criminals were all upper-level successful men, political bureaucrats, and Nazi Party members facing a possible death sentence. How representative were these war criminals to the larger universe of psychopaths, bureaucrats, prisoners, and others? To whom should they be compared?

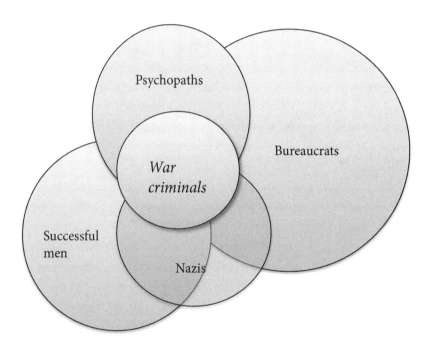

Fig. 23. Relation of Nuremberg war criminals to other relevant groups. (Adapted with permission from Gerald L. Borofsky and Don J. Brand, "Personality Organization and Psychological Functioning of the Nuremberg War Criminals: The Rorschach Data," in *Survivors, Victims, and Perpetrators: Essays on the Nazi Holocaust*, ed. Joel E. Dimsdale [Washington, DC: Hemisphere, 1980])

Harrower made a surprising choice, selecting two very different comparison groups—psychiatric outpatients and Unitarian ministers. If blind raters could not distinguish the Nazis from these two groups, there had to be something very wrong with Miale and Selzer's analysis! She selected records across a range of functioning within each group. That way, if there were group differences, they would not result from accidentally having more low-functioning people in one group as opposed to another. After matching tests across the three groups and omitting all identifying information from these tests, she asked ten Rorschach experts an ingenuously simple question: "Would you mind sorting these Rorschach responses into three groups using whatever information you could glean from the tests?" The experts were quick to sort the tests according to level of functioning. They recognized *common* features in all of the high-functioning records from the Nazi war criminals, Unitarian ministers, and medically ill patients. Similarly, they accurately sorted the medium-functioning individuals and the low-functioning individuals into separate groups. Before the sorting, Harrower had wondered if the Rorschachs would be readily identifiable as belonging to one group or another. Now she had an answer. There was no evidence that the Nazi Rorschachs (or the Unitarians' Rorschachs, for that matter) had some *special* features as a group.

She then gave the experts a second task, informing them that the records had been completed by various groups, such as "members of the clergy, cross section of middle class population, war criminals, [and] civil rights leaders," and asking the experts to guess what sorts of patients completed the cards.[17] Again, the expert Rorschach raters could not identify the groups, even when they were offered possible group identifiers. All in all, this was hardly a ringing endorsement for the ability of the Rorschach to characterize a unique mind-set of the Nazi war criminal.

It just got worse and worse for Miale and Selzer's position. Barry Ritzler used a different technique for scoring and compared Gilbert's set of Rorschachs with a set from a different comparison group. He found although the Nuremberg Rorschachs were not normal, they were certainly *not* those of monsters as described by Miale and Selzer.[18] Six more studies, some even using the Exner Comprehensive Scoring System, also failed to reveal a specific mental disorder in the Nuremberg defendants.[19]

Then, there was the business about the chameleons. Five of the defendants made an unusual identification on Card VIII, labeling a portion of the blot as a chameleon. To have a chameleon pop up five times was striking, but what did it mean? Could it imply that the war criminals were careful to fit in with their surroundings? One scholar commented: "The Nazi elite differed from most people in one respect; they possessed a 'chameleonlike' personality that allowed them to adopt the beliefs and objectives of whatever leadership was in power at that moment, rather than to base their judgments on an 'internal compass.'"[20]

How unusual was this chameleon response? Each image has expected and unexpected responses, given that many thousands of patients have completed the test. Thus, we actually have data on the frequency of chameleon responses. For instance, in a sample of 568 Johns Hopkins medical students, chameleons were found in only 1.7 percent of the responses, as compared to 37 percent of the Nazi defendants' responses.[21] The chameleon response, though unusually common among the war criminals, is actually a good Form response (F+), which suggests good reality testing. Miale and Selzer, however, were not content with pointing out the unusual frequency of chameleon responses. They went on to emphasize that because the chameleons were described as *climbing up,* it implied that the war criminals were consumed by opportunism. Borofsky and Brand were unconvinced about that interpretation, so they surveyed a number of experienced Rorschach examiners, none of whom could recall anyone describing the animals as *climbing downward.*[22] So much for the inference that climbing upward was unusual and opportunistic! In other words, as the cards were examined more closely, especially blindly, many of the purported monstrous abnormalities simply evaporated.

Conclusions?

The Nuremberg Rorschachs were finally on public view. But the light of day revealed chaos rather than enlightenment. Ten years after Hermann Rorschach died, the Nazis began their rule, devouring the lives of millions of people. Twenty-one years after Hermann Rorschach died, his inkblot test was used to diagnose what kind of people ruled Nazi Germany.

Seventy years after the Nuremberg trial, we are still fighting over what these Rorschachs mean. If you knew what you were looking at, you could discern a menace lurking in the prisoners' responses. If not, well, they were just— more inkblot responses. Seventy years after they were administered, the question remains: What if anything can these Rorschach tests tell us about the nature of malice?

11

Malice on a Continuum:
The Social Psychologists' Perspective

> The Holocaust, after all, is a story with far too few heroes and all too
> many perpetrators and victims.
> —Christopher Browning, *Ordinary Men*, 1998

THE TRIBUNAL CONCLUDED IN 1946. The struggles between Kelley and Gilbert ended with Kelley's suicide in 1958. And then the trail of the psychological examinations at Nuremberg seemed to grow cold until the Eichmann trial in 1961. In the ensuing ten years a series of stunning social psychological observations emerged that followed in the intellectual footsteps of Douglas Kelley.

Kelley's perspective was clear: the Nazi leaders were not anomalies. All they needed was "overweening ambition, low ethical standards, [and] strongly developed nationalism."[1] Kelley came home in 1946 to a United States still steeped in racism, and he worried that Nazi ideology could flourish on new soil. His conviction that malice could develop anywhere shaped the development of social psychological interpretations of malice. Following Nuremberg, four enormously influential investigations examined the implications of this social psychological point of view.

Hannah Arendt

On May 11, 1960, Adolf Eichmann, the head of the Gestapo's Division of Jewish Affairs, was captured by Israeli agents outside of Buenos Aires, where he had been living under the name of Ricardo Klement. Somewhere along the way, he had his SS tattoo removed, and he blended well into the German émigré community as the owner of a small laundry business. One evening as he got off a bus, Israeli agents captured him, drugged him, and headed for the airport days later. They got him through Argentinian passport control dressed as an El Al crewman who'd had too much to drink the night before and flew him to Israel.

Eichmann's trial started the following April, and he was convicted in December 1961. The trial riveted audiences around the world and shattered the silence surrounding the concentration camps. Fifteen years after the Nuremberg judgment, here was a new opportunity to scrutinize a Nazi leader. Eichmann had meticulously planned the seizure and transportation of the Jews to the concentration camps, and his organizational skills were literally murderous in their consequences.

The social philosopher Hannah Arendt (fig. 24) sat in the Jerusalem courtroom gallery, observing and listening keenly to the testimony. This intense, chain-smoking woman had been imprisoned by the Gestapo before she managed to emigrate to the United States. She had personal knowledge of the Nazi cataclysm. So when she published her penetrating essay, initially in the *New Yorker,* with its explosive message and tone, her observations stung deeply. Arendt was a brilliant gadfly who posed maddeningly provocative questions: Wouldn't the death count have been much lower if the concentration camp inmates had resisted? Didn't the Judenrat's collaboration with the Nazis make things worse for the Jews? Did some of the survivors act dishonorably? Was Eichmann's trial even legal? At a time when people were just beginning to talk about their concentration camp experiences, Arendt seemed to suggest that the survivors had brought their imprisonment on themselves and that their survival itself may have come at the cost of other less fortunate inmates.

A storm of denunciations and threats followed the publication of her book *Eichmann in Jerusalem*. The eminent historian Barbara Tuchman eloquently gave voice to the public anger: "There is a peculiar stridency about those who, having remained safe outside, now seize eagerly on the thesis that the Jews submitted too easily and were somehow responsible for their own slaughter. The attractiveness of the thesis is that by shifting guilt onto the victim, it relieves everyone else."[2]

Fig. 24. Hannah Arendt in 1966. (Copyright © Fred Stein Archive, fredstein.com)

Another strand of Arendt's observations particularly infuriated people. To her way of thinking, Eichmann was no monster at all but rather a banal civil servant who relished the technical aspects of his work and removed himself from any emotional or moral involvement. Throughout the trial Eichmann sat in his glass booth, looking weak, colorless, and shabby. He certainly did not *appear* to be a monster. According to Nazi hunter Simon Wiesenthal, "There was nothing demonic about him; he looked like an accountant who was afraid to ask for a raise."[3]

Eichmann denied responsibility for killing the Jews and emphasized that he was not one of the deciders at all, that he had his hands full just in arranging the details of the deportations and transportation. To Arendt, this drab, almost invisible man embodied the banality of evil.

The trouble with Eichmann was precisely that so many were like him, and that the many were neither perverted nor sadistic, that they were, and still are, terribly and terrifyingly normal. From the viewpoint of our legal institutions and of our moral standards of judgment, this normality was much more terrifying than all the atrocities put together, for it implied . . . that this new type of criminal, . . . commits his crimes under circumstances that make it well-nigh impossible for him to know or to feel that he is doing wrong.[4]

Arendt considered Eichmann not only relatively normal but so preoccupied with his job and getting promoted that he failed to see the brutal consequences of his actions:

Except for an extraordinary diligence in looking out for his personal advancement, he had no motives at all. . . . He *merely . . . never realized what he was doing.* . . . He was not stupid. It was sheer thoughtlessness . . . that predisposed him to become one of the greatest criminals of that period. And if this is "banal," . . . if . . . one cannot extract any diabolical or demonic profundity from Eichmann, that is still far from calling it commonplace. . . . That such remoteness from reality and such thoughtlessness can wreak more havoc than all the evil instincts taken together . . . that was, in fact, the lesson one could learn in Jerusalem.[5]

Eichmann's prosecutor Gideon Hausner disagreed sharply with Arendt's characterization and regarded Eichmann as a moral monster and savage psychopath. But even Hausner acknowledged that there was a peculiarity about Eichmann's robotic meticulousness in following rules: "One morning he was given by mistake six slices of bread for breakfast, instead of the usual two. He ate all six. When the guard asked him whether he would like to have six slices in the future, he replied, 'Oh, no. Two are quite enough. But when you give me six, I have to eat them.'"[6]

When interrogated about his work, Eichmann stated: "It gave me uncommon joy. I found it fascinating to deal with these matters. . . . I worked 100 percent. To obey is the highest command. Obedience was my ideal in life."[7] He put a premium on the joys of obedience, commenting sadly: "[When the war ended,] I sensed I would have to live a leaderless and difficult individual life, I would receive no directives from anybody, no orders or commands would any longer be issued to me, no pertinent ordinances would be there to consult."[8]

Trial observers were also struck by Eichmann's tortuous syntax and logic. He twitched when he spoke, and his testimony was often convoluted. The following examination by Israeli interrogator Avner Less is typical:

> LESS: You sent people to Auschwitz only?
> EICHMANN: Auschwitz, and there was once a transport conference, though I, my God, never took part in any such conferences. It went somewhere else, so it seems to me, so it seems. But I don't know, did it go to Treblinka, into a ghetto, into one of the big ghettos? I really can't say now, Mr. Chief Inspector, I never had any contact with the Economic Office. This was Guenther's job, and I never took part in a transport conference. This was the assignment of Captain Novak, and several times, I think, Guenther was present. I never participated.[9]

Arendt thought that this convoluted testimony accurately reflected Eichmann's thinking itself. "*Officialese* became his language because he was genuinely incapable of uttering a single sentence that was not a cliché. . . . His inability to speak was closely connected with an inability to *think* . . . from the standpoint of somebody else."[10]

Having sat through the long trial, Arendt concluded that Eichmann was an automaton who never stopped to consider the moral implications of his actions. There was contradictory testimony to suggest his fanatical hatred, but Arendt downplayed it.[11] She hadn't said that Eichmann was innocent; what she said was that he was not a monster. Eichmann exemplified not radical demonic evil or depravity but rather the consequences of a lack of empathy—sheer thoughtlessness. He had no moral compass.

Communication scholar Valerie Hartouni has commented thoughtfully about the implications of Arendt's writings. While noting that Arendt understated Eichmann's devotion to his work, Hartouni concluded that Arendt's assessments of Eichmann—that he acted without thought—were "somewhere in the general vicinity of truth." She artfully summarized the dialectic between Arendt and Gideon Hausner as follows: "Where Arendt saw . . . the embodiment of something she described as *evil in its total banality,* the prosecution . . . pursued a diabolically wicked, morally monstrous Nazi official whose hatred of the Jews was relentless."[12]

During the Nuremberg trial Arendt had corresponded with the German philosopher and psychiatrist Karl Jaspers concerning the nature of evil, and that correspondence influenced her later thinking about Eichmann. She was deeply troubled by Nuremberg, but Jaspers cautioned her against overemphasizing the magnitude of the Nazis' satanic or demonic qualities. Instead, he suggested, "we have to see these things in their total banality, in their prosaic triviality. . . . Bacteria can cause epidemics that wipe out nations, but they remain merely bacteria." In other words, demonic intentions are not a requirement for causing suffering. Simple thoughtlessness can be as destructive as malevolence. In post-Eichmann debates (this time with the Jewish scholar Gershom Scholem), Arendt recalled Jaspers's analogy but shifted from talking about bacteria to fungi. "Evil was . . . very much like a fungus, laying waste, it was without depth or demonic dimension." "[I] no longer speak of 'radical evil.' . . . It is . . . my opinion now that evil . . . possesses neither depth nor any demonic dimension. It can overgrow and lay waste the whole world precisely because it spreads like a fungus on the surface. . . . That is its 'banality.'"[13]

A series of provocative social psychology experiments emerged from the aftermath of the Nuremberg trial and from Arendt's observations of the Eichmann trial. Their scientific lineage is impeccable, originating from Yale, Columbia, Princeton, and Stanford. Arguably, it all began at Yale University in the laboratory of young professor Stanley Milgram. His studies and those of John Darley, Bibb Latané, and Philip Zimbardo offer an explosive view of what we are all capable of.

Obedience: Stanley Milgram (1963)

Psychologist Stanley Milgram began his studies on obedience to authority in 1961, the year of the Eichmann trial. Adolf Eichmann maintained that he was not responsible for the killing because he was only following orders. Milgram wondered, "How far will normal people go in following orders?" His research, first published in 1963 and with many subsequent iterations, exploded across the academic landscape and public consciousness.[14]

Milgram's advertisement seeking volunteers could not have sounded more benign: "Persons needed for a study of memory. Each person who participates will be paid $4.00 (plus 50 cents carfare) for approximately 1 hour's time. . . . Fill out the coupon below and mail it now to Professor Stanley Milgram, Department of Psychology, Yale University, New Haven."[15]

As the expression goes, there is no such thing as a free lunch. By the time each subject had completed the study, he would have been asked to nearly electrocute another human being.

The subject of the experiment arrived at the lab and was greeted by a professor who explained that the purpose of the study was to examine whether learning could be enhanced by aversive stimuli—electric shocks. The subject was told to test the memory of a learner (another subject) who was wired up in an adjacent room. The learner was actually Milgram's confederate. The two subjects communicated via intercom. Every time the learner made a mistake, the subject was instructed to administer an electric shock. The more mistakes, the higher the voltage.

In reality, no shocks were administered, but the subject did not know that. Instead, he was treated to a carefully scripted charade. How far would he go? The schedule of responses below gives a sense of the study. As the learner makes more and more mistakes, the subject administers shocks of ever-higher magnitude.

90 VOLTS: Ugh!!!

120 VOLTS: Ugh!!! Hey, *this* really hurts.

150 VOLTS: Ugh!!! Experimenter! That's all. Get me out of here. I told you I had heart trouble. My heart's starting to bother me now. Get me out of here, please. My heart's starting to bother me. I refuse to go on. Let me out.

180 VOLTS: (*Shouting*) Ugh!!! I can't stand the pain. Let me out of here!

210 VOLTS: Ugh!! Experimenter! Get me out of here. I've had enough. I won't be in the experiment any more.

270 VOLTS: (*Agonized scream*) Let me out of here. Let me out of here. Let me out of here. Let me out. Do you hear? Let me out of here. . . .

300 VOLTS: (*Agonized scream*) I absolutely refuse to answer any more. Get me out of here. You can't hold me here. Get me out. Get me out of here.

330 VOLTS: (*Intense and prolonged agonized scream*) Let me out of here. Let me out of here. My heart's bothering me. Let me out, I tell you. (*Hysterically*) Let me out of here. Let me out of here. You have no right to hold me here.[16]

If the subject hesitated to administer the increasingly severe shocks, the professor would respond, "Please continue," or "The experiment requires that you continue," or "It is absolutely essential that you continue," or "You have no other choice; you must go on."

How far would people go? *All* of the subjects administered shocks up to the 300-volt point and two-thirds continued to the maximum voltage. Milgram noted that although many of the subjects showed signs of considerable stress and uncertainty, the point was that ostensibly normal people could be ordered to do horrible things and that they *would* in fact do so. You did not have to be depraved or evil or monstrous to give painful shocks to people even when their screams were loud and imploring. Normal people would indeed "follow orders."[17]

Milgram repeatedly drew the analogy to the mass killing in the concentration camps. Indeed, the concentration camps were very much on his mind. Portrait photos often reveal surprises in their periphery. A photograph of Milgram reveals his preoccupation with the Holocaust (fig. 25). At eye level, his office bookshelves hold Raul Hilberg's *Destruction of the European Jews*, Albert Speer's *Inside the Third Reich*, Hannah Arendt's *Eichmann in Jerusalem*, and Bruno Bettelheim's *The Informed Heart*. One can infer that Milgram thought a great deal about the horrors of the mass killings. The books confronted him every day as he sat at his desk.

Years later, in discussing his work, Milgram concluded: "The question arises as to whether there is any connection between what we have studied in the laboratory and the forms of obedience we so deplored in the Nazi epoch. . . . The essence of obedience consists in the fact that a person comes to view himself as the instrument for carrying out another person's wishes, and he therefore no longer regards himself as responsible for his actions."[18]

Fig. 25. Stanley Milgram at CUNY. The degree of his engagement
with the Holocaust may be inferred by the books on his shelf. At his
eye level are key texts relating to the Third Reich and the Holocaust.
(Courtesy of Graduate Center, City University of New York)

Bystander Apathy: John Darley and Bibb Latané (1968)

The very public murder of young Kitty Genovese in New York City motivated the next social psychology exploration on the nature of malice. On the
night of March 13, 1964, Genovese left work and was walking on a street in
Kew Gardens, Queens, when she was chased down and stabbed. The murder was doubly horrific. She didn't die suddenly; rather, her assailant kept
chasing her, stabbing and slashing her over and over again in an attack that
lasted more than thirty minutes. She called out in terror: "Please help me!
Please help me!" But no one did.

Although murders like this are not rare, what made the Genovese kill-ing unusual was that thirty-eight individuals witnessed the attack and did nothing to intervene: they didn't try to stop the assault; they didn't shout at the assailant; they didn't even call the police.[19] One witness said defensively: "I didn't want to get involved." The witnesses' apparent indifference was the occasion for considerable soul searching across the nation, and com-parisons with Nazi Germany were readily made. Indifference indeed could be lethal. Ian Kershaw commented years later that public opinion in Nazi Germany was shaped less by "the creation of dynamic hatred than of lethal indifference towards the fate of the Jewish population."[20]

Two investigators, John Darley and Bibb Latané, designed a series of ex-periments to find out why people do not intervene even in life-threatening situations. If Milgram conducted his studies on the influence of authority, looking over his shoulder at Nazi Germany, Darley and Latané wanted to learn what accounts for bystander apathy. Why did no one intervene to save Genovese's life? Why did so many people stand by and do nothing to save the lives of Nazi victims? It was a topic Hannah Arendt had wrestled with in another context: "Under conditions of terror most people will comply but *some people will not*. . . . No more is required, and no more can reasonably be asked, for this planet to remain a place fit for human habitation."[21] Sadly, the number of people who resist complying is small.

To be fair, emergency situations are often sudden, ambiguous, and out of the typical life experience of the beholder. But, as Darley and Latané would learn, there was something about the social environment itself that influences how a person would respond to emergencies. Painstakingly, first at Columbia University and New York University and then at Prince-ton University, the investigators grappled with this problem in multiple experiments.[22]

Darley and Latané confronted their subjects with a threatening situation and assessed how the subjects would respond. Then, in an ingenious twist, Darley and Latané studied the subject alone or else in small groups. How would a subject respond to an emergency in the presence of other people who appeared to ignore what was happening?

In one experiment, subjects reported to a room to talk about the problems of urban life while smoke poured from the room's heating register—not just a few puffs, but so much smoke that by the end of the session "vision was obscured in the room by the amount of smoke present." When subjects waited alone, 75 percent of them quickly reported the smoke, but when they entered a room with two other seated people who studiously ignored the smoke, the subjects' behavior was strikingly different. Only 10 percent of these subjects reported the smoke even though they "coughed, rubbed their eyes, and opened the window."[23]

In another experiment, subjects arrived at the lab and were greeted by a receptionist who stood up, drew a curtain, and noisily clambered up on a chair to grab some folders. The receptionist surreptitiously turned on a tape recorder, which played the sound of a loud crash, a scream, and the following script: "Oh, my God, my foot . . . I . . . can't move . . . it. Oh . . . my ankle, I can't get this . . . thing . . . off me." The tape played sounds of weeping and moaning. Here again, the question was simple: Would anyone check on the receptionist, and how long would it take? It may be comforting that 70 percent of the subjects who waited alone checked on the receptionist. It will not be comforting to learn that when the subjects were waiting with a stranger who ignored the receptionist's plight, only 7 percent of the subjects intervened.[24]

A third experiment revealed even more indifference. In this setting, subjects were ushered into individual cubicles and asked to talk via intercom with other subjects about the problems they experienced in college. One subject, secretly a confederate of the investigators, revealed that in addition to all the usual stresses of college, he was embarrassed because he had a seizure disorder. He then grew increasingly incoherent, saying: "I-er-um-I think I-I need-er-if-if could-er-er-somebody er-er-er-er-er-er-er give me a little-er-give me a little help here because-er-I-er-I'm-er-er h-h-having a-a-a real problem-er-right now and I-er-if somebody could help me out it would-it would-er-er s-s-sure be-sure be good . . . because-er-there-er-er-a cause I-er-I-uh-I've got a-a one of the-er sei----er-er-things coming on and-and-and I could really-er-use some help so if somebody would-er give me a little h-help-er-uh-uh-uh (choking sounds). . . . I'm gonna die-er-er I'm . . . gonna die-er-help-er-er-seizure-er (chokes, then quiet)."[25]

When subjects were alone in the cubicle, 85 percent got up within a minute to check on the subject who was presumably having a seizure. Subjects were then tested with other people in the same cubicle. If the subject was paired with one person who had been secretly instructed to ignore the situation, 62 percent of the subjects got up to check on the presumably ill student. If however, the subject was tested with four confederates who ignored the apparent seizure, then the chance of the subject responding fell to only 31 percent, and it took such people, on average, three minutes to check on their fellow student.[26]

There have been countless variations on the design, but the inherent message remains the same: in social situations, there is a diffusion of responsibility. If a bystander sees that other witnesses are doing nothing, then he or she will also do nothing—"bystander apathy," as Darley and Latané put it so pungently.

The Stanford Prison Experiment: Philip Zimbardo (1971)

So far, social psychologists had observed that normal people would obey orders to do dreadful things and that bystanders would rarely stop to help others who were in obvious distress. It got worse.

In 1971, Stanford University professor Philip Zimbardo designed the Stanford Prison Experiment.[27] Volunteers were told that Stanford was studying prison behaviors and that they would be randomly assigned to be either prisoners or guards in a simulated prison environment. Years later, Zimbardo reminisced about the beginning of the experiment: "Sunday, August 14, 1971, 9:55 a.m. The temperature is in the seventies, the humidity is low, as usual, the visibility is unlimited; there is a cloudless azure blue sky above. Another picture-perfect summer day begins in Palo Alto, California."[28]

Suddenly, the volunteer prisoners were picked up in police cars, handcuffed, blindfolded, and transported to a makeshift jail that was actually in the basement of the psychology building. Zimbardo gave considerable attention to the details of the study to make the experiment more realistic. Prisoners were booked, they were strip-searched, and their mug shots were taken. The jail's volunteer guards were given uniforms, dark sunglasses, handcuffs, and batons and told to make the prisoners feel powerless without physically harming them.[29] Meanwhile, Zimbardo observed the emerging behaviors in what was supposed to have been a two-week experiment.

Rather quickly, the experiment spun out of control. Guards began brutally harassing the prisoners, and they wouldn't stop, even after the prisoners shouted, screamed, or wept. Over the course of the week, the guards increased their harassment. They stripped the prisoners naked in retaliation for apparent rule violations, deprived them of food, and limited their access to rest rooms. The prisoners in turn became increasingly submissive, and some of them fell apart. The experiment was halted after six days.

On being debriefed, one guard said he started to regard the prisoners as cattle. Another said, "I was surprised at myself. I made them . . . clean the toilets out with their bare hands." Yet another confessed, "Acting authoritatively can be fun. Power can be a great pleasure." Tellingly, one guard commented: "Looking back I am impressed by how little I felt for them." All in all, about a third of the guards went over to the dark side by tormenting the prisoners.[30]

Although there were major questions about the ethics of this research, Zimbardo's experiment brought to light another disturbing conclusion: social context alone could foment a phenomenal amount of nastiness. Simply being assigned the role of prison guard could intoxicate a person to the extent that he would lord it over and abuse the prisoners in his charge. These were college students with no history of sociopathic behaviors or psychiatric problems, yet when they were randomly assigned to their roles, their behaviors changed to reflect their role assignments. Power corrupted, and brutality emerged.

Critics have argued that such studies cannot generalize to the Third Reich. They argue that the Zimbardo study was like a fraternity hazing gone bad and that surely, after a longer period of time, these young men would have come to their senses. That is of course an untestable proposition. From the accounts of the Nazi killers, the opposite seems to be the case—the longer the killing went on, the easier it became.

There is an interesting coda to the Zimbardo study, which brings us back to the observations of Darley and Latané. In repeated interviews Zimbardo has acknowledged that he would have continued the study, even in the face of the brutality, had it not been for the intervention of a colleague, Christina Maslach.[31] That she intervened and that he listened is to their credit. However, in a little-known interview from 1997, Zimbardo commented that more than fifty people had observed the study in progress and none objected.[32]

Summing Up

Hannah Arendt was an observer of human nature rather than an experimentalist. She was a self-assured, confrontational woman who made some missteps in her analysis of Eichmann. Her accounts about Eichmann's "thoughtlessness" are overstated, given his hatreds, but her image that evil is like a fungus is brilliant. A fungus oozes and spreads and destroys even if it doesn't have the intention to wreak havoc. There are ghosts of Plato and Augustine in this perspective—that evil represents the absence of good. For Arendt, Eichmann and his companions were evil because they didn't think through the ramifications of their actions, rather like drunken hit-and-run drivers. There is something about such thoughtlessness that allows it to spread inexorably, like a fungus.

The experimentalists took up the issue of how this spreading occurred. The experimentalists reflected on Nuremberg and on life around them, and they came up with dispiriting conclusions about human nature itself. Milgram pointed out that people will all too readily suspend their judgment about right and wrong behavior. Given an authority figure who tells them to torture and potentially kill another human being, most people will in fact do so promptly. Latané and Darley observed that good intentions can be silenced in social settings. With increasing numbers of indifferent people around us, our sense of individual responsibility is diffused and we lack the courage to intervene. Zimbardo introduced another dimension of thoughtless evil. Put a person in a role and he will start to adopt that role unthinkingly. He will summon up observations from literature, from movies, from growing up and he will start imitating those behaviors, even to the extent of assuming a mantle of brutality.

All of these studies follow in the tradition of Douglas Kelley's observations. Evil happens all too easily, given the "right" social situation. But there is one LARGE assumption behind all of these studies—that we come into the world tabula rasa, a blank slate to be shaped by our interactions with others. What if some of us don't have blank slates at all? What if the basic default position of some human beings is not neutral at all but much darker than that? We take up these troubling questions in the next chapter.

Malice as Categorically Different: Encounters with "the Other"

Most men are bad.

— Bias, Greek philosopher, sixth century BCE

I have found little that is "good" about human beings on the whole. Most of them are trash.

— Sigmund Freud to Oskar Pfister, September 10, 1918

THE BATTLE LINES WERE ALREADY DRAWN. On one side, there was Douglas Kelley, who thought there was a bit of malice in everyone and that it was socially determined. On the opposite side, Gustave Gilbert believed that the Nazi leaders' malice constituted a special category of evil. Gilbert's view has roots in surprisingly diverse fields—theology, psychopathology, neuroscience, and law. If the Nuremberg trial were held today, the prosecution would portray the defendants as categorically evil and the defense would argue that their sentences should be mitigated because the defendants had psychopathic personality disorder and/or brain damage. There are long traditions supporting these arguments and some surprising insights from contemporary neuroscience research.

What Is the Nature of Man?

Even Hermann Göring was drawn to this question. One evening, surrounded by the gloom in his prison cell, he confided in Gilbert that man is the biggest beast of prey there is, "because he has the brains for large-scale destruction, while other beasts-of-prey merely kill to eat when they are hungry."[1]

In a way, questions about the nature of man anticipate the problem of theodicy, how a morally perfect and omnipotent God permits bad things to happen. Many religious traditions regard life as a battleground between luminous good and brooding evil. In this context, evil is not just sin (that is, man's fault) but a manifestation of a Malicious Intentionality. One finds traces of this perspective, for instance, in Norse mythology, and it is of course well developed in Zoroastrianism. Even contemporary Catholicism struggles with a Manichean legacy dating back to the third century that recognizes a dualistic struggle between good and evil.

Peter tells us: "Your adversary the devil prowls around like a roaring lion, seeking someone to devour" (1 Pet. 5:8). Paul shares that view, noting: "For we wrestle not against flesh and blood, but against principalities, against powers, against the rulers, the darkness of this world, against spiritual wickedness in high places" (Eph. 6:12). As so many popes have reminded us, "The devil is real." Augustine subtly stepped back from Manichaeism by suggesting that evil, rather than being a force in its own right, was the absence of good.[2] But secular thinkers like Einstein have also recognized the tangibility of evil by noting, "It is easier to denature plutonium than to denature the evil spirit of man."[3]

Years ago, when I graduated from college, the commencement speaker—discouraged by the riots, assassinations, and wars of the 1960s—offered a dark view of our future by quoting the sixth-century BCE philosopher Bias, who summed up his view of the nature of man in just four words: "Most men are bad." These words have haunted me from time to time whenever I've encountered malice, but then I ran into Bias, literally, when I was in the Vatican's Hall of Philosophers, where his bust is prominently displayed.

It seems odd that the Vatican honors a man whose opinion of humanity was so dark and pessimistic, but Bias summarized a worldview that is still widely felt. Two thousand years later, Thomas Hobbes shared Bias's pessimism about the nature of man and concluded in his Leviathan (1651) that in the state of nature, man's life is "poor, nasty, brutish and short," and Freud, of all people, shared that point of view as well ("Most men are trash"). Such views imply that the social psychologists are wrong and that we are not born with a blank slate. Worse than that, some people's default position is neither benign nor neutral but malevolent.

Our prevailing positivism and optimism incline us to view evil as symbolic or inner, and we think that only eccentrics view evil as palpably external.[4] Theology and philosophy are not alone, however, in considering malice as a distinct presence. Psychiatry and psychology recognize its unique signature in psychopaths, and Gilbert saw them everywhere he looked in Nuremberg.

The Psychopaths' Lack of Empathy

When people were starting to think about the Nazi leaders as psychopaths, they were anticipating maniacs, monstrous psychopaths who enjoyed their violence. This assumption that the war criminals would be sadistic psychopaths caused no end of trouble at Nuremberg because there are other types of psychopaths who are far more common, individuals who are corrupt, occasionally charming, and vicious only when necessary. These psychopaths claw their way to the top and leave mayhem in their wake, not out of thrill-seeking or sadistic pleasure but because others were simply "in their way." Even more common are the black sheep found in any family, psychopaths who "defy all norms, reject authority, and act only out of blind selfishness."[5] All of them have in common a lack of empathy.[6]

Psychopaths have been described under different names for centuries. Psychiatrist Donald Black beautifully described how the term has evolved over the years.[7] Around 1800, the French physician Philippe Pinel observed patients who had cloudbursts of violence and rage but were not delusional or confused. He called these outbursts *manie sans delire,* mania without delirium. About the same time, the American psychiatrist Benjamin Rush described patients with chronic, willful bad behavior, which he attributed to a defect in the mind. In 1850, the diagnosis had morphed into *moral insanity,* where intellect was preserved but habits and behaviors had run amok. By 1890, individuals who manifested such behavior chronically were called "psychopaths." The nineteenth-century Italian criminologist Cesare Lombroso felt that in addition to their unsavory behavior, psychopaths were marked by anomalies in their physical appearance such as facial asymmetries. They were indeed "other."

In 1941, American psychiatrist Hervey M. Cleckley published *The Mask of Sanity,* which suggested that a profound mental disorder lurked behind the psychopath's seemingly normal facade—thus, the "mask of sanity."[8] Given the date of the publication, Cleckley's work was influential when the Nuremberg Tribunal convened. Cleckley asserted that the psychopath appeared normal but in fact had profound impairment in the ability to understand emotions and interpersonal loyalties. He emphasized that psychopaths were typically unreliable people who could be superficially charming but had poor judgment. They were self-absorbed and had few emotional commitments. They broke rules and laws frequently and without remorse or guilt. Importantly, Cleckley did not think them insane because they knew right from wrong, acted with intentionality, and were free from psychosis. But they were VERY peculiar.

Numerous studies support Cleckley's observations. Psychopaths have subtle deficits in the way they perceive the world and the people around them. They slough off blame because it's always somebody else's fault. For such people, "remorse" is a word in a foreign dictionary. Truth is fungible and deceit is the norm.

Cleckley noted that the psychopath's aberration is more pronounced than just breaking rules. After all, illegal activities and rule breaking are common; however, the psychopath's transgressions are different.[9] First off, their record of rule breaking is lifelong, with onset in childhood, and is evident during good times and bad, peacetime and wartime. Second, psychopaths feel no guilt, shame, or empathy. Lots of us break rules, but we put ourselves in other's places and feel empathy for those we have hurt. Oddly, the psychopath has none of this. To the psychopath, we are all mere krill. A shark has no feelings about eating krill; it kills and eats. The psychopath's victim is in the way or has something the psychopath wants, like money or sex. Again, this does not happen just once or twice; it is an enduring pattern of predation.[10]

Psychopaths are also notorious for their rashness and impulsivity. It is providential for the rest of us that most criminal psychopaths get caught because of their recklessness. Although some psychopaths can be very calculating, such individuals, fortunately, are rare. Instead, most psychopaths do not learn well from their experiences. As a result, prisons are filled with careless psychopaths like bank robbers who left their cell phones behind at the scene of the crime.

Numerous studies show that psychopaths are indeed "different" in their response to stressors. Their impulsivity trips them up, and many of them may appear dumb although their IQ is typically normal. Normal people respond to a stressor with increased sympathetic nervous system activity; their heart rate increases, they start to sweat, and the stress is aversive to them. They *learn*. Psychopaths, however, are "blind" to stress; they respond in a wooden or blunted way, and they do not feel the aversive effects of their behavior. Put them in a stressful situation and their body shakes it off—no increase in heart rate, no increase in sweating.[11] This may sound advantageous, but it has a dark consequence: psychopaths do not get feedback from their own bodies about dangerous behaviors. Some investigators feel that this defect in stress responsivity hampers learning and accounts for psychopaths' puzzling lack of guilt and impulsivity.

Over time, psychiatrists began to differentiate among various types of psychopaths. First there were "inadequate" types—cheats and vagrants who weren't particularly aggressive. Then there were "aggressive" psychopaths who were dangerous and violent. There were also "creative" psychopaths— eccentrics who ignored society's rules; today, this category is now included in narcissistic personality disorder.[12]

The diagnostic territory of psychopathic personality, thus, has constantly shifted. When the first DSM was published in 1952, the overall term was "sociopathic personality disturbance." At that point psychiatry recognized four variants. "Antisocial reaction" patients were described as "always in trouble, profiting neither from experience nor punishment, and maintaining no real loyalties . . . frequently callous and hedonistic, showing marked emotional immaturity, with lack of sense of responsibility, lack of judgment, and an ability to rationalize their behavior so that it appears warranted, reasonable, and justified."[13]

That edition of the DSM distinguished between antisocial reaction and dissocial reaction. People in the latter group showed a disregard for the usual social codes because of living in an abnormal moral environment.

They might well be predatory, but they had loyalties. Sexual deviation, the third variant of sociopathic personality disturbance, included sadism, homosexuality, fetishism, and pedophilia. Addiction was the fourth variant of sociopathic personality disturbance described in this early DSM.[14]

In 1945, one can thus see that witnesses found a special meaning in Göring's red nail polish and his drug addiction. To psychiatric observers, this buttressed his diagnosis as a psychopath. Today, a man wearing nail polish might be regarded as eccentric, and drug abuse would be so commonplace that it would not, by itself, lead to a diagnosis of psychopathic personality (or antisocial personality disorder, as it is technically referred to now).

Today, the term "psychopath" is reserved for people with severe antisocial personality disorder, and the diagnosis is typically based on a commonly used twenty-item checklist.[15] In 1945, the checklist approach was not available, and the Rorschach was considered a preeminent technique for diagnosing psychopathy and was recognized as such by the OSS and of course by Kelley and Gilbert.

Even though psychopaths are callous and emotionally shallow, they can be haunted, later in life, by the shadow of lives they have ruined. They can and do get depressed and frequently seek solace in drugs and alcohol. Psychiatrists have a lot of familiarity with psychopaths because they are referred to us by their disconsolate spouses or by the courts. Psychopaths can respond to intensive psychotherapy, but the course is difficult. There is no pill for treating them, but some medications decrease impulsive irritability. If they come to the courts' attention, the legal system tries to help *us* by trundling them off to jail. From Gilbert's point of view, the best treatment for the Nuremberg psychopaths was a hemp noose.

Neuropsychiatry's Quest for "the Bad Brain"

Psychiatry and psychology provide a clear description of psychopaths but refrain from attributing a cause to the disorder. All of the usual suspects are blamed for psychopathy—crowded slums, bad parenting, bad genes, and brain injury. Numerous studies support each of these potential pathways, but ultimately, it comes down to the brain.[16]

There is a long tradition linking brain pathology to violence and criminal behavior. Mary Shelley anticipated this research in her novel about Frankenstein and his poorly cobbled together Creature with a defective brain who commits unspeakable crimes. But outside of fiction, there is also a centuries-old medical literature documenting, for instance, how syphilis or mercury toxicity could affect the brain, leading to irritability, dementia, and megalomania. It is no wonder that Nuremberg observers were on the lookout for neuropathology in the war criminals.

The brain isn't just a three-pound, gelatinous adding machine; it has multiple parts that are organized topographically. In the 1930s physicians recognized that the innermost part of the brain oversees the vital turbines of the body—breathing, heart rate, digestion—whereas the outermost part of the brain, the cortex, is in charge of thinking and evaluating. Sandwiched between these two areas is the limbic system, which helps us "feel" in response to the world. We would all be like a *Tyrannosaurus rex* if our limbic system had its way; fortunately, those limbic rages and lusts are modulated by our cortex. The large prefrontal cortex presides over it all—a traffic cop between thinking and feeling. If the prefrontal cortex is damaged, the brain's deeper structures acquire a louder voice; the timbre of behavior changes, and people become more impulsive, irritable, and morally lax. Whatever the cause of the injury—automobile accidents, athletic injuries, military combat—there is a link to impulsivity and violence, depending on the extent and location of the brain injury.[17] Neuroscientists have reasoned that violence and psychopathy can emerge when either the top-down inhibitory action of the cortex is weakened or the bottom-up activity of the limbic system is enhanced.[18]

The brain has an elegant origami design with layers of the brain folded in on themselves and deep crevasses that result from all of that folding. Many of the folds, or sulci, provide landmarks that help us identify features of the brain more precisely. But in a way, the brain is also a complex macramé design with neurons twisting and weaving around one another like an oddly designed freeway with on-ramps and exits that materialize willy-nilly.

In 1848, an American railroad worker's accident led to one of the most influential case reports on brain injury and moral behavior. A forty-three-inch-long tamping iron with a diameter of one and a quarter inches blasted through Phineas Gage's head in an explosion, yet surprisingly, he survived. But "he" wasn't the same. As his doctor famously observed:

> The equilibrium or balance, so to speak, between his intellectual faculties and animal propensities, seems to have been destroyed. He is fitful, irreverent, indulging at times in the grossest profanity (which was not previously his custom), . . . impatient of restraint or advice when it conflicts with his desires, at times pertinaciously obstinate, yet capricious and vacillating. . . . A child in his intellectual capacity and manifestations, he has the animal passions of a strong man. . . . His mind was radically changed, so decidedly that his friends and acquaintances said he was "no longer Gage."[19]

Neuroscientists reconstructed the trajectory of the injury and inferred that the tamping iron had profoundly damaged Gage's left and right prefrontal cortex (located roughly behind the forehead on each side).[20] Patients with such an injury have difficulties planning complex tasks that require flexibility and multitasking; their emotional regulation is damaged; and they become moody and impulsive while at the same time appearing indifferent in the wake of their outbursts. This starts to sound a bit like psychopathic behavior.

Neural Imaging

In 1945, it was difficult to study the brains of psychopaths. When patients like Robert Ley died, their brains could be sent for biopsy, but the tools for tracking the brain damage were somewhat coarser than today's. At the time of the Nuremberg trials, there were few instruments available to examine a living brain. One could observe the patient closely or else wait for the eventual autopsy. There was little in between. Thus, when we try to second-guess the neuropathologists who examined Ley's brain, we must keep in mind what was knowable in 1945. Today, we can use neural imaging to scrutinize neural circuitry. Not surprisingly, investigators have leapt at the opportunity to use such tools to study psychopaths' brains.[21]

From studies on brain-injured patients, we have a sense for regions of the brain that are involved in decision-making and emotional expression. The question arises: Are these areas eroded in psychopaths? A growing literature suggests that psychopaths have defects in their prefrontal cortex, which contribute to their lack of judgment, difficulties in planning, and greater impulsivity. They also have reductions in the medial aspect of their temporal lobe (the amygdala, to be precise), an area that helps regulate fear, emotionality, and threat perception.[22] Many studies support these conclusions, but one by Martina Ly and colleagues gives a sense for the general approach.[23] The investigators used structural magnetic resonance imaging to compare the brains of psychopathic and nonpsychopathic prisoners. They found significant thinning in the cerebral cortex in the psychopaths, particularly in the areas of the brain that oversee planning and emotionality (fig. 26). It is almost as if one can see the reptilian brain burning through areas of the thinned cortex in the psychopaths.

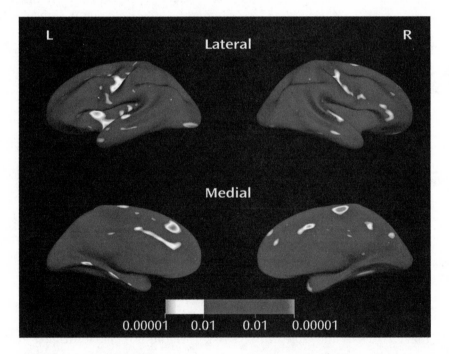

Fig. 26. Comparison of brain structure of psychopaths and normal controls. Lighter areas denote significant differences across the two groups. Psychopaths had thinner cortex in L insula and dorsal anterior cingulate cortex, L and R precentral gyri, L and R anterior temporal cortices, R inferior frontal gyrus. The color grid marks the degree of significance. (Reprinted with permission from Martina Ly et al., "Cortical Thinning in Psychopathy," *American Journal of Psychiatry* 169 [2012]: 743–749)

Functional imaging is slightly more complicated to grasp than structural imaging. In functional magnetic resonance imaging (fMRI), one examines how different areas of the brain function, or respond, to certain tasks. The choice of tasks is important. If you contrasted eyes open versus eyes closed, that contrast would not be particularly informative for understanding psychopaths. However, if you used a task that examined impulsivity, that might be more useful. To examine impulsivity, one can ask a subject to perform a task—pressing a button every time he or she sees an "X"—and notice how often the subject jumps the gun by pressing the button when the "X" hasn't appeared on the screen. Similarly, scrutinizing how the brain responds to a task requiring an emotional judgment (empathy) can be informative. Obviously, there are many such tasks that could be employed and many regions of the brain to be scanned. However, studying areas of the brain that serve emotional regulation, decision-making, and empathy might be highly informative for understanding how psychopaths think.

In one study, seventy prisoners were divided into groups on the basis of high or low psychopathy scores. Then, the investigators showed the prisoners movie clips of people being intentionally hurt—struck, cut, crushed (fingers in a car door). Would the psychopaths show any response of empathy? More important, would their brain regions involved in emotional regulation respond normally? In fact, the high scorers on the psychopathy scale differed profoundly. Their lack of empathy was not just on the surface; instead, in the depths of their brains, they were dead to watching another person's pain.[24] Other studies have pointed out that psychopaths are poor in reading other people's emotional cues, and the brain region that is normally activated by such tasks stays ominously quiet in psychopaths.[25]

This neural imaging literature is fascinating, but it faces unique research challenges. Brain scans are so expensive that researchers rarely can afford to study large numbers of patients. In studies with small samples, random noise or confounding factors like drug abuse can complicate the inferences. Scientists are trained to be skeptical unless findings can be replicated, and precise replications in terms of type of scan, type of task, and area of the brain studied remain all too rare. Even subtle variations in the task can have major effects on the findings. For instance, asking patients to press a button with their left hand versus their right hand can affect the findings, thereby confusing the interpretation.

What are the chances that an observation may be a fluke? When one examines large numbers of regions of interest in the brain, there is a chance of misidentifying a finding as significant when it is just a coincidence. One solution is to perform specialized meta-analyses that summarize findings across many studies while controlling for subtle differences in design. Researchers are just beginning to use such techniques to understand the neural imaging literature on psychopaths.[26]

I am an amateur photographer. Getting useful data from functional imaging experiments is a lot like taking a photo with a powerful telephoto lens; unless you have a tripod, your pictures will be blurry. The tripod in the case of neural imaging is a precise research design. Without such precision, whatever pictures or insight we might get from such studies will be blurry. Mairead Dolan, one of the leading researchers in this area, summarized the problem succinctly: "At present, too few methodologically sound brain imaging studies in those who have engaged [in] anti-social violence exist for definitive conclusions to be drawn."[27] That sober assessment hasn't stopped the arguments in the courts.

Neuroendocrine Physiology

Neuroendocrine research examines how neurons communicate with each other, and recent studies suggest that the psychopath's neuronal communication signals are unusual. Two neurotransmitters—serotonin and oxytocin—have stirred considerable interest because of their peculiar regulation in psychopaths.

Serotonin is involved in mood regulation, aggression, and impulsivity.[28] Murderers, for instance, have lower levels of serotonin in their nervous system.[29] It is interesting that medications like fluoxetine, which increase the bioavailability of serotonin, have been used informally to treat irritability and impulsivity.[30]

While disturbance in serotonin metabolism may contribute to psychopaths' impulsiveness and irritability, that disruption does not explain their callous indifference to others. An entirely different compound—oxytocin—

may have relevance here. We used to think that oxytocin's main role was to increase uterine contractility, but research in the past thirty years has suggested a much broader role for oxytocin. Sites in the hypothalamus that produce oxytocin have neural links to the brain's emotional regulatory centers as well as to the pituitary, which regulates much of the body's stress response.

Initial research on oxytocin and emotion was performed on small, burrowing rodents called voles, which are about seven inches long. It turns out that male *prairie* voles are strictly monogamous, help take care of their young, and are gregarious. In contrast, *meadow* voles are loners, but if you treat them with oxytocin, their behavior changes dramatically and they start to resemble prairie voles in behavioral style.[31]

It is a considerable stretch from voles to humans, but people release oxytocin during activities when they are close to another person—close in ways as diverse as prayer, sexual intimacy, or even team sports. However, some people do not release oxytocin under such conditions. Not only that, they share many of the characteristics of psychopaths: they are callous and indifferent to others' feelings.[32] Hormones like oxytocin work in conjunction with receptors, and some individuals have a genetic modification in their receptors that make them relatively poor in binding oxytocin. These individuals manifest more callous behaviors, even in childhood.[33] Thus, studies are starting to suggest that callous behaviors emerge when the oxytocin level is low or when it is poorly bound to its receptor. The obvious next step has been to manipulate oxytocin levels.

When oxytocin is administered, it has direct effects on social behavior, and individuals become more trusting and generous.[34] This was demonstrated in ingenious experiments that employed game theory models.[35] Imagine, for instance that two subjects are studied in adjacent rooms and allowed to communicate through the computer. Each is given ten dollars. Subject A is told that he or she can donate money to Subject B and that the money will be tripled when it arrives in B's account. B is told that he or she can keep the money or donate some of it back to A. In this case, there will be no tripling of funds. Thus, if A donates two dollars to B, B will have sixteen dollars, and if subject B gives three dollars back to A, both will be ahead (A will have eleven dollars and B will have thirteen dollars).

How much money will A give to B (or B to A)? That question starts to get at issues of trust and generosity. After receiving oxytocin, subject As were 80 percent more generous.[36] A small percentage of subject Bs were untrustworthy and indifferent to their partner; they kept all the money to themselves. Interestingly, these subjects appeared to have abnormal oxytocin receptors.[37]

Such observations have led investigators to speculate that psychopaths and patients with other personality disorders might benefit from taking oxytocin. Could their indifference toward others improve with oxytocin? One study compared healthy controls and personality disorder patients in terms of their response to emotional stimuli. When viewing angry faces, patients with personality disorder fixated on the angry faces more rapidly, and this intense focus was related to increased activity in their amygdalae. However, when these patients were treated with oxytocin, such differences in response patterns disappeared.[38]

Even if psychopaths could be reliably diagnosed by their unusual brain structure and function, and even if they have peculiarities in their neuro-endocrine physiology, how does this help define their legal responsibility? If Julius Streicher met the criteria for psychopathy, should he have been treated more leniently at Nuremberg? How would a latter-day Streicher be viewed by the courts of today?

Forensic Views of Malice

Euripides' *Oresteia* focuses on the evolution of law. Without law, the Furies foment an endless cycle of revenge and retribution, and there is no escape until all the involved parties are dead. With law, the perspective changes. Society acts as an impartial judge and imposes terms of settlement or punishment. Should such judgments consider a defendant's mental illness? When patients with mental illness commit crimes, the courts are interested in the defendant's mental state at the time of the crime and also whether the person can meaningfully participate in the trial. Those are two separate matters, and the rules for deciding such matters vary greatly in different jurisdictions. The Nuremberg Tribunal grappled with this problem, particularly in the case of Rudolf Hess, but this controversial issue has much older legal precedents.

Daniel McNaughton had been delusional for years before he shot and killed Edmund Drummond in 1843. We would not remember this case except that Drummond was Prime Minister Robert Peel's assistant, and it wasn't clear which of the two men was actually McNaughton's target. Even back in the nineteenth century, the courts were prepared to exonerate Mc-Naughton if it could be shown that he was mentally ill, but that entailed demonstrating that he was raving mad, impulsive and unreachable to human discourse. McNaughton, however, was quietly psychotic and was convinced that unnamed others were watching him and bothering him. He had lashed out at Drummond, who just happened to be in the wrong place at the wrong time. The court found the evidence of his "partial insanity" persuasive, and rather than pronounce McNaughton guilty and hang him, they sent him to a psychiatric hospital where he was locked up for the rest of his life. The judges wrote that in McNaughton's case: "Reason is not driven from her seat, but distraction sits down upon her. . . . [A] delusion carried him away beyond the power of his own control . . . over acts which had connexion with his delusion."[39] Queen Victoria was so furious about this decision that she wrote a friend, "What did the jury mean by saying he was *not guilty?* I will *never* believe that anyone could be 'not guilty' who wanted to *murder* a conservative Prime Minister!"[40]

The storm died down, and for the next hundred years some variant of the McNaughton rule was accepted by many courts. "Insanity" meant that a person's mental illness prevented the defendant from understanding the nature of his or her actions, and the defendant was "not guilty by virtue of insanity." In many jurisdictions today, a mental illness defense is limited to mitigating the verdict. Instead of being ruled "not guilty by virtue of mental illness," one is judged "guilty *and* mentally ill." The sentence might be shorter or the person might be sent to a special prison for the criminally insane, but he or she would still be convicted and sequestered.

In Chapter 4, I mentioned Justice Robert Jackson's reservations about psychological testing of the war criminals. He feared that this might open up a Pandora's box of controversy, that dueling psychiatric experts would derail the trial. It was a prescient observation. For years, the courts have been struggling with such issues, particularly in cases of severe personality disorders, and certainly some of the Nuremberg defendants seemed to fall in this category. Given the diverse associations between psychopathy and the brain, one can anticipate EXACTLY how the defense might have argued. Even back in 1962, prominent forensic psychiatrist Bernard Diamond contended: "Their appearance of normalcy, their apparent ability to exercise free will, [and] choice . . . is purely a façade, an artifact that conceals the extent to which they are victims of their own brain pathology."[41]

When the American serial killer John Wayne Gacy came to trial in 1980, many psychiatric witnesses were called by the defense, testifying about his psychiatric disorders and his abusive childhood. They argued that he was a "pseudo-neurotic paranoid schizophrenic," or a "borderline personality organization with a subtype of antisocial or psychopathic personality manifested by episodes of an underlying condition of paranoid schizophrenia," or that he was paranoid, obsessive, narcissistic, "polymorphously perverse," and fearful of his sexuality. In short, "he was eaten up by his raging illness." The prosecution was more succinct: Gacy was evil. The jury agreed with the prosecution.[42]

The contemporary studies of neural imaging, brain hormones, and psychopathy are inevitably making their way into the courts and have led to a new field in criminal cases: "neuro-law." If the brain of a psychopathic defendant is unusual, should this inform deliberations about criminal responsibility, culpability, or punishment? A study published in *Science* examined the impact of the "bad brain" defense on sentencing. Judges were asked to determine the sentence of a hypothetical criminal described to some as a violent psychopath and to others as a psychopath with defective brain functioning. Being described as a psychopath with its characteristic features of lack of remorse or empathy led to a long jail sentence. In contrast, being described as a psychopath with a "bad brain" was regarded as a mitigating factor. The judges imposed a lighter sentence, reasoning that the defendant lacked control and it wasn't entirely the defendant's "fault"—that is, he or she had a "sick brain."[43]

Neuro-law antedates the advent of fMRI machines by millennia. After all, in *Timaeus,* Plato argued: "No man is voluntarily bad; but the bad becomes the bad by reason of an ill disposition of the body."[44] To use Rebecca Goldstein's felicitous rephrasing of Plato, the twenty-first-century neuro-law argument would be: "My amygdala made me do it."[45]

Conclusion

At Nuremberg, there was a clash of ideology between those who regarded malice as categorically distinct and those who saw it on a continuum of behavior. This chapter has summarized the intellectual strands that regard malice as categorically distinct. How well do these descriptions fit the four war criminals? Hermann Göring was viewed as a classical, charming, narcissistic psychopath whose actions were premeditated and cold-blooded. Julius Streicher was almost demonic in his hot-blooded impulsivity. Robert Ley certainly had a brain injury that altered his behavior, but paradoxically, he was also the most remorseful defendant at Nuremberg. Rudolf Hess was an enigma, but most observers thought that he suffered from a delusional disorder. As far as the court was concerned, Göring's and Streicher's diagnoses were irrelevant for their sentencing. Because Ley killed himself before the trial started, the tribunal never ruled in his case. The tribunal considered psychiatric status as a mitigating factor for Hess alone.

At Nuremberg, we naively believed that there would be *answers* if psychiatrists and psychologists could examine the defendants. In fact, what emerged were *diagnoses,* but they were hardly revelatory about the origins of malice. Today, there is an International War Crimes Tribunal at The Hague. To my knowledge, neuro-law arguments have not been introduced at The Hague. It's only a matter of time.

Conclusion

You will say I have robbed you of your sleep. But these are things which have turned the stomach of the world.

—Justice Robert Jackson, testimony, International
Military Tribunal, November 21, 1945

Looking Back

FORTY YEARS AGO, I PROMISED THE Nuremberg executioner that I would study the Nazi perpetrators. I dodged the task for years. I had other responsibilities—patients to treat, students to teach, research to do, a family to raise. Yet I kept running into malice and suffering in the lives of my patients and in the news of the day. By happenstance, along the way I met some extraordinary people who were witnesses to it all. They're gone now, and I realized that if I didn't start writing, their stories would disappear with me.

Since I have done research most of my professional life, my first impulse was to delve into archives. Research is inherently unpredictable, and archival research is particularly so because archives are typically uncataloged, unexplored, and frequently located in unusual locations. Of course, the Library of Congress and the National Archives have vaults of information about Nazi war crimes, but my search also took me to improbable places like the University of Akron, attics in Berkeley, coffeehouses in San Diego, living rooms in Jerusalem, Rohnert Park, California, and Silver Spring, Maryland.

I became steeped in documents from the mid-1940s. As World War II was drawing to a close, the world was haunted. How could a civilized country undertake such a concerted plan of mass killing? How could Nazi leaders continue on this lethal business even when it wasn't in Germany's best interest? It seemed mad. Even before the war ended, psychiatry and psychology began promising to study the psychology of the Nazi leaders. Rudolf Hess's behavior was so bizarre that it suggested profound mental illness. Hermann Göring had a past history of psychiatric hospitalization and continuing drug abuse. Julius Streicher's rap sheet of depravity was *very* long, and he was so self-destructive that he antagonized everyone. Robert Ley's alcoholism and brain injury led to aberrant behavior, and he was crippled by depression. All of this was obvious to everyone, but there was an expectation that professional study would somehow reveal more.

At Nuremberg, two brilliant young doctors—as different as night is from day—stepped into that arena to scrutinize the war criminals. I think each of them found what he was looking for, even if it wasn't the same thing. Douglas Kelley found a collection of hoodlums and moral cripples who— had luck been with the world—would have led their shabby lives as private citizens and not governmental leaders. Luck was not with us, and they used their skills to orchestrate mass killing. Gustave Gilbert found not hoodlums but depraved psychopaths who bore the mark of Cain.

Kelley and Gilbert spoke with great assurance, ignoring the fact that they were extrapolating on the basis of a small sample. The Nuremberg defendants were ideologically committed opportunists, upper-level managers who designed, facilitated, and fomented the deaths of millions but had little to do with the day-to-day operations. As Justice Robert Jackson observed, "These defendants were men of a station and rank which does not soil its own hands with blood. They were men who knew how to use lesser folk as tools."[1] Kelley's and Gilbert's findings might have been different had they examined those men—and women—whose fingers were on the triggers. That, however, is a different question.[2]

Neither Kelley nor Gilbert took into account that psychological testing in a dank prison might have influenced their observations. The prisoners had witnessed the total defeat of their regime and personal hopes. They were imprisoned in solitary cells for months and faced probable death sentences.

How much confidence can we have in a Rorschach test administered under such circumstances? Would the testing results in Nuremberg really explain what the defendants were like while they were in power? In his opening statement, prosecutor Jackson soberly noted: "In the prisoners' dock sit twenty-odd broken men. Reproached by the humiliation of those they have led, almost as bitterly as by the desolation of those they have attacked, their personal capacity for evil is forever past. It is hard now to perceive in these miserable men as captives the power by which as Nazi leaders they once dominated much of the world and terrified most of it."[3] Jackson's observation pointed out the challenges that faced the psychiatrists and psychologists of Nuremberg. Under the circumstances, how valid would their observations be?

Kelley and Gilbert were certainly aware that their testing conditions were nonstandard, but they pragmatically continued as best as they could. This is hardly the stuff of modern research—no randomized clinical trials here. It was, however, a step in the right direction. For millennia, cultures have speculated about why people do despicable things. Traditional explanations have included possession by the gods or madness. At Nuremberg, "possession" did not seem a creditable explanation, and "madness" did not seem a very accurate descriptor, in the technical sense of the word, for most of the prisoners. Psychiatry and psychology offered a new way of examining the prisoners, and the Rorschach test in particular promised a glimpse into their unconscious. But the test itself was so sensitive to the interpreter's judgment that no consensus could be reached about the Nazi leaders. People were expecting malice to be monochromatic. What emerged instead was a *spectrum* of behaviors and disorders as the basis of malice. Observers were taken by surprise and responded with vituperative disagreement.

Cultural Templates for Malice

While it may be more reassuring to think that the war criminals were a diabolical and homogeneous group, that belief is an illusion. It doesn't even work that way in film. Our iconic images of monsters in film and literature—*Frankenstein* (1818), *Dracula* (1897), and *Jekyll and Hyde* (1886) may all share the name "monsters," but they differ profoundly from one another.[4]

In Mary Shelley's *Frankenstein,* the monster was man-made. Dr. Victor Frankenstein was misguided, but he was ultimately responsible for the actions of his Creature. In a similar vein, the Nuremberg war criminals brought the mass killing to life by fomenting mass murder, and they were held responsible for the ensuing carnage.[5] This was the view of Justice Jackson and the tribunal.

Bram Stoker's Dracula, however was an entirely different monster, definitely an alien "other." He was not man-made, and although his origin was ultimately unclear, his essence was distinctly demonic. This representation of a monster who was "other" corresponds to Gustave Gilbert's view of the war criminals as psychopaths, so distinctly "other" that they shared nothing in common with the rest of us.

Last, the monster in Robert Louis Stevenson's story of *The Strange Case of Dr. Jekyll and Mr. Hyde* is neither created by man nor an alien other but lies within. This is perhaps the most terrifying monster of all, because if the monster Hyde can lurk within Jekyll, then Hyde can lurk in *anyone.* This was the alarming conclusion that Douglas Kelley propounded. Anyone—any *one* of us—could become a war criminal, given the wrong set of circumstances.

Speculations on a Latter-Day Nuremberg

So the battle raged at Nuremberg and beyond to define the contours of malice. Recently, I began to wonder how these points would be argued in contemporary war crimes trials. In 2012, forensic psychologists reviewed recent International War Crimes Trials and commented with surprise that so far "there are no empirical psychological studies in the persons convicted of war crimes."[6]

Today, we could employ vastly better tools than our colleagues had in 1945. We could use structured psychiatric interviews to define more precisely the nature of the defendants' psychiatric history and diagnosis. That may sound like a simple change, but such standardization represents a profound advance in psychiatry and psychology. In addition, we could use neural imaging to characterize the defendants' brain structure and response to tasks that elicit impulsivity or empathy. All this information would surely be introduced as evidence.

Even if the tribunal had such new evidence, my hunch is that the judgments would have been the same as those reached in 1946. Hess might have been confined for life in a psychiatric hospital as opposed to a Spandau-like prison. Göring would have been executed or sentenced to life imprisonment, although he still might have killed himself with contraband drugs. Streicher would have been executed or imprisoned for life, but given his abrasive tactlessness, he probably would not have lasted long in prison. Ley is the great mystery. A tribunal today would hesitate over his fate because he was so profoundly remorseful. That remorse, combined with a documented record of his severe head injury, might have resulted in a shorter prison sentence.

While these more contemporary analyses will surely be used in future war crimes trials, the question is: Will anyone bother to do the research? Nuremberg represented a rare convergence of unusual elements. First, there was an international consensus that the trials were necessary. Second, physicians and social scientists, as well as officials at the highest levels of government, all agreed that study of the war criminals was crucial. Last, that agreement would have come to naught were it not for the serendipitous presence of two gifted, stubborn, argumentative individuals (Kelley and Gilbert) who led that inquiry. Will we ever see such an improbable confluence at The Hague on the occasion of future war crimes trials?

Afterword

I was on another improbable quest for answers. What is it about this topic that leads to archives in such improbable places? This time, I was back home in California, walking through the redwood trees that stand like sentinels around the library at UC Santa Cruz. A subdued light filtered through the moist early morning air, and the groves were filled with the scent of the redwoods and caws from the Steller's jays.

I had come to the library in the hopes of learning more about malice. For unclear reasons, its archives held some of Douglas Kelley's papers.[7] The files were useful in revealing more information about Kelley—magician, astronomer, television producer, raconteur—but included few new documents pertinent to Nuremberg.

I was of course disappointed, but then I started to reflect. Would any archives have answered my questions about malice? The Bible says pointedly "The dark places of the earth are full of the habitations of cruelty" (Ps. 74:80). The poet Pablo Neruda concludes more hopefully: "The earth is a bed / blooming for love, soiled in blood."[8]

Kelley found some darkness in every person. Gilbert found a unique darkness in some. They were both right.

NOTES

Introduction

Epigraphs: Niccolò Machiavelli, *The Prince and the Discourses*, trans. Luigi Ricci (New York: Modern Library, 1950), 117; attributed to Edmund Burke (1729–1797).

1. See, e.g., John Steiner, whose excellent work on rank-and-file SS members is based on close personal observation and questionnaires.

2. Interestingly, Rudolf Höss, commandant of Auschwitz, used this very argument in a letter to his wife shortly before he was executed. "[I was] a cogwheel in the monstrous German machinery of destruction, [an] automaton who blindly obeyed every order." Thomas Harding, *Hanns and Rudolf: The True Story of the German Jew Who Tracked Down and Caught the Kommandant of Auschwitz* (New York: Simon and Schuster, 2013), 271.

3. Douglas Kelley, *22 Cells in Nuremberg* (New York: Greenberg, 1947; reprint ed., New York: MacFadden, 1961), and G. M. Gilbert, *Nuremberg Diary* (New York: Farrar, Straus and Giroux, 1947; reprint ed., New York: Da Capo, 1995), are foundational. On the Rorschachs, Eric A. Zillmer, Molly Harrower, Barry A. Ritzler, and Robert P. Archer, *The Quest for the Nazi Personality: A Psychological Investigation of Nazi War Criminals* (Hillsdale, NJ: Lawrence Erlbaum, 1995), and Florence R. Miale and Michael Selzer, *The Nuremberg Mind: The Psychology of the Nazi Leaders* (New York: Quadrangle, 1995), are pivotal. Jack El-Hai, *The Nazi and the Psychiatrist: Hermann Göring, Dr. Douglas M. Kelley, and a Fatal Meeting of Minds at the End of WWII* (New York: Public Affairs, 2013), provides a much-needed insight into Kelley's life.

4. Special thanks to University of California, San Diego; University of California, Santa Cruz; National Museum of Health and Medicine; US Army Military History Institute; US Air Force Academy McDermott Library; University of Akron Center for the History of Psychology; Columbia University archives; University

of California, Berkeley; Yale University archives; Cornell University archives; Graduate Center of CUNY; New York University; University of Florida; Library of Congress; National Archives; and United States Holocaust Memorial Museum.

5. E. H. Carr, *What Is History?* (Cambridge: Cambridge University Press, 1961).

6. Joel E. Dimsdale, ed., *Survivors, Victims, and Perpetrators: Essays on the Nazi Holocaust* (Washington, DC: Hemisphere, 1980), 284–287.

7. Rose Macauley, *The Towers of Trebizond* (New York: Farrar, Straus and Giroux, 1956), 226.

8. J. E. Exner, *The Rorschach Systems* (New York: Grune and Stratton, 1969).

9. Valerie Hartouni, *Visualizing Atrocity: Arendt, Evil, and the Optics of Thoughtlessness* (New York: New York University Press, 2012), 66.

Chapter 1. How Was This Genocide Different from All the Rest?

Epigraphs: Anna Akhmatova, *The Poetry of Anna Akhmatova: Living in Different Mirrors*, trans. Alexandra Harrington (New York: Anthem Press, 2006), 98; Timothy Snyder, *Bloodlands: Europe between Hitler and Stalin* (New York: Basic Books, 2010), 205.

1. The border between psychiatry and history has been contentious. On the one hand, psychiatry and psychology have frequently overreached with jargon-filled psychohistories. British psychiatrist Henry Dicks, for instance, described the Nazis as "men of markedly pregenital or immature personality structure in which libido organization followed a sado-masochistic pattern based on a repression of the tender tie with the mother and resulting typically in a homo-sexual paranoid . . . relation to a harsh and ambivalently loved and hated father figure." Henry V. Dicks, "Personality Traits and the National Socialist Ideology: A War-Time Study of German Prisoners of War," *Human Relations* 3, no. 2 (1950): 113–114. On the other hand, as Judith Hughes put it so succinctly, "Biography without psychology is not possible." Judith M. Hughes, *The Holocaust and the Revival of Psychological History* (New York: Cambridge University Press, 2015), 10.

2. Ian Kershaw, *Hitler, the Germans, and the Final Solution* (New Haven: Yale University Press, 2008), 363, 364.

3. Snyder, *Bloodlands*, 227.

4. The veracity of the quotation is debatable.

5. Charles Y. Glock, Gertrude J. Selznick, and Joe L. Spaeth, *The Apathetic Majority: A Study Based on Public Responses to the Eichmann Trial* (New York: Harper and Row, 1966), 26.

6. Raul Hilberg, "The Development of Holocaust Research," in *Holocaust Historiography in Context: Emergence, Challenges, Polemics, and Achievements*, ed. David Bankier and Dan Michman (Jerusalem: Yad Vashem, 2008), 33.

7. For a thoughtful discussion of these motivations, see Alon Confino, *A World without Jews: The Nazi Imagination from Persecution to Genocide* (New Haven: Yale University Press, 2014).

8. Yitzhak Katzsnelson as quoted in Dan Michman, "Introduction," in Bankier and Michman, *Holocaust Historiography in Context*, 11.

9. Patrick Girard, "Historical Foundations of Anti-Semitism," in *Survivors, Victims, and Perpetrators: Essays on the Nazi Holocaust*, ed. Joel E. Dimsdale (Washington, DC: Hemisphere, 1980).

10. Robert H. Jackson, testimony, November 21, 1945, *Trial of the Major War Criminals before the International Military Tribunal, Nuremberg, 14 November 1945–1 October 1946*, 22 vols. (Nuremberg: International Military Tribunal, 1947), 2:104.

11. Kershaw, *Hitler, the Germans, and the Final Solution*.

12. Zygmunt Bauman, *Modernity and the Holocaust* (Ithaca, NY: Cornell University Press, 1989), 26.

13. Translation of document 20, *Documents of the Persecution of the Dutch Jewry, 1940–1945*, Joods Historisch Museum Amsterdam (Amsterdam: Athenaeum-Polak en Van Gennep, 1960), 139.

14. Raul Hilberg, *The Destruction of the European Jews* (Chicago: Quadrangle Books, 1967), 152.

15. Among the many musicians, Gustav Mahler's niece Alma Rose was forced to direct the prison orchestra at Auschwitz until her death in the camp.

16. On street signs at Treblinka, see Samuel Rajzman, testimony, February 27, 1946, *Trial of the Major War Criminals*, before the International Military Tribunal, February 27, 1946, 8:325; on the entrance to the gas chambers, see Snyder, *Bloodlands*, 270.

17. Snyder, *Bloodlands*, 271.

18. Günther Schwarberg, *The Murders at Bullenhuser Damm: The SS Doctor and the Children* (Bloomington: Indiana University Press, 1984).

19. Major Elwyn Jones, testimony, August 8, 1946, *Trial of the Major War Criminals*, 20:519.

20. Hilberg, *Destruction of the European Jews*, 249.

21. Christopher R. Browning, *Ordinary Men: Reserve Police Battalion 101 and the Final Solution in Poland* (New York: Harper Perennial, 1998), 159.

22. George M. Kren and Leon Rappoport, *The Holocaust and the Crisis of Human Behavior* (New York: Homes and Meier, 1994), 82.

23. David Bankier, *The Germans and the Final Solution: Public Opinion under Nazism* (Oxford: Blackwell, 1992).

24. Hilberg, *Destruction of the European Jews*, 216.

25. The gas itself was cheap, costing the equivalent of half a cent per person. See the calculations in Irving Greenberg, "Cloud of Smoke, Pillar of Fire: Judaism, Christianity, and Modernity after the Holocaust," in *Auschwitz: Beginning of a New Era? Reflections on the Holocaust*, ed. Eva Fleischner (New York: KTAV, 1977), 11.

26. Hilberg, *Destruction of the European Jews*, 645.

27. Fritz Sauckel, quoted in Joseph E. Persico, *Nuremberg: Infamy on Trial* (New York: Penguin, 1994), 164.

28. Snyder, *Bloodlands*, 257.

29. Hilberg, *Destruction of the European Jews*, 218.

30. Hans Frank quoted in Snyder, *Bloodlands*, 214.

31. Otto Ohlendorf, testimony, January 3, 1946, *Trial of the Major War Criminals*, 4:321–323.

32. Browning, *Ordinary Men*, 25.

33. Hannah Arendt, *Eichmann in Jerusalem* (New York: Viking, 1964), 106.

34. Hilberg, *Destruction of the European Jews*, 595–596.

35. Mortality estimates vary for all of these groups.

36. The straight-line distance from San Diego to Berlin is 5,837 miles.

37. George Steiner, *In Bluebeard's Castle: Some Notes towards the Redefinition of Culture* (New Haven: Yale University Press, 1971), 30–31, 53–54.

Chapter 2. The Gathering at Ashcan

Epigraph: John Kenneth Galbraith, "The 'Cure' at Mondorf Spa," *Life*, October 22, 1945.

1. Ashcan contained many other war criminals, but they are not a focus of this book.

2. Code names are whimsical. A comparable British POW camp near Frankfurt was named Dustbin.

3. John E. Dolibois, *Pattern of Circles: An Ambassador's Story* (Kent, OH: Kent State University Press, 1989), 85.

4. Biography, Burton C. Andrus Collection, US Army Military History Institute.

5. Joseph E. Persico, *Nuremberg: Infamy on Trial* (New York: Penguin, 1994), 49.

6. Burton C. Andrus, *The Infamous of Nuremberg* (London: Leslie Frewin, 1969), 22.

7. "Hermann Goering 'Too Heavy' for US Plane Transport after Capture," *Telegraph*, January 31, 2011.

8. Andrus, *Infamous of Nuremberg*, 29–30.

9. Eugene Davidson, *The Trial of the Germans: An Account of the Twenty-Two Defendants before the International Military Tribunal at Nuremberg* (New York: Macmillan, 1966; reprint ed., Columbia: University of Missouri Press, 1997), 66.

10. Dolibois, *Pattern of Circles*, 86.

11. Ibid., 169.

12. Andrus, *Infamous of Nuremberg*, 29.

13. Ibid., 31.

14. Ibid., 34.

15. Jack El-Hai, *The Nazi and the Psychiatrist: Hermann Göring, Dr. Douglas M. Kelley, and a Fatal Meeting of Minds at the End of WWII* (New York: Public Affairs, 2013), 23.

16. Douglas M. Kelley personal papers.

17. Galbraith, "'Cure' at Mondorf Spa."

18. Dolibois, *Pattern of Circles*, 118.

19. Ronald Smelser, *Robert Ley: Hitler's Labor Front Leader* (Oxford: Berg, 1988), 2.

20. Ibid., 112.

21. Ibid., 113.

22. Judgment of the International Military Tribunal, "Judgement: Streicher," available at http://avalon.law.yale.edu/imt/judstrei.asp.

23. Julius Streicher, personal statement (translated), June 16, 1945, Julius Streicher Collection, folder 1, Center for Jewish History, Leo Baeck Institute.

24. Andrus, *Infamous of Nuremberg*, 53.

25. Ibid., 39.

26. Dolibois, *Pattern of Circles*, 113.

27. Ibid., 116.

28. Ibid., 111.

29. Ibid.

30. Ibid., 104.

31. Quoted in George Tucker, "Doomsday for the Guilty," *Collier's*, September 22, 1945.

32. Dolibois, *Pattern of Circles*, 123.

33. Ibid., 129.

34. Andrus, *Infamous of Nuremberg*, 39; El-Hai, *Nazi and Psychiatrist*, 63.

35. Associated Press, "Rolling Your Own Is Rugged—Just Ask Herr Goering," *Maple Leaf*, August 1, 1945.

36. Galbraith, "'Cure' at Mondorf Spa."

37. On Camp Ashcan, see http://en.wikipedia.org/wiki/Camp_Ashcan.

38. George McDonald, *Frommer's Belgium, Holland and Luxembourg* (Hoboken, NJ: Wiley, 2011).

Chapter 3. The Nuremberg War Crimes Trial

Epigraphs: Rebecca West, "Extraordinary Exile," *New Yorker*, September 7, 1946, 45; Robert Jackson, testimony, November 21, 1945, *Trial of the Major War Criminals before the International Military Tribunal, Nuremberg, 14 November 1945–1 October 1946*, 22 vols. (Nuremberg: International Military Tribunal, 1947), 2:99.

1. Werner Maser, *Nuremberg: A Nation on Trial*, trans. Richard Barry (New York: Scribner's, 1979), 25.

2. Joseph E. Persico, *Nuremberg: Infamy on Trial* (New York: Penguin, 1994), 8.

3. Joseph Pulitzer, quoted in "Urges Executions of 1,500,000 Nazis," *New York Times*, May 23, 1945.

4. Seymour Peyser, quoted in Bruce M. Stave and Michele Palmer, *Witnesses to Nuremberg: An Oral History of American Participants at the War Crimes Trials* (New York: Twayne, 1998), 145.

5. A. N. Trainin, quoted in A. Neave, *Nuremberg: A Personal Record of the Trial of the Major Nazi War Criminals in 1945–6* (London: Hodder and Stoughton, 1978), 229.

6. Telford Taylor, *The Anatomy of the Nuremberg Trials: A Personal Memoir* (New York: Alfred A. Knopf, 1992), 43.

7. Ibid., 44, 45.

8. Robert H. Jackson, *Report to the President on Atrocities and War Crimes; June 7, 1945,* http://avalon.law.yale.edu/imt/imt_jack01.asp.

9. Taylor, *Anatomy of the Nuremberg Trials,* 64.

10. Telford Taylor recounts how touchy some of the interpreters were. One Russian interpreter did not want to translate the expression "to throw the baby out with the bath water," and, blushing, declared, "It eez not *nice.*" Taylor, *Anatomy of the Nuremberg Trials,* 101.

11. Francis Biddle, quoted in Stave and Palmer, *Witnesses to Nuremberg,* 5.

12. Jackson, testimony, July 26, 1946, *Trial of the Major War Criminals,* 19:432.

13. Maser, *Nuremberg,* 273.

14. He is commonly known as "Wild Bill" Donovan, a reference to his nickname when he played football for Columbia University.

15. Christopher Dodd, *Letters from Nuremberg: My Father's Narrative of a Quest for Justice* (New York: Crown, 2007), 255.

16. He later became Senator Dodd. Dodd, *Letters from Nuremberg,* 103.

17. Maser, *Nuremberg,* 253.

18. Iona Nikitchenko, quoted in Eugene Davidson, *The Trial of the Germans: An Account of the Twenty-Two Defendants before the International Military Tribunal at Nuremberg* (New York: Macmillan, 1966; reprint ed., Columbia: University of Missouri Press, 1997), 18.

19. Persico, *Nuremberg,* 204.

20. Ibid., 82–84; Douglas M. Kelley personal papers.

21. Davidson, *Trial of the Germans,* 165.

22. G. M. Gilbert, *Nuremberg Diary* (New York: Farrar, Straus and Giroux, 1947; reprint ed., New York: Da Capo, 1995), 192, 193.

23. Joseph Maier, quoted in Stave and Palmer, *Witnesses to Nuremberg,* 115.

24. Fritz Sauckel was Gauleiter of Thuringia and plenipotentiary of labor deployment; quoted in Gilbert, *Nuremberg Diary,* 75.

25. Dodd, *Letters from Nuremberg,* 229.

26. Hermann Göring, quoted in Gilbert, *Nuremberg Diary,* 113.

27. Douglas Kelley, *22 Cells in Nuremberg* (New York: Greenberg, 1947; reprint ed., New York: MacFadden, 1961), 56.

28. National Archives, Record Group 238: National Archives Collection of World War II War Crimes Records, 1933–1949, Series: Documents Primarily Relating to the Defendants at the International Military and Trials at the Military Tribunals at Nuremberg and Replevined from James P. Atwood, 1945–1947.

29. Ursula Sherman, quoted in Leslie Katz, "Nuremberg—50 Years after Trial of Nazi Horrors," *Jewish Bulletin of North Carolina,* November 17, 1995.

30. Brady Bryson, quoted in Hilary Gaskin, *Eyewitnesses at Nuremberg* (London: Arms and Armour, 1991), 172, 173.

31. There is an ironic coda to this chapter. Many of the documents in the National Archives bear witness to the corrosive effect of Nuremberg on the participants' judgment. There was a crucial file in the archives containing psychiatric records from

Nuremberg that was labeled as "replevined documents." "Replevined"? Archives can have idiosyncratic classification schemes, but this was too much. The word means recovered property that was unlawfully taken. One of the Americans assigned to Nuremberg internal security helped himself to scores of these documents without authorization and took them home as souvenirs. He wasn't normally a thief. Indeed, his officer efficiency report in 1950 describes him as "an active officer with fine military bearing and high moral qualities. Intelligent, expresses himself clearly. Strict, industrious, accepts responsibility willingly." National Archives, Record Group 238: National Archives Collection of World War II War Crimes Records, 1933–1949, Series: Documents Primarily Relating to the Defendants at the International Military and Trials at the Military Tribunals at Nuremberg and Replevined from James P. Atwood, 1945–1947. Replevined indeed and filled with information.

Chapter 4. War Criminals with Psychiatrists and Psychologists?

Epigraph: Douglas Kelley, *22 Cells in Nuremberg* (New York: Greenberg, 1947; reprint ed., New York: MacFadden, 1961), 18.

1. Rudolf Hess, unpublished document, Douglas M. Kelley personal papers.
2. Hess, quoted in *The Case of Rudolf Hess: A Problem in Diagnosis and Forensic Psychiatry*, ed. J. R. Rees (New York: W. W. Norton, 1948), ix.
3. J. Gibson Graham, quoted in ibid., 17.
4. Henry Dicks, quoted in ibid., 34.
5. Gibson Graham, quoted in ibid., 21.
6. Ibid., 25.
7. Dicks, quoted in ibid., 28, 29.
8. Ellis Jones, N. R. Phillips, and Dicks, quoted in ibid., 71.
9. Jones, Phillips, and Dicks, quoted in ibid., 72.
10. Hess, quoted in ibid., 82.
11. Ibid., 88.
12. Ibid., 16.
13. Winston Churchill, quoted in Stephen McGinty, *Camp Z: The Secret Life of Rudolf Hess* (London: Quercus, 2011), 149.
14. In later years, Dolibois had an illustrious career as a university administrator at Kent State University and ambassador to Luxembourg.
15. John E. Dolibois, *Pattern of Circles: An Ambassador's Story* (Kent, OH: Kent State University Press, 1989), 187.
16. Eric A. Zillmer, Molly Harrower, Barry A. Ritzler, and Robert P. Archer, *The Quest for the Nazi Personality: A Psychological Investigation of Nazi War Criminals* (Hillsdale, NJ: Lawrence Erlbaum, 1995), 41.
17. Gustave Gilbert, quoted in Ian Bevan, "Finding How the Nazi Mind Works," *Sydney Morning Herald*, December 19, 1945.
18. Joseph E. Persico, *Nuremberg: Infamy on Trial* (New York: Penguin, 1994), 232.
19. The American Association on Mental Deficiency, the American branch of the International League against Epilepsy, the American Neurological Association, the

American Orthopsychiatric Association, the American Psychiatric Association, the American Society for Research in Psychosomatic Problems, and the National Committee for Mental Hygiene. Today, it would be almost unheard of for such organizations to agree to a common statement on ANYTHING, perhaps with the exception of more funding for the National Institutes of Health.

20. Robert Houghwout Jackson Papers, box 107, Library of Congress (hereafter cited as Jackson Papers).

21. Ibid.

22. Although the test looks very unstructured, it is in fact a carefully choreographed interaction between tester and patient. The tester presents the patient with ten cards and asks, "What does this card remind you of?" and then, "Can you point out what parts of the card made you say that?" Some cards are black and white, while others have bursts of color. Patients typically offer multiple interpretations of each card, and the number of such interpretations is tracked carefully. The examiner writes down verbatim what the patient says about each inkblot picture. While the examiner analyzes what content themes are present in the patient's interpretation, the scoring is far more extensive than that. The examiner notes how long it takes the patient to make a response and whether the patient responds to the whole card or just a piece of it. Does the person attend to color or shading in the blot, the black of the ink versus the white space on the card? How good is the form? Can the examiner "see" how the patient identified a certain part of a card as dancing people, for instance, or does it require a major leap of imagination to see such a form in the card?

23. Jackson to John Millet, June 23, 1945, Jackson Papers.

24. Ibid.

25. Millet to Jackson, August 16, 1945, Jackson Papers.

26. Jackson to Millet, October 12, 1945, ibid.

27. Memo to commanding officer, Internal Security Detachment, ibid.

28. Mind you, given Hess's prior experience with Amytal, the utility of a second interview would have been questionable.

29. Memo to Colonel Paul Schroeder, December 17, 1945, Jackson Papers.

30. Millet to Jackson, June 3, 1946, ibid.

31. Erich Fromm, *Anatomy of Human Destructiveness* (New York: Holt, Rinehart and Winston, 1973), chapter 13.

32. For a fine discussion of the role of anthropology in the war efforts, see Peter Mandler, *Return from the Natives: How Margaret Mead Won the Second World War and Lost the Cold War* (New Haven: Yale University Press, 2013).

33. The British were also interested in psychology, tapping the expertise of Wilfred Bion and John Bowlby, among others, who were to become so central to the growth of psychiatry and psychology after the war.

34. The Hitler biography ultimately was declassified and published in 1972. W. Langer, *The Mind of Adolf Hitler: The Secret Wartime Report* (New York: Basic Books, 1972).

35. Daniel Pick's fine book *The Pursuit of the Nazi Mind: Hitler, Hess, and the Analysts* (Oxford: Oxford University Press, 2012) details some of Donovan's schemes; see esp. 117–120.

36. "Rehabilitation" has regrettably been dropped as a goal from most American prisons.

37. Burton Andrus, quoted in Ann Tusa and John Tusa, *The Nuremberg Trial* (New York: Skyhorse, 2010), 232.

38. Gustave Gilbert, transcript, The Trial of Adolf Eichmann, session 55, May 29, 1961, The Nizkor Project, http://www.nizkor.org/hweb/people/e/eichmann -adolf/transcripts/Sessions/Session-055-01.html.

39. Persico, *Nuremberg*, 186, 189.

40. Kelley, *22 Cells in Nuremberg*, 17.

41. Kelley to Donovan, undated, Donovan Nuremberg Trials Collection, Cornell University Law Library.

42. David Irving, *Nuremberg: The Last Battle* (London: Focal Point, 1996), 212.

43. They also administered the Thematic Apperception Test (TAT) but rarely discussed this, and their later writings focused solely on IQ and Rorschach.

44. "Talk of the Town," *New Yorker*, June 1, 1946, 19.

45. Lewis Terman was a Stanford psychologist who longitudinally tracked California children with high IQs.

46. D. M. Kelley, "Preliminary Studies of the Rorschach Records of the Nazi War Criminals," *Rorschach Research Exchange and Journal of Projective Techniques* 10 (1946): 45–48.

47. This fact is a bit unusual because Rorschach testing is more valid when patients have not seen the stimulus cards before.

48. James Owen, *Nuremberg: Evil on Trial* (London: Headline Review, 2006), 115.

49. Jack El-Hai, *The Nazi and the Psychiatrist: Hermann Göring, Dr. Douglas M. Kelley, and a Fatal Meeting of Minds at the End of WWII* (New York: Public Affairs, 2013), 141.

50. Zillmer, Harrower, Ritzler, and Archer, *Quest for the Nazi Personality*, xvii.

51. L. Davis, "Hitler Gang Just Ordinary Thugs, Psychiatrist Says," *Nashville Tennessean*, January 29, 1946.

52. Persico, *Nuremberg*, 170.

53. Gilbert also gave unauthorized interviews to the press, but he was less quotable.

54. Howard Whitman, "What Goering & Co. Talk about in Their Cells as Told by Dr. Douglas M. Kelley," *Sunday Express*, August 25, 1946; Burton C. Andrus Collection, box 33, folder 91, US Army Military History Institute.

55. A. Rosenberg, cited in El-Hai, *Nazi and Psychiatrist*, 142.

Chapter 5. Defendant Robert Ley

Epigraphs: Robert Ley, autobiographic statement, p. 4, Douglas M. Kelley personal papers; Thomas Dodd, quoted in Christopher Dodd, *Letters from Nuremberg: My Father's Narrative of a Quest for Justice* (New York: Crown, New York, 2007), 198.

1. Robert Houghwout Jackson Papers, box 107, Library of Congress (hereafter cited as Jackson Papers).

2. From a scientific point, it is a pity, but there were concerns that if the war criminals were buried, their graves would become shrines to neo-Nazis.

3. Ronald Smelser, *Robert Ley: Hitler's Labor Front Leader* (Oxford: Berg, 1988), 18.

4. Robert Ley, quoted in ibid., 62.

5. Ibid., 19.

6. Associated Press, "German Criminal Makes Gallows of Towel and Pipe," Nuremberg, October 25, 1945.

7. Smelser, *Robert Ley*, 144.

8. Ibid., 2.

9. Ibid., 211.

10. Hermann Göring, quoted in ibid., 257.

11. Ian Kershaw, *The End: The Defiance and Destruction of Hitler's Germany, 1944–1945* (New York: Penguin, 2011).

12. Smelser, *Robert Ley*, 18.

13. Cited in ibid., 114.

14. AP, "German Criminal Makes Gallows."

15. Douglas Kelley, *22 Cells in Nuremberg* (New York: Macfadden, 1947), 125.

16. Robert Ley, quoted in Robert Overy, *Interrogations: The Nazi Elite in Allied Hands* (New York: Viking, 2001), 491, 498.

17. Interrogation of Robert Ley, National Archives, Record Group 238: National Archives Collection of World War II War Crimes Records, Microfilm Collection M1270: Interrogation Records Prepared for War Crimes Proceedings at Nuernberg, 1945–1947 (hereafter cited as Interrogation Records), roll 12.

18. Overy, *Interrogations*, 167.

19. John E. Dolibois, *Pattern of Circles: An Ambassador's Story* (Kent, OH: Kent State University Press, 1989), 118.

20. Kelley, *22 Cells in Nuremberg*, 114.

21. Interrogation of Ley, October 6, 1945, Interrogation Records, roll 12.

22. Ibid., October 11, 1945.

23. Ibid., October 18, 1945.

24. Burton Andrus, quoted in Dodd, *Letters from Nuremberg*, 181.

25. Quoted in Burton C. Andrus, *The Infamous of Nuremberg* (London: Leslie Frewin, 1969), 90.

26. Lieutenant Colonel Rene H. Juchli to Major General Donovan, November 2, 1945, Donovan Nuremberg Trials Collection, Cornell University Law Library.

27. Douglas Kelley, memo, October 26, 1945, ibid.

28. D. M. Kelley, "Preliminary Studies of the Rorschach Records of the Nazi War Criminals," *Rorschach Research Exchange and Journal of Projective Techniques* 10 (1946): 46.

29. Kelley, quoted in Dolibois, *Pattern of Circles*, 119.

30. Kelley, "Preliminary Studies of the Rorschach Records," 45–48.

31. Stefan Link, "Rethinking the Ford-Nazi Connection," *Bulletin of the GHI* 49 (2011): 135–150.

32. Kelley, "Preliminary Studies of the Rorschach Records," 45–48.

33. Webb Haymaker Collection, box 10, Otis Historical Archives, National Museum of Health and Medicine, Armed Forces Institute of Pathology.

34. "Doctors Find Brain of Ley, Nazi Suicide, Diseased for Years," *Evening Star* (Washington, DC), January 18, 1946.

35. "Dr. Robert Ley's Brain," *Medical Record* 159 (1946): 188.

36. Smelser, *Robert Ley*, 30.

37. Douglas Kelley, telex note, Webb Haymaker Collection, box 10.

38. "Dr. Robert Ley's Brain," Medical Record, 159:188, 1946.

39. Molly Harrower Papers, box M3208, folder 9, Archives of the History of American Psychology, The Center for the History of Psychology, University of Akron.

   Thin slices of cells are difficult to see through microscopy, so one stains the tissue with various dyes. The dyes are also advantageous because different types of cells or parts of cells take up the coloring distinctively. There is always a risk of tearing or distorting the appearance of the ultra-thin slice of tissue when it is embedded on a slide.

40. Eric A. Zillmer, Molly Harrower, Barry A. Ritzler, and Robert P. Archer, *The Quest for the Nazi Personality: A Psychological Investigation of Nazi War Criminals* (Hillsdale, NJ: Lawrence Erlbaum, 1995), 32.

Chapter 6. Defendant Herman Göring

Epigraph 1: Thomas Dodd, quoted in Christopher Dodd, *Letters from Nuremberg: My Father's Narrative of a Quest for Justice* (New York: Crown, 2007), 237; Hermann Göring, as quoted by G. M. Gilbert, *Nuremberg Diary* (New York: Farrar, Straus and Giroux, 1947; reprint ed., New York: Da Capo, 1995), 67.

1. Douglas Kelley, *22 Cells in Nuremberg* (New York: Greenberg, 1947; reprint ed., New York: MacFadden, 1961), 52.

2. John E. Dolibois, *Pattern of Circles: An Ambassador's Story* (Kent, OH: Kent State University Press, 1989), 130.

3. Kelley, *22 Cells in Nuremberg*, 51.

4. Eugene Davidson, *The Trial of the Germans: An Account of the Twenty-Two Defendants before the International Military Tribunal at Nuremberg* (New York: Macmillan, 1966; reprint ed., Columbia: University of Missouri Press, 1997), 63.

5. Dolibois, *Pattern of Circles*, 129.

6. Interrogation of Herman Göring, National Archives, Record Group 238: National Archives Collection of World War II War Crimes Records, Microfilm Collection M1270: Interrogation Records Prepared for War Crimes Proceedings at Nuernberg, 1945–1947 (hereafter cited as Interrogation Records), roll 5.

   There are rules for deportment in research libraries—no pens, no briefcases, and, above all, no noise. I am afraid I broke the last rule and snorted with laughter as I read this long-forgotten transcript. The adjacent scholars glared at me.

7. Dolibois, *Pattern of Circles*, 130.

8. Interrogation of Göring, Interrogation Records, roll 5.

9. Ibid.

10. Dolibois, *Pattern of Circles*, 130.

11. Leon Goldensohn, *The Nuremberg Interviews*, ed. Robert Gellately (New York: Alfred A. Knopf, 2004), 131.

12. Ibid., 131–132.

13. Joseph Maier, quoted in Bruce M. Stave and Michele Palmer, *Witnesses to Nuremberg: An Oral History of American Participants at the War Crimes Trials* (New York: Twayne, 1998), 115–116.

14. Werner Maser, *Nuremberg: A Nation on Trial*, trans. Richard Barry (New York: Scribner's, 1979), 91; Burton C. Andrus, *The Infamous of Nuremberg* (London: Leslie Frewin, 1969), 113–114.

15. Hermann Göring, quoted in Andrus, *Infamous of Nuremberg*, 136.

16. Göring, quoted in Gilbert, *Nuremberg Diary*, 114.

17. Ibid., 137.

18. Kelley, *22 Cells in Nuremberg*, 58.

19. Janet Flanner (aka Genêt), "Letter from Nuremberg," *New Yorker*, March 23, 1946, 80.

20. Except for Albert Speer, who viewed Göring as lazy and corrupt, Gilbert, *Nuremberg Diary*, 201.

21. Schacht, quoted in ibid., 186.

22. Harold Burson, quoted in Stave and Palmer, *Witnesses to Nuremberg*, 185.

23. Göring, testimony, March 18, 1946, *Trial of the Major War Criminals before the International Military Tribunal, Nuremberg, 14 November 1945–1 October 1946*, 22 vols. (Nuremberg: International Military Tribunal, 1947), 9:454.

24. Davidson, *Trial of the Germans*, 61.

25. Göring, quoted in Gilbert, *Nuremberg Diary*, 208.

26. Göring, quoted in ibid., 12.

27. D. M. Kelley, "Preliminary Studies of the Rorschach Records of the Nazi War Criminals," *Rorschach Research Exchange and Journal of Projective Techniques* 10 (1946): 45–48.

28. Zillmer, Harrower, Ritzler, and Archer, *Quest for the Nazi Personality*, 81.

29. Kelley, *22 Cells in Nuremberg*, 44.

30. Göring, cited in Jack El-Hai, *The Nazi and the Psychiatrist: Hermann Göring, Dr. Douglas M. Kelley, and a Fatal Meeting of Minds at the End of WWII* (New York: Public Affairs, 2013), 78.

31. Ibid., 60–61.

32. Dukie Kelley, note, Douglas M. Kelley personal papers.

33. Zillmer, Harrower, Ritzler, and Archer, *Quest for the Nazi Personality*, 82.

34. Kelley, *22 Cells in Nuremberg*, 44.

35. Ibid., 53.

36. August 8, 1945, Kelley personal papers.

37. Kelley, *22 Cells in Nuremberg*, 49. Others dispute whether Kelley deserves much credit here. The prison food was terrible, and Warden Andrus maintained that he had put Göring on a mandatory diet.

38. Kelley, *22 Cells in Nuremberg*, 49.

39. Kelley, cited in El-Hai, *Nazi and Psychiatrist*, 95.

40. National Archives, Record Group 238: National Archives Collection of World War II War Crimes Records, 1933–1949, Series: Documents Primarily Relating to the Defendants at the International Military and Trials at the Military Tribunals at Nuremberg and Replevined from James P. Atwood, 1945–1947.

41. Ibid., box 8.

42. G. M. Gilbert, *The Psychology of Dictatorship: Based on an Examination of the Leaders of Nazi Germany* (New York: Ronald Press, 1950), 96.

43. Ibid., 89.

44. Gilbert, *Nuremberg Diary*, 216.

45. Göring, quoted in ibid., 278.

46. Ibid., 312.

47. Gustave Gilbert, quoted in Andrus, *Infamous of Nuremberg*, 95.

48. Gilbert, *Psychology of Dictatorship*, 115.

49. Göring, as per Gustave Gilbert, Rorschach test report, December 9, 1949, The Center for the History of Psychology, University of Akron, Archives of the History of American Psychology, Molly Harrower Papers (hereafter cited as Harrower Papers), box M3100, folder 2.

50. Harrower Papers, box M3199, folder 2.

51. Gilbert, *Psychology of Dictatorship*, 108.

52. Gilbert, *Nuremberg Diary*, 435.

53. Harrower Papers, box M3199, folder 2.

54. Joseph E. Persico, *Nuremberg: Infamy on Trial* (New York: Penguin, 1994), 408–409.

55. Harrower Papers, box M3199, folder 2.

56. Gilbert, *Psychology of Dictatorship*, 109.

57. G. M. Gilbert, "Hermann Goering: Amiable Psychopath," *Journal of Abnormal Social Psychology* 43 (1948): 211–229.

58. William H. Dunn, quoted in Persico, *Nuremberg*, 412.

59. Göring, quoted in Dolibois, *Pattern of Circles*, 208.

60. Göring, quoted in Persico, *Nuremberg*, 419.

61. Kingsbury Smith, Associated Press, October 16, 1946, as quoted in Smith Obituary, *Los Angeles Times*, February 6, 1999.

62. Kelley, *22 Cells in Nuremberg*, 61.

63. Gilbert, *Nuremberg Diary*, 435.

64. Christine Goeschel, *Suicide in Nazi Germany* (Oxford: Oxford University Press, 2009), 158.

65. Gitta Sereny, *Albert Speer: His Battle with Truth* (New York: Alfred A. Knopf, 1995), 543; Roger Forsgren, "The Architecture of Evil," *New Atlantis*, no. 36 (2012): 44–62.

66. Bob Pool, "Former GI Claims Role in Goering's Death," *Los Angeles Times*, February 7, 2005.

67. Petronella Wyatt, "The Quality of Mercy," *Spectator*, February 1, 2003, 48.

68. "War Crimes: Night without Dawn," *Time*, October 28, 1946, 35.

69. Andrus, *Infamous of Nuremberg*, 15.

70. Burton C. Andrus, quoted in Persico, *Nuremberg*, 449.

Chapter 7. Defendant Julius Streicher

Epigraphs: Julius Streicher, quoted in John E. Dolibois, *Pattern of Circles: An Ambassador's Story* (Kent, OH: Kent State University Press, 1989), 115; testimony, April 29, 1946, *Trial of the Major War Criminals before the International Military Tribunal, Nuremberg, 14 November 1945–1 October 1946*, 22 vols. (Nuremberg: International Military Tribunal, 1947), 12:348; Joseph Goebbels, cited in Ronald Smelser, *Robert Ley: Hitler's Labor Front Leader* (Oxford: Berg, 1988), 55.

1. Eugene Davidson, *The Trial of the Germans: An Account of the Twenty-Two Defendants before the International Military Tribunal at Nuremberg* (New York: Macmillan, 1966; reprint ed., Columbia: University of Missouri Press, 1997), 43.

2. Julius Streicher, quoted in G. M. Gilbert, *Nuremberg Diary* (New York: Farrar, Straus and Giroux, 1947; reprint ed., New York: Da Capo, 1995), 36.

3. Burton C. Andrus, *The Infamous of Nuremberg* (London: Leslie Frewin, 1969), 103.

4. Douglas M. Kelley personal papers.

5. Davidson, *Trial of the Germans*, 54.

6. Ibid., 46.

7. Margaret Eastwood, *The Nuremberg Trial of Julius Streicher: The Crime of "Incitement to Genocide"* (Lewiston, NY: Edwin Mellen, 2011), 53.

8. Joseph E. Persico, *Nuremberg: Infamy on Trial* (New York: Penguin, 1994), 56.

9. Andrus, *Infamous of Nuremberg*, 105.

10. Airey Neave, *Nuremberg: A Personal Record of the Trial of the Major Nazi War Criminals in 1945–6* (London: Hodder and Stoughton, 1978), 86, 87, 93.

11. Joel Sayre, "Letter from Nuremberg," *New Yorker*, July 14, 1945, 51–52.

12. Rebecca West, "Extraordinary Exile," *New Yorker*, September 7, 1946, 34.

13. Interrogation of Julius Streicher, National Archives, Record Group 238: National Archives Collection of World War II War Crimes Records, Microfilm Collection M1270: Interrogation Records Prepared for War Crimes Proceedings at Nuernberg, 1945–1947 (hereafter cited as Interrogation Records), roll 21.

14. Davidson, *Trial of the Germans*, 44, 45.

15. Testimony of Julius Streicher, October 17, 1945, in Office of United States Chief Counsel for Prosecution of Axis Criminality, *Nazi Conspiracy and Aggression: Supplement B* (Washington, DC: US Government Printing Office, 1948), 1428.

16. Julius Streicher, quoted in Dolibois, *Pattern of Circles*, 186.

17. Robert Ley, interestingly, had requested a Jewish lawyer to defend him.

18. James Owen, *Nuremberg: Evil on Trial* (London: Headline Review, 2006), 220.

19. Eric A. Zillmer, Molly Harrower, Barry A. Ritzler, and Robert J. Archer, *The Quest for the Nazi Personality: A Psychological Investigation of Nazi War Criminals* (Hillsdale, NJ: Lawrence Erlbaum, 1995), 158.

20. Deputy Chief Prosecutor of USSR Pokrovsky, memo, November 16, 1945, *Trial of the Major War Criminals,* 1:151.

21. Jean Delay, Eugene Krasnushkin, and Paul Schroeder, psychiatric reports, ibid., 153.

22. Streicher, quoted in Eastwood, *Nuremberg Trial of Streicher,* 61.

23. Streicher, quoted in Davidson, *Trial of the Germans,* 50.

24. Streicher, testimony, April 29, 1946, *Trial of the Major War Criminals,* 12:328.

25. Hermann Göring, quoted in G. M. Gilbert, *Nuremberg Diary* (New York: Farrar, Straus and Giroux, 1947; reprint ed., New York: Da Capo, 1995), 118. As the trial was nearing an end, it was "payback time," and Streicher told Gilbert that he was "elated that those who had helped the prosecution had gotten it in the neck anyway." Eastwood, *Nuremberg Trial of Streicher,* 217.

26. Streicher, quoted in Eastwood, *Nuremberg Trial of Streicher,* 176.

27. Ibid., 98.

28. Robert Jackson, closing argument, July 26, 1946, *Trial of the Major War Criminals,* 19:427.

29. Gustave Gilbert, quoted in Andrus, *Infamous of Nuremberg,* 104.

30. Ibid., 15.

31. Ibid., 41.

32. Gilbert, *Nuremberg Diary,* 125–126. I empathize with Gilbert. It must have been incredibly trying to sit on a cot with this man. If I had to spend time with any of the Nuremberg defendants, Streicher would definitely be my last choice as well. After an hour with Streicher, I think I would go home and take a shower with Phisohex.

33. Ibid., 411.

34. Persico, *Nuremberg,* 117.

35. Gilbert, *Nuremberg Diary,* 74.

36. Streicher, quoted in Persico, *Nuremberg,* 366.

37. Douglas Kelley, *22 Cells in Nuremberg* (New York: Greenberg, 1947; reprint ed., New York: MacFadden, 1961), 106.

38. Ibid., 105.

39. Streicher, quoted in ibid., 111–112.

40. National Archives, Record Group 238: National Archives Collection of World War II War Crimes Records, 1933–1949, Documents Primarily Relating to the Defendants at the International Military and Trials at the Military Tribunals at Nuremberg and Replevined from James P. Atwood, 1945–1947 (hereafter cited as Atwood documents), box 3.

41. Dolibois served as Kelley's interpreter for this testing session.

42. Zillmer, Harrower, Ritzler, and Archer, *Quest for the Nazi Personality,* 164, 169.

43. Atwood documents, box 8.
44. Leon Goldensohn, *The Nuremberg Interviews*, ed. Robert Gellately (New York: Alfred A. Knopf, 2004), 253–254.
45. Streicher, autobiography, Kelley personal papers.
46. Julius Streicher to Douglas Kelley, October 9, 1945, Kelley personal papers, kindly translated by Professor Frank Biess.
47. Cicero, *Tusculan Disputations* 3.1, 3.3, 3.2.
48. Andrus, *Infamous of Nuremberg*, 197.
49. Werner Maser, *Nuremberg: A Nation on Trial* (New York: Scribner's, 1979), 13.

Chapter 8. Defendant Rudolf Hess

Epigraphs: Rebecca West, "Greenhouse with Cyclamens I" (1946), in *A Train of Powder* (New York: Viking, 1955); Douglas Kelley, *22 Cells in Nuremberg* (New York: Greenberg, 1947; reprint ed., New York: MacFadden, 1961), 33.

1. G. M. Gilbert, *The Psychology of Dictatorship* (New York: Ronald Press, 1950), 122.
2. Seaghan Maynes, quoted in Hilary Gaskin, *Eyewitnesses at Nuremberg* (London: Arms and Armour, 1990), 77.
3. Editorial comment, "The Case of Rudolf Hess," *Lancet* 246 (1946): 750.
4. J. R. Rees, quoted in Eugene Davidson, *The Trial of the Germans: An Account of the Twenty-Two Defendants before the International Military Tribunal at Nuremberg* (New York: Macmillan, 1966; reprint ed., Columbia: University of Missouri Press, 1977), 119.
5. There are countless other examples from other times and cultures. Lucius Junius Brutus, one of the founders of the Roman Republic, feigned slow-wittedness to avoid execution by Tarquin. The sixteenth-century Dominican priest Tommaso Campanella was charged with treason but escaped the death sentence by feigning mental illness and setting his cell on fire. Ernst Germana, *Tommaso Campanella* (Amsterdam: Springer, 2010).
6. Interrogation of Rudolf Hess, Interrogation Records Prepared for War Crimes Proceedings at Nuernberg, 1945–1947, Record Group 238: National Archives Collection of World War II War Crimes Records, 1933–1949, Microfilm Collection M1270, roll 7, National Archives (hereafter cited as Interrogation Records).
7. Ibid.
8. Ibid.
9. Andrus, *Infamous of Nuremberg*, 72.
10. Ibid., 73.
11. Ibid., 118.
12. Burton Andrus to Douglas Kelley, November 15, 1945, SMS 1285, series 5, folder 1, US Air Force Academy McDermott Library.
13. Ibid.
14. Hermann Göring, quoted in G. M. Gilbert, *Nuremberg Diary* (New York: Farrar, Straus and Giroux, 1947; reprint ed., New York: Da Capo, 1995), 36.
15. Interrogation of Hermann Göring, Interrogation Records, roll 5.

16. Leon Goldensohn, quoted in Daniel Pick, *The Pursuit of the Nazi Mind: Hitler, Hess, and the Analysts* (Oxford: Oxford University Press, 2012), 163.

17. Ibid.

18. Ibid., 161.

19. Andrus, *Infamous of Nuremberg*, 133.

20. Pick, *Pursuit of the Nazi Mind*, 159.

21. "Current Comment: Psychiatric Examination of Rudolf Hess," *JAMA* 130 (1946): 790.

22. Pick, *Pursuit of the Nazi Mind*, 158.

23. Andrus, *Infamous of Nuremberg*, 119–120.

24. Ibid., 121.

25. Eugene Krasnushkin, Eugene Sepp, and Nicolas Kurshakov, report of November 17, 1945, *Trial of the Major War Criminals before the International Military Tribunal, Nuremberg, 14 November 1945–1 October 1946*, 22 vols. (Nuremberg: International Military Tribunal, 1947), 1:163.

26. Robert Jackson, testimony of November 30, 1945, ibid., 2:304.

27. West, *Train of Powder*, 69.

28. Hess, testimony of November 30, 1945, *Trial of the Major War Criminals before the International Military Tribunal*, 2:495.

29. Douglas Kelley, quoted in Rees, *Case of Rudolf Hess*, 171.

30. Gilbert, "Report of Prison Psychologist on Mental Competence of Defendant Hess," August 17, 1946, *Trial of the Major War Criminals*, vol. 1.

31. Kelley, *22 Cells in Nuremberg*, 31–32. I have my doubts that Kelley's recounting is verbatim accurate. Gilbert was with him at the time, and all that Gilbert says was that Hess was in high spirits.

32. Gilbert, *Nuremberg Diary*, 133.

33. Julius Streicher, quoted in Rees, *Case of Rudolf Hess*, 169.

34. Göring, quoted in John E. Dolibois, *Pattern of Circles: An Ambassador's Story* (Kent, OH: Kent State University Press, 1989), 175.

35. Göring, quoted in Gilbert, *Nuremberg Diary*, 60.

36. Whitney Harris, quoted in Gaskin, *Eyewitnesses at Nuremberg*, 90.

37. His assertion was almost out of Joseph Heller's *Catch-22:* "If he says he's sane, he must be crazy."

38. Kelley, cited in Jack El-Hai, *The Nazi and the Psychiatrist: Hermann Göring, Dr. Douglas M. Kelley, and a Fatal Meeting of Minds at the End of WWII* (New York: Public Affairs, 2013), 118.

39. National Archives, Record Group 238: National Archives Collection of World War II War Crimes Records, 1933–1949, Documents Primarily Relating to the Defendants at the International Military and Trials at the Military Tribunals at Nuremberg and Replevined from James P. Atwood, 1945–1947 (hereafter cited as Atwood documents), box 9.

40. Atwood documents, box 2.

41. Atwood documents, box 8.

42. Quoted in Andrus, *Infamous of Nuremberg*, 166.

43. Pick, *Pursuit of the Nazi Mind*, 160.

44. Hess, quoted in Douglas Kelley personal papers.

45. Kelley, quoted in Rees, *Case of Rudolf Hess*, 135.

46. Atwood documents, box 8.

47. Kelley, quoted in Rees, *Case of Rudolf Hess*, 174.

48. Atwood documents, box 8; when Kelley says "no evidence of psychopathology," he was applying a strict forensic standard. Obviously, he thought Hess had major psychiatric issues but believed that these were forensically irrelevant.

49. Kelley, *22 Cells in Nuremberg*, 7, 34, 33.

50. Gilbert, *Psychology of Dictatorship*, 131.

51. Andrus, *Infamous of Nuremberg*, 119.

52. Gilbert, *Nuremberg Diary*, 11.

53. Report by Dr. Gilbert, in Rees, *Case of Rudolf Hess*, 176.

54. Hjalmar Schacht, quoted in ibid., 177.

55. Ibid.

56. Kelley, *22 Cells in Nuremberg*, 29.

57. Atwood documents, box 8.

58. Kelley, *22 Cells in Nuremberg*, 30.

59. Kelley personal papers.

60. Gilbert, "Report by Dr. Gilbert," 187.

61. Gilbert, in Rees, *Case of Rudolf Hess*, 175.

62. D. L. Rosenhan, "On Being Sane in Insane Places," *Science* 179 (1973): 250–258.

63. Shakespeare, *Hamlet*, 4.5.78–79.

64. Lara Braff and David L. Braff, "The Neuropsychiatric Translational Revolution: Still Very Early and Still Very Challenging," *JAMA Psychiatry* 70 (2013): 777–779.

65. Charles L. Scott, "Evaluating Amnesia for Criminal Behavior: A Guide to Remember," *Psychiatric Clinics of North America* 35 (2012): 797–819.

66. Dean C. Delis and Spencer R. Wetter, "Cogniform Disorder and Cogniform Condition: Proposed Diagnoses for Excessive Cognitive Symptoms," *Archives of Clinical Neuropsychology* 22 (2007): 589–604.

67. David Irving, *Hess: The Missing Years, 1941–1945* (London: Macmillan, 1987).

68. Ewen Cameron, one of the psychiatrists who examined him for the tribunal, later worked on the CIA's mind-control program MKUltra.

69. Rudolf Hess, Nuremberg trial transcript, quoted in James Owen, *Nuremberg: Evil on Trial* (London: Headline Review, 2006), 306–307.

70. West, *Train of Powder*, 46–47.

Chapter 9. A Collaboration from Hell

Epigraphs: Douglas Kelley, *22 Cells in Nuremberg* (New York: Greenberg, 1947; reprint ed., New York: MacFadden, 1961), 11; G. M. Gilbert, "The Mentality of SS Murderous Robots," *Yad Vashem Studies* 5 (1963): 35–41.

1. Joseph E. Persico, *Nuremberg: Infamy on Trial* (New York: Penguin, 1994), 293.

2. Ibid., 240.

3. Kelley had every intention of publishing a book on racial prejudice and his publisher's files (Greenberg) are filled with such references but Kelley never got around to it.

4. Howard Whitman, interview with Douglas Kelley, "What Goering & Co. Talk About in Their Cells," *Sunday Express* (London), August 25, 1946.

5. Howard Whitman, "Squeal, Nazi, Squeal," *Collier's*, August 31, 1946, 21ff.

6. Burton C. Andrus, "To public relations officer, war department, regarding the misconduct of Dr. Douglas M Kelly, former Major, Medical Corp, US Army, 6 Sept 1946," Burton C. Andrus Collection, box 33, folder 91, US Army Military History Institute.

7. D. M. Kelley, "Preliminary Studies of the Rorschach Records of the Nazi War Criminals," *Rorschach Research Exchange and Journal of Projective Techniques* 10 (1946): 45–48.

8. "Talk of the Town," *New Yorker,* June 1, 1946, 19–20.

9. Persico, *Nuremberg,* 373.

10. February 13, 1947, Greenberg Publisher Records, series 4, box 48, Columbia University Libraries Rare Book and Manuscript Library.

11. December 23, 1946, ibid.

12. Press release, January 15, 1947, ibid.

13. G. M. Gilbert, *Nuremberg Diary* (New York: Farrar, Straus and Giroux, 1947; reprint ed., New York: Da Capo, 1995).

14. Kelley, *22 Cells in Nuremberg,* 7, 8.

15. Gilbert, *Nuremberg Diary* (acknowledgments).

16. February 18, 1947, Greenberg Publisher Records.

17. Kelley, *22 Cells in Nuremberg,* 171.

18. G. M. Gilbert, *The Psychology of Dictatorship* (New York: Ronald Press, 1950), 109.

19. Edmund Burke, *The Writings and Speeches of Edmund Burke,* ed. Paul Langford and William B. Todd, vol. 2 (Oxford: Oxford University Press, 1981), 282.

20. Parenthetically, this dispute about whether behavioral disturbances fall on a continuum versus whether there are distinct categories of behavior underlies most of the contemporary debates concerning psychiatric diagnosis.

21. Letter from Douglas Kelley, undated, Greenberg Publisher Records.

22. Molly Harrower Papers, box M3208, folder 4, Archives of the History of American Psychology, The Center for the History of Psychology, University of Akron (hereafter cited as Harrower Papers).

23. Ibid.

24. Goldensohn, the psychiatrist who succeeded Kelley, was someone Gilbert disdained as well.

25. Eric A. Zillmer, Molly Harrower, Bruce A. Ritzler, and Robert P. Archer, *The Quest for the Nazi Personality: A Psychological Investigation of Nazi War Criminals* (Hillsdale, NJ: Lawrence Erlbaum, 1995), 60.

26. Harrower Papers, box M3208, folder 11.

27. Molly Harrower, "Rorschach Records of the Nazi War Criminals: An Experimental Study after 30 Years," *Journal of Personality Assessment* 40 (1976): 342.

28. Molly Harrower, "Were Hitler's Henchmen Mad?," *Psychology Today*, July 1976, 76–80.

29. Zillmer, Harrower, Ritzler, and Archer, *Quest for the Nazi Personality*, 62.

30. Ibid., 64.

31. Ibid., 65.

32. Gilbert, *Psychology of Dictatorship*.

33. Zillmer, Harrower, Ritzler, and Archer, *Quest for the Nazi Personality*, 67.

34. Letter to Molly Harrower, Harrower Papers, box M3208, folder 18.

35. Ian Kershaw, *Hitler, the Germans, and the Final Solution* (Jerusalem: International Institute for Holocaust Research, Yad Vashem, 2008), 321. Kershaw was alluding to the attacks on Christopher Browning's thoughtful work, *Ordinary Men: Reserve Police Battalion 101 and the Final Solution in Poland,* by Daniel Goldhagen, author of *Hitler's Willing Executioners: Ordinary Germans and the Holocaust.* It is interesting to note a recurring theme here. Browning, like a latter-day Kelley, asserted that typical Nazi killers were in fact ordinary people who made accommodations to the orders coming from above and that, by implication, genocidal killing was in all of our cultural repertoires. Goldhagen, like Gilbert, regarded the killers as demonic homicidal maniacs who loved their work and was so insulted by Browning's perspective that he attacked it repeatedly. I know of few areas of scholarship that are characterized by more polemics.

36. He famously observed that in the 1950s one third of the Oakland police department was psychologically unfit for duty, but he was so engaging that the police *still* liked him.

37. Lewis Terman to Douglas Kelley, quoted in Jack El-Hai, *The Nazi and the Psychiatrist: Hermann Göring, Dr. Douglas M. Kelley, and a Fatal Meeting of Minds at the End of WWII* (New York: Public Affairs, 2013), 205.

38. Quoted in ibid., 198.

39. "UC's Dr. Kelley, Crime Expert, Commits Suicide," *San Francisco Chronicle*, January 2, 1958.

40. *New York Times*, January 2, 1958.

41. Molly Harrower, Grand Rounds Presentation at Massachusetts General Hospital, May 10, 1977, Harrower Papers, box M3208, folder 16.

42. El-Hai, *Nazi and Psychiatrist*.

43. Barbara Nemiroff, personal communication, 2013; Zillmer, Harrower, Ritzler, and Archer, *Quest for the Nazi Personality*, 89.

44. G. M. Gilbert, "The Mentality of SS Murderous Robots," *Yad Vashem Studies* 5 (1963): 35–41.

45. Florence R. Miale and Michael Selzer, *The Nuremberg Mind: The Psychology of the Nazi Leaders* (New York: Quadrangle, 1995), 14.

46. Zillmer, Harrower, Ritzler, and Archer, *Quest for the Nazi Personality*, 83–88.

47. By coincidence, Kennedy was working in Boston with Samuel Beck's son, who interceded with the institute on Kennedy's behalf so that she could access his father's papers.

48. The seventh Rorschach is in Kelley's personal papers.

Chapter 10. A Message in the Rorschachs?

Epigraphs: Abraham J. Heschel, *The Prophets* (New York: Harper and Row, 1962), xv; Raul Hilberg, "The Significance of the Holocaust," in *The Holocaust: Ideology, Bureaucracy, and Genocide,* ed. Henry Friedlander and Sybil Milton (Millwood, NY: Kraus International, 1980), 181.

1. For example, specialized terms such as *Erlebnistypus* (EB), *introversive, extratensive,* and *ambitent* are commonly used by Rorschach specialists. EB refers to the patient's problem-solving style, a ratio between responses to human movement and color. When movement responses dominate, the patient is described as *introversive* and more likely to solve problems from an analytic perspective. Conversely, when color responses dominate, the subject is *extratensive* and more likely to make choices based on a gut feeling. The *ambitent* shows more of a balance between movement and color (thinking versus feeling), but this balance is not necessarily advantageous because *ambitents* are slower in problem solving. See Eric A. Zillmer, Molly Harrower, Bruce A. Ritzler, and Robert P. Archer, *The Quest for the Nazi Personality: A Psychological Investigation of Nazi War Criminals* (Hillsdale, NJ: Lawrence Erlbaum, 1995), 97, for more details.

2. John E. Exner, *The Rorschach: A Comprehensive System,* vols. 1 and 2 (New York: Wiley, 1974, 1978); Exner, *The Rorschach: A Comprehensive System,* 2nd ed., vol. 1, *Basic Foundations* (New York: Wiley, 1986).

3. Douglas Kelley, quoted in Zillmer, Harrower, Ritzler, and Archer, *Quest for the Nazi Personality,* 203.

4. Gustave Gilbert, cited in Florence R. Miale and Michael Selzer, *The Nuremberg Mind: The Psychology of the Nazi Leaders* (New York: Quadrangle, 1995), 86.

5. Ibid., 86–87.

6. Kelley, quoted in Zillmer, Harrower, Ritzler, and Archer, *Quest for the Nazi Personality,* 205.

7. Ibid., 209.

8. Molly Harrower Papers, box M3199, folder 17, Archives of the History of American Psychology, The Center for the History of Psychology, University of Akron (hereafter cited as Harrower Papers).

9. Gilbert, cited in Miale and Selzer, *Nuremberg Mind,* 102.

10. Ibid., 102, 103.

11. Ibid.

12. Richard Rubinstein, review of Florence R. Miale and Michael Selzer, *The Nuremberg Mind: The Psychology of the Nazi Leaders, Psychology Today,* July 1976, 83–84.

13. Miale and Selzer, *Nuremberg Mind,* 22.

14. Ibid., 277, 287.

15. Harrower Papers, box M3199, folder 12.

16. Molly Harrower, "Rorschach Records of the Nazi War Criminals: An Experimental Study after Thirty Years," *Journal of Personality Assessment* 40 (1976): 341–351.

17. The list was actually more extensive than that.

18. Barry A. Ritzler, "The Nuremberg Mind Revisited: A Quantitative Approach to Nazi Rorschachs," *Journal of Personality Assessment* 47 (1978): 344–353. There were some intriguing findings in the Nuremberg Rorschachs, but a word of caution is needed. Although *ambitents* were slightly overrepresented in the war criminals, a chance response by one or two patients can get overemphasized in such a small group. Nonetheless, there is a small literature suggesting that *ambitents* are slower at making decisions and have difficulties coping. See, e.g., Exner, *Rorschach: A Comprehensive System*, vol. 1, *Basic Foundations*, 2nd ed.

19. Zillmer, Harrower, Ritzler, and Archer, *Quest for the Nazi Personality*, 95.

20. Ibid., 98.

21. Ibid., 116.

22. Gerald L. Borofsky and Don J. Brand, "Personality Organization and Psychological Functioning of the Nuremberg War Criminals: The Rorschach Data," in *Survivors, Victims, and Perpetrators: Essays on the Nazi Holocaust*, ed. Joel E. Dimsdale (Washington, DC: Hemisphere, 1980).

Chapter 11. Malice on a Continuum

Epigraph: Christopher Browning, *Ordinary Men: Reserve Police Battalion 101 and the Final Solution in Poland* (New York: Harper Perennial, 1998), 158.

1. Douglas Kelley, *22 Cells in Nuremberg* (New York: Greenberg, 1947; reprint ed., New York: MacFadden, 1961), 171.

2. Barbara Tuchman, in Gideon Hausner, *Justice in Jerusalem* (New York: Schocken Books, 1968), xx.

3. Valerie Hartouni, *Visualizing Atrocity: Arendt, Evil, and the Optics of Thoughtlessness* (New York: New York University Press, 2012), 135.

4. Hannah Arendt, *Eichmann in Jerusalem* (New York: Viking, 1964), 276.

5. Ibid., 287–288.

6. Hausner, *Justice in Jerusalem*, 8.

7. Ibid., 9, 11.

8. Arendt, *Eichmann in Jerusalem*, 32.

9. Hausner, *Justice in Jerusalem*, 280.

10. Arendt, *Eichmann in Jerusalem*, 48, 49.

11. After all, years earlier Eichmann had stated, "I will jump into my grave laughing, because the fact that I have the death of five million Jews . . . on my conscience gives me extraordinary satisfaction." Quoted in Arendt, *Eichmann in Jerusalem*, 46. See also Bettina Stagneth, *Eichmann before Jerusalem* (New York: Alfred A. Knopf, 2014).

12. Hartouni, *Visualizing Atrocity*, 23, 25.

13. Ibid., 39, 117 (quoting Arendt).

14. Stanley Milgram, "Behavioral Study of Obedience," *Journal of Abnormal and Social Psychology* 67 (1963): 371–378; Milgram, *Obedience to Authority: An Experimental View* (New York: Harper and Row, 1974).

15. Milgram, *Obedience to Authority*, 15.

16. Ibid., 56–57.

17. These studies are marked by controversy. Were they ethical? Were the reports of the studies distorted? Can you extrapolate from a short laboratory experiment to real life? Nonetheless, Milgram's studies seared the landscape of social psychology and reverberated in Holocaust studies.

18. Milgram, *Obedience to Authority*, xii.

19. Recent reports question whether the witnesses were in fact as passive as originally described, but it was the original reports that captivated and troubled John M. Darley and Bibb Latané and inspired them to study bystander apathy.

20. Ian Kershaw, *Hitler, the Germans, and the Final Solution* (Jerusalem: International Institute for Holocaust Research, Yad Vashem, 2008), 130.

21. Arendt, *Eichmann in Jerusalem*, 233.

22. Bibb Latané and John M. Darley, "Bystander 'Apathy,'" *American Scientist* 57 (1969): 244–268.

23. Bibb Latané and John M. Darley, *The Unresponsive Bystander: Why Doesn't He Help?* (Englewood Cliffs, NJ: Prentice Hall, 1970), 48.

24. Ibid., 58–60.

25. John M. Darley and Bibb Latané, "Bystander Intervention in Emergencies: Diffusion of Responsibility," *Journal of Personality and Social Psychology* 8 (1968): 377–383, quotation at 379.

26. Latané and Darley, *Unresponsive Bystander*, 94–98.

27. Interestingly, Zimbardo and Milgram were childhood friends from the Bronx.

28. Philip Zimbardo, *The Lucifer Effect* (New York: Random House, 2007), 21.

29. Ibid. For photos and more information about the experiment, see the Stanford Prison Experiment website at http://www.prisonexp.org/.

30. Craig Haney, Curtis Banks, and Philip Zimbardo, "A Study of Prisoners and Guards in a Simulated Prison," *Naval Research Review* 30 (1973): 4–17.

31. See, e.g., Romesh Ratnesar, "The Menace Within," *Stanford Magazine*, July–August 2011.

32. Kathleen O'Toole, "The Stanford Prison Experiment: Still Powerful after All These Years," Stanford University News Service, January 8, 1997. It is interesting to note the diversity of these non-intervening bystanders: "parents and friends of the students, . . . a Catholic priest, a public defender, professional psychologists, graduate students, and staff of the psychology department."

Chapter 12. Malice as Categorically Different

Epigraph: Sigmund Freud to Oskar Pfister, quoted in Paul Roazen, *Freud and His Followers* (New York: Da Capo, 1992), 146.

1. Herman Göring, quoted in G. M. Gilbert, *Nuremberg Diary* (New York: Farrar, Straus and Giroux, 1947; reprint ed., New York: Da Capo, 1995), 194.

2. Augustine converted from Manichaeism to Christianity in the fourth century.

3. Albert Einstein, "The Real Problem Is in the Hearts of Men," *New York Times Magazine,* June 23, 1946.

4. Anthropologists argue passionately about viewing human nature as innocent ("noble savage"—J.-J. Rousseau) or evil ("Nature, red in tooth and claw"—Alfred, Lord Tennyson). See, e.g., Serena Golden's article about the Marshall Sahlins versus Napoleon Chagnon controversy. Golden, "A Protest Resignation," *Inside Higher Education,* February 25, 2013.

5. Donald W. Black, *Bad Boys, Bad Men: Confronting Antisocial Personality Disorder* (Oxford: Oxford University Press, 1999), 199.

6. It is interesting that empathy can be lost in humans because it is evident even in animals. Animals can understand when another animal is suffering, particularly if they have experienced the same adversities. Rats will rescue a fellow rat that is drenched in water. They rescue their peers particularly quickly if they themselves have previously been in similar unpleasant water chambers. Not only will they rescue another rat, but they will do that even in preference to getting food. See Nobuya Sato, Ling Tan, Kazushi Tate, and Maya Okada, "Rats Demonstrate Helping Behavior toward a Soaked Conspecific," *Animal Cognition,* published online, May 12, 2015, DOI 10.1007/s10071–015–0872–2.

7. Black, *Bad Boys, Bad Men.*

8. Hervey M. Cleckley, *The Mask of Sanity: An Attempt to Clarify Some Issues about the So-Called Psychopathic Personality* (Saint Louis, MO: Mosby, 1941).

9. A Saint Louis study, for instance, found that 45 percent of men admitted three or more extramarital affairs and 43 percent disclosed holding illegal jobs like drug dealing at some point in their lives. Lee N. Robins, "The Epidemiology of Antisocial Personality," in *Psychiatry,* vol. 3, ed. Robert O. Michels and Jesse O. Cavenar (Philadelphia: J. B. Lippincott, 1988). There is no reason to believe that Saint Louis is a latter-day Sodom; we are all guilty of various wrongdoings, but the pattern is more extensive among psychopaths.

10. J. Reid Meloy, "Predatory Violence and Psychopathy," in *Psychopathy and Law: A Practitioner's Guide,* ed. Helinä Häkkänen-Nyholm and Jan-Olof Nyholm (New York: Wiley-Blackwell, 2012), 159–175.

11. Adrian Raine et al., "Reduced Prefrontal Gray Matter Volume and Reduced Autonomic Activity in Antisocial Personality Disorder," *Archives of General Psychiatry* 57 (200): 119–127.

12. Black, *Bad Boys, Bad Men,* 19. The border between psychopathy and narcissistic personality disorder is a hazy one. Narcissistic personality disorder is characterized more by grandiosity and self-preoccupation, but that border can shift easily.

13. American Psychiatric Association, *Diagnostic and Statistical Manual: Mental Disorders* (Washington, DC: American Psychiatric Association, 1952), 38.

14. Later editions of the DSM moved addiction and deviant sexuality to different diagnostic categories, and homosexuality was dropped as a psychiatric disorder in 1974.

15. Robert D. Hare, *Manual for the Revised Psychopathy Checklist*, 2nd ed. (Toronto, ON: Multi-Health Systems, 2003).

16. Even if the psychopath's brain is different, that does not mean he or she is incurable. The brain heals; new learning triggers the development of fresh neural pathways.

17. J. Grafman et al., "Frontal Lobe Injuries, Violence, and Aggression: A Report of the Vietnam Head Injury Study," *Neurology* 46 (1996): 1231–1238; M. C. Brower and B. H. Price, "Neuropsychiatry of Frontal Lobe Dysfunction in Violent and Criminal Behavior: A Critical Review," *Journal of Neurology, Neurosurgery, and Psychiatry* 71 (2001): 720–726.

18. S. M. Stahl, "Deconstructing Violence as a Medical Syndrome: Mapping Psychotic, Impulsive, and Predatory Subtypes to Malfunctioning Brain Circuits," *CNS Spectrums* 19 (2014): 357–365.

19. John M. Harlow, "Recovery from the Passage of an Iron Bar through the Head," *Bulletin of the Massachusetts Medical Society* 2 (1868): 327–347.

20. Hanna Damasio et al., "The Return of Phineas Gage: Clues about the Brain from the Skull of a Famous Patient," *Science* 264 (1994): 1102–1105.

21. S. Pridmore, A. Chambers, and M. McArthur, "Neuroimaging in Psychopathology," *Australian and New Zealand Journal of Psychiatry* 38 (2005): 856–865.

22. Nathaniel E. Anderson and Kent A. Kiehl, "The Psychopath Magnetized: Insights from Brain Imaging," *Trends in Cognitive Science* 16 (2012): 52–60.

23. Martina Ly et al., "Cortical Thinning in Psychopathy," *American Journal of Psychiatry* 169 (2012): 743–749.

24. Jean Decety, Laurie R. Skelly, and Kent A. Kiehl, "Brain Response to Empathy-Eliciting Scenarios Involving Pain in Incarcerated Individuals with Psychopathy," *JAMA Psychiatry* 70 (2013): 638–645.

25. Sherrie Williamson, Timothy J. Harpur, and Robert D. Hare, "Abnormal Processing of Affective Words by Psychopaths," *Psychophysiology* 28 (1991): 260–273.

26. Yaling Yang and Adrian Raine, "Prefrontal Structural and Functional Brain Imaging Findings in Antisocial, Violent, and Psychopathic Individuals: A Meta-Analysis," *Psychiatry Research* 174 (2009): 81–88.

27. Mairead C. Dolan, "What Imaging Tells Us about Violence in Anti-Social Men," *Criminal Behaviour and Mental Health* 20 (2010): 199–214.

28. Andrea L. Glenn and Adrian Raine, "The Neurobiology of Psychopathy," *Psychiatric Clinics of North America* 31 (2008): 463–475; Daniel R. Russell and Larry J. Siever, "The Neurobiology of Aggression and Violence," *CNS Spectrums* 20 (2015): 254–279.

29. L. Lidberg et al., "Homicide, Suicide and CSF 5-HIAA," *Acta Psychiatrica Scandinavica* 71 (1985): 230–236.

30. E. Hollander and J. Rosen, "Impulsivity," *Journal of Psychopharmacology* 14, suppl. 1 (2000): S39–S44. Some investigators report that patients even acquire better emotional recognition skills when they have been treated with such medications. Caroline Moul, Simon Killcross, and Mark R. Dadds, "A Model of Differential Amygdala Activation in Psychopathy," *Psychological Review* 119 (2012): 789–806.

31. Paul J. Zak, *The Moral Molecule: The Source of Love and Prosperity* (New York: Dutton, 2012).

32. Rachel Bachner-Melman and Richard P. Ebstein, "The Role of Oxytocin and Vasopressin in Emotional and Social Behaviors," in *Clinical Neuroendocrinology,* ed. Eric Fliers, Marta Korbonits, and J. A. Romijn, vol. 124 of *Handbook of Clinical Neurology* (Amsterdam: Elsevier, 2014), 53–68.

33. Mark R. Dadds et al., "Polymorphisms in the Oxytocin Receptor Gene Are Associated with the Development of Psychopathy," *Development and Psychopathology* 26 (2013): 21–31.

34. Manuela Kanat, Markus Heinrichs, and Gregor Domes, "Oxytocin and the Social Brain: Neural Mechanisms and Perspectives in Human Research," *Brain Research* 1580 (2014): 160–171.

35. Zoe R. Donaldson and Larry J. Young, "Oxytocin, Vasopressin, and the Neurogenetics of Sociality," *Science* 322 (2008): 900–904.

36. Paul J. Zak, Angela A. Stanton, and Sheila Ahmadi, "Oxytocin Increases Generosity in Humans," *PLoSOne* 2 (2007): e1128.

37. Paul J. Zak, "The Neurobiology of Trust," *Scientific American,* June 2008, 88–95.

38. Katja Bertsch et al., "Oxytocin and Reduction of Social Threat Hypersensitivity in Women with Borderline Personality Disorder," *American Journal of Psychiatry* 170 (2013): 1169–1177. There are many studies suggesting that chromosome anomalies or excess testosterone may also be relevant to psychopathic behavior. However, the serotonin and oxytocin papers have captured the most contemporary interest. It is obviously a burgeoning literature.

39. M'Naughton's Case, 8 Eng. Rep. 718 (H.L. 1843), quoted in Matthew M. Large, "Treatment of Psychosis and Risk Assessment for Violence," *American Journal of Psychiatry* 171 (2014): 258.

40. Richard Ciccone, "Daniel McNaughton and the Evolution of the Insanity Defense," American Psychiatric Association Isaac Ray Lecture, New York, May 5, 2014, emphasis in original.

41. Bernard L. Diamond, "From M'Naghton to Currens, and Beyond," *California Law Review* 50 (1962): 189–205.

42. Black, *Bad Boys, Bad Men,* 177–178.

43. Greg Miller, "In Mock Case, Biological Evidence Reduces Sentences," *Science* 337 (2012): 788.

44. Plato, *Timaeus,* in *The Dialogues of Plato,* trans. Benjamin Jowett (Chicago: Encyclopedia Britannica, 1952), 474.

45. Rebecca Goldstein, *Plato at the Googleplex: Why Philosophy Won't Go Away* (New York: Pantheon, 2014), 410.

Conclusion

Epigraph: Robert Jackson, testimony, November 21, 1945, *Trial of the Major War Criminals before the International Military Tribunal, Nuremberg, 14 November 1945–1 October 1946,* 22 vols. (Nuremberg: International Military Tribunal, 1947), 2:129.

1. Ibid.

2. The International Military Tribunal at Nuremberg focused on the Nazi leaders, those who had the least chance of arguing that they were mere cogs in the machine. There are many studies on the Nazi rank and file, including even Rorschach studies of two hundred Danish collaborators unearthed by Michael Selzer and Barry Ritzler. See Eric A. Zillmer, Molly Harrower, Bruce A. Ritzler, and Robert P. Archer, *The Quest for the Nazi Personality: A Psychological Investigation of Nazi War Criminals* (Hillsdale, NJ: Lawrence Erlbaum, 1995).

3. Jackson, testimony, November 21, 1945.

4. I am indebted to Stuart Voytilla for this insight.

5. Although their motivations may have been different (Victor Frankenstein was trying to create immortality, whereas Hitler aimed for a thousand-year Reich), such motivations were irrelevant to their culpability.

6. Helinä Häkkänen-Nyholm and Jan-Olof Nyholm, "Psychopathy in Economical Crime, Organized Crime, and War Crimes," in *Psychopathy and Law: A Practitioner's Guide* (New York: Wiley-Blackwell, 2012), 193.

7. There isn't even a record of who gave them the files. Indeed, in all the years of the library's stewardship of these files, I was only the second visitor to request access to these sleepy, unexplored files.

8. Pablo Neruda, "Oda a la cama" (Ode to the bed), 1959, trans. Cary Ratcliff, Conspirare Company of Voices, Austin, TX, September 18, 2014, http://conspirare .org/wp-content/uploads/The-Poet-Sings-Pablo-Neruda-program-booklet.pdf.

ACKNOWLEDGMENTS

MANY PEOPLE HELPED to make this book possible. To the extent that it is readable and accurate, they deserve the credit; for the lapses, I deserve the blame. My wife, Nancy, endured my musings on this topic for years and helped me to focus my embarrassingly rough early drafts. My son, Jonathan, helped me understand what the next generation needs to know about Nuremberg.

My editor at Yale University Press, Jennifer Banks, offered valuable advice about the structure of the book. Sandy Dijkstra is a superb agent and helped bring this book to life. My assistant, Gary Lyasch, was, as always, patient and meticulous.

Books like this depend on research libraries and a cadre of archivists. From the University of California, San Diego, I thank Brian Schottlaender, Lynda Claasen, and Peter Devine for their sustained interest and assistance. Beth Remak-Honnef guided me through the archives at University of California, Santa Cruz. Adrianne Noe and Eric Boyle helped from the National Museum of Health and Medicine. Richard Baker cheerfully retrieved documents from the US Army Military History Institute, and Mary Elizabeth Ruwell searched the archives at the US Air Force Academy McDermott Library. Lizette Royer Barton was an invaluable resource at the University of Akron Center for the History of Psychology. Raphael and Elizabeth Rosen took time from their studies to retrieve documents from the Columbia University archives; Martha Winnacker found files for me at University of

California, Berkeley; Susan Berishaj helped me with the Yale University archives; and Cornell University provided its online archives in an easy-to-use format. Tanya Domi at the Graduate Center of CUNY, Peter Stein at New York University, and Nina Stoyan-Rosenzweig at the University of Florida helped me retrieve photographs. Last but certainly not least, I wish to acknowledge the resources of the Library of Congress, the National Archives, and the United States Holocaust Memorial Museum. They are all national treasures.

Excerpts from the *Nuremberg Diary* are reprinted by permission of Da Capo Press, a member of the Perseus Books Group.

My friends supported me with advice, even when their own projects were clamoring for attention. I would like to thank my colleagues in history (Frank Biess, Jack Fisher, Debora Hertz, Susanne Hillman, Judith Hughes, the late John Marino, and Eric van Young), literature (Steve Cox), communications (Valerie Hartouni), neuropathology (Henry Powell and Lawrence Hansen), psychology (Dean Delis and William Perry), psychiatry (David Braff, Lewis Judd, Scott Matthews, Robert Nemiroff, Steve Ornish, and Steve Stahl), film studies (Stuart Voytilla), and law (Mark Evans). I am also grateful for the insights shared in conversations with Barbara Nemiroff, Kurt Shuler, and Judge Norbert Ehrenfreund. I am deeply indebted to Douglas Kelley, who kindly shared his father's personal papers. Michelle Williamson skillfully redrew the map in Chapter 1.

All of you constitute that rarest of commodities—a community of scholars who provided encouragement, insight, and guidance on a difficult task. Thank you.

INDEX

Page numbers in *italics* indicate illustrations.